The New Rules of Retirement

The New Rules of Retirement

Strategies for a Secure Future

Robert C. Carlson

WILEY

John Wiley & Sons, Inc.

Published by John Wiley & Sons, Inc., Hoboken, New Jersey.
Published simultaneously in Canada.

For general information on our other products and services, or technical support, please contact our Customer Care Department within the United States at 800-762-2974, outside the United States at 317-572-3993 or fax 317-572-4002.

Wiley also publishes its books in a variety of electronic formats. Some content that appears in print may not be available in electronic books.

For more information about Wiley products, visit our web site at www.wiley.com.

Library of Congress Cataloging-in-Publication Data:

Carlson, Robert, 1957–
  The new rules of retirement : strategies for a secure future/ Robert Carlson.
      p. cm.
  Includes index.
  ISBN 0-471-68346-9 (cloth)
  1. Retirement—United States—Planning. I. Title.

  HQ1063.2.U6C37   2004
  332.024'014—dc22

                                    2004013746

Printed in the United States of America

10 9 8 7 6 5 4 3 2 1

To my parents,
Ed and Muriel

CONTENTS

ABOUT THE AUTHOR

Robert C. Carlson is editor of the monthly newsletter, *Retirement Watch*. He is also the managing member of Carlson Wealth Advisors, L.L.C. Mr. Carlson is Chairman of the Board of Trustees of the Fairfax County Employees' Retirement System, which has over $2 billion in assets, and is a member of the Board of Trustees of the Virginia Retirement System, which oversees $40 billion in assets.

Mr. Carlson is an attorney and certified public accountant. He received his J.D. and an M.S. (Accounting) from the University of Virginia and received his B.S. (Financial Management) from Clemson University. He also is an intrument-rated private pilot. He is listed in the fifty-seventh Edition of *Who's Who in America* (2003 Edition).

The New Rules of Retirement

Retirement and retirement planning are changing. They were changing before the bear market of 2000–2002, the recession of 2001, and before September 11, 2001. Significant trends were already afoot that transformed many aspects of retirement and retirement planning: the cost of retirement, pensions, health care, housing, the financial markets, estate planning, tax planning, and many more facets of the years after middle age. In the future, there will be more changes to retirement, and the changes will occur much more rapidly.

A force that is bigger than anything that has tested retirement plans so far is causing these changes. This force is coming. You cannot stop it. Neither can the government.

This force is known as the Age Wave.

Virtually everyone's future safety and comfort will be affected. Whether you are 40 or 80, you will feel the effects of the Age Wave. Even those who already are retired have felt these forces and will continue to feel them. Many of the changes will be positive. Yet, not everyone will enjoy riding the Wave. To take advantage of the coming retirement opportunities, you have to adapt. You must plan and prepare for the consequences of the new trends.

Three key, unstoppable trends that already are in place combine to make up the Wave.

Trend #1—The Boomers Again

The biggest influence behind the Wave is the Baby Boomers —that generation of 76 million people born between 1946 and 1964. The generation before the Boomers numbered only 55 million, and the Boomers' grandparents' generation in the U.S. was just 44 million. The generation following the Boomers is estimated at 41 million (those born between 1965 and 1976), and the following generation (called the Echo Boom, born from 1977 to 1993) is numbered at 64 million.

More precisely, the important trend is the aging of the Baby Boomers. The first Boomers are past age 50. In 2005 they will reach age 59 1/2, the age at which penalty-free distributions can be taken from retirement plans. In 2008, they will be 62, the age at which they are eligible to begin receiving Social Security retirement benefits. Some already are retired. Soon, they will retire in droves. The Wave probably will hit with full force between 2010 and 2014.

As they aged, the surge of Boomers changed much in America: primary education, higher education, housing, health care, and retail. The Gerber baby food company had sales double just from 1948 to 1950. Sales steadily increased through the early 1960s before leveling off. Mattel and Toys 'R Us also were popular growth stocks during the Boomers' early years, only to fall on hard times as the Boomers got older. Next was a surge in school building and an emergency call for people to become teachers to educate this enormous generation. Then college enrollment, along with tuition costs, exploded. Colleges and universities enjoyed a building explosion, only to enter the 1980s scrambling for enough students to fill their dorms after the Boomers graduated and moved on.

As the Boomers entered their adult years, housing was the new growth industry. Homes of all kinds were built around the country, and real estate values steadily increased. Some analysts believe interest rates increased steadily during the 1960s and 1970s because the Boomers were borrowing to buy homes, cars, and home furnishings. There's not much doubt that unemployment increased steadily during this period because so many Boomers entered the job market at the same time. The financial market boom began in 1982—about the same time that the Boomers were entering the peak saving and investing period of life.

Demographics might not be destiny, as some contend. But the size of the post-World War II generation definitely had an impact on the economy and markets. The Baby Boomers already have changed retirement and will change it more dramatically in the coming years. While other forces will be at work, the influence of the Boomers reaching their retirement years will be great.

The repercussions of the Boomers on retirement will be amplified by two other trends. These three factors are working together to transform retirement.

Trend #2—Medical Miracles

The second trend is that people are living longer. Around 1890, German Chancellor Otto von Bismarck set age 65 as the retirement age in his government-provided retirement plan, earning him credit for establishing 65 as the traditional retirement benchmark in the western economies. The average life span in Bismarck's day was about 46, so few actually lived to receive their retirement benefits. In 1960, average life expectancy in the United States was 70 years, leaving the first generation of American retirees to spend, on average, only about five years in retirement. By 2000, U.S. life expectancy was up to 78 years. It is estimated that it will be almost 84 years by 2050. The "old old," those ages 85 or older, are the fastest growing portion of the population.

Here's another way to look at life expectancy. Those who were 20 years old in 1954 can expect to spend on average 13 years, or about 24 percent of their lives, in retirement if they retire at 65. Because that is only an average, many retirees will spend 20 years in retirement, and some will have retirement stretch for 25 or 30 years—and even longer for a small but growing percentage.

Even these estimates might be low. During the twentieth century, developments in health care doubled the average life expectancy. It is not unreasonable to expect that further medical developments could dramatically increase life expectancy for the Boomers.

The result is that there are more Boomers than any other generation. The Boomers are likely to live longer than any previous generation.

Trend #3—Fewer Offspring

The third trend is what the demographers call the replacement rate. It has been declining for decades. The Boomers simply were not as prolific as prior generations. They married later and had fewer children. Birth rates dropped after the 1950s, producing smaller new generations. Demographers say that for a population to be stable, it needs to produce an average of 2.1 children for each woman of childbearing age. A higher fertility rate means that the population will grow. A lower fertility rate leads to a shrinking population. In the United States, the fertility rate was 3.3 in 1960. It now is 2.0, and is estimated to be 2.2 in 2050.

Thus these three trends make up the Wave: an unusually large population segment that is past midlife, longer overall life expectancy, and a low population replacement rate. Compounded, these make for an aging population. There will be fewer younger people for each older person, and each year a higher percentage of the population will be over age 65. In 2000, the United States had four workers for each person over age 65. In 2015 this number is estimated to drop to 3.4, and by 2050 it is estimated that there will be 2.3 workers for each American over 65. The U.S. population is getting older, and it will continue to get older if these trends continue to dominate.

The United States is not the only country with an aging population. These trends are occurring in most developed countries. Europe is aging faster than the United States, and Japan is aging the fastest of all countries.

In 50 years, Japan is estimated to have one person over age 65 for each person under 65.

Because of longer life spans, the very elderly population will increase dramatically. Not long ago it was unusual for someone to live past age 85. But the over-85 crowd is the fastest growing section of the population and is getting ready to be a significant portion of the United States. This segment of the population often requires a disproportionate amount of resources for financial support, health care, and assistance with the activities of daily living.

Where Will the Wave Take Us?

An aging population has consequences. A number of books and reports have ventured to forecast the consequences of the Age Wave. We'll discuss the possible consequences in some detail in Chapter 1. Keep in mind, though, that no matter how diligent the research behind a forecast is, things can change. Sometimes new trends intervene to change the consequences of older trends. Also, while current forecasts agree on some consequences of the Wave (which doesn't mean those parts of the forecasts will be correct), they disagree on others. Population aging on this scale is new. Since the dawn of man, aging certainly hasn't occurred in combination with longer life expectancies and the accompanying need for retirement income and medical care.

Yet, the consequences of the Baby Boomers passing through the earlier phases of their lives were anticipated fairly accurately. It makes sense to sketch probable implications of the graying post-World War II generation by starting with the needs and activities of current and previous generations of senior Americans. Then, we should try to anticipate the likely effects from the influx of Boomers.

The worst-case scenario of an aging population is indeed bleak. Some analysts believe that the extended depression Japan has experienced since 1989 is what is in store for the United States. An aging population can lead to lower economic growth rates and higher inflation. Government programs will be increasingly strained as the number of nonproductive workers drawing government benefits dwarfs the number of taxpayers. The cost of goods and services demanded by older Americans will soar unless there is an offsetting increased supply.

Some analysts are forecasting tumbling home prices. They believe as Americans age, they will sell larger homes to move into smaller homes or retirement housing. There will not be enough younger buyers for the larger homes, so prices will fall. Likewise, some forecast that older Americans will sell stocks and bonds to pay living expenses, and there won't be enough younger people in the saving stage of life to buy these stocks and bonds. The combination could cause meltdowns in the housing and financial markets.

No Time to Panic

It is easy to paint a disaster scenario of the consequences of an aging population, as we have just seen and will examine in more detail in Chapter 1. But don't start packing your bags and looking for some other place to retire just yet. I won't join the chorus of doomsayers.

People tend to foresee and adapt to changes. Most of the financial disasters and near disasters of the past did not have the severe adverse consequences that were predicted at the onset. Consider the horrifying scenarios that were predicted after the Asian financial crisis of 1997, the Russian debt default of 1998, and the anticipated year 2000 computer glitch. Even the terrorist attacks on the World Trade Center and the Pentagon, while killing thousands and inflicting serious damage on the economy, did not have nearly the negative effects on the economy and financial markets that many expected. The Depression of the 1930s and the stagflation of the 1970s were the only modern periods in which people took a long time to learn or adapt well. The economic consequences of those periods were as bad as most people anticipated. Even so, we recovered from the 1970s fairly rapidly once government policies were changed. Those who bought gold and stored food in anticipation of a collapsing society did so unnecessarily.

In addition, the Age Wave is not occurring in a vacuum. There are a number of other factors, which we'll review in Chapter 1, that could intervene to change or ameliorate the effects of the Wave.

Retirement Night and Day

We know the Wave has changed retirement and will change it further. We don't know if the best-case or worst-case scenarios—or something in between—will be realized. Yet, we do know many of the changes the Wave is likely to have on individual retirees. We also know we must be alert to the possibility of additional changes in the future and to be ready to adapt to them.

We know that retirement in the future will be as different from the retirement of the past as night is from day. Those who planned for retirement only 15 or 20 years ago would be shocked by the task faced by their counterparts in the early twenty-first century. Many of the issues and questions to be addressed today weren't even on the radar screen not long ago.

The first real generation of American retirees, those who retired in the 1960s and 1970s, developed the image of retirement that many Americans hold today. They retired at age 65 with company pensions, Social Security, investments, and paid-off mortgages. They also had Medicare to cover many of their health care bills. Soaring real estate values from the 1950s through the 1970s enabled them to sell their homes for tremendous profits.

They could buy luxurious retirement homes in sunny climes, move into retirement communities, or simply buy a smaller home and bank the rest of the profits. Retirement seemed to be set.

For most of the second, third, and fourth retirement generations, things will be different. Sometimes they will be shockingly different. Here are the key changes we know have been caused by the trends that make up the Age Wave.

Longer and Healthier

It used to be that a 65-year-old was elderly and beginning to get frail. The first generation of retirees lived an average of only five years in retirement. But most 65-year-olds today are healthy and vigorous. Also, people are retiring before 65, often long before 65. On average, men retire at 63 while women retire at 60. Many, of course, retire much younger than these averages.

The combination of longer life spans and earlier retirement means that retirement can last a long time. It is not unusual now for someone to spend 20 or 30 years in retirement. This should become even more common in the next few decades.

A healthier generation of older Americans also means that for many people retirement no longer means kicking back and doing nothing or simply playing. It means starting new, fulfilling activities, such as beginning a second or third career, starting a business, learning a new hobby, going to school, traveling, volunteering, spending more time with the family, or a host of other activities. Retirement can only get better as health care improves, life spans increase, people stay active longer, and America becomes wealthier.

Rising Costs and Expectations

Retirement is becoming more expensive. It takes a lot of money to spend 20 or 30 years in retirement or semiretirement. In addition, with more people reaching retirement age, demand for the goods and services typically purchased by retirees is likely to rise. The supply of those goods and services probably will rise. But if supply does not rise at least as much as demand, prices could rise—perhaps faster than the general inflation rate.

Price increases are not the only reason the cost of retirement is likely to rise. The expectations for retirement are higher. Americans are expecting to have more luxuries in retirement and to participate in more activities that cost money—such as travel and golf—than they did during their working years. They expect to enjoy some things that they postponed while raising their children and putting them through college.

On Your Own

Retirees increasingly must rely on their own resources to fund their lifestyles. The first generation of retirees, those who retired in the 1960s and 1970s, could count on employer pensions, known as defined benefit plans, that guaranteed a stream of payments for life. Under these plans, the income payments are fixed, and the retiree cannot outlive the money. Today, only about 20 percent of retirees are covered by such pensions. Male workers born in 1964 will derive about 17 percent of their retirement pension wealth from defined benefit plans, while those who were already retired in 2000 received about 44 percent of their retirement plan benefits from such plans. More and more retirees depend on 401(k) accounts or other defined contribution plans and their own savings for retirement income. Younger Baby Boomers and subsequent generations will get about three-quarters of their retirement income from sources that they could outlive, such as 401(k) plans.

Defined contribution plans, such as the 401(k), can be adequate when the stock markets are doing well, the accounts are invested primarily in stocks, employees are contributing the maximum amount possible, and employers make matching contributions to their employees' accounts. They also have the advantage of giving the employee freedom of choice. An employee who begins contributing to a 401(k) plan early in his working life and invests well could end up with far more wealth than through a defined benefit plan.

But stocks don't always do well. Few employees contribute the maximum amount for most of their careers or invest for long-term growth. In addition, the recession of 2001 caused employers to start reducing their matching contributions to 401(k) plans. Companies also increased the share of plan expenses that are borne by employees through direct deductions from their accounts. Some studies say these expenses are, on average, almost 3 percent of the account value.

Employers that do make matching contributions might do so only in company stock, not cash. Employees might be required to hold the company stock until a certain age or for a minimum time. That works out well when returns from the company's stock are as high or higher than the market indexes. But it became a big problem for employees of Enron, Kodak, Polaroid, Xerox, and a host of other companies. Shares of these companies declined substantially in short periods of time, and employees were unable to sell those stocks from their 401(k) accounts.

More Medical Care, Less Insurance

Health care is becoming a more costly responsibility for most retirees. Frequently, as one gets older, medical expenses increase. More treatment and care is required. Also, a host of new pharmaceuticals and medical procedures now treat a range of previously untreatable conditions. These drugs and procedures generally are expensive. Even when they are not expensive, they are more likely to be treatments rather than cures. A drug treatment needs to be taken regularly for life to keep the medical condition under control. On average, someone over age 64 has health care expenses three to five times those of a younger person.

The first generation of retirees had employer–paid health care that covered most medical expenses. Retirees paid only a small percentage of their health care costs. A majority of large-company retirees still are covered by employer–paid health care coverage. However, the percentage covered is declining rapidly. According to Hewitt Associates, in 1991, 88 percent of companies with 1,000 or more employees offered health benefits to future retirees under age 65. That percentage fell to 72 percent by 2000. Those offering health care coverage to retirees age 65 or older shrank from 80 percent in 1991 to 62 percent in 2000. This percentage will continue to decline.

Also, retirees who are covered by employer plans are having their benefits cut. Employers are increasing the share of premiums that retirees must pay, raising copayments and deductibles, reducing lifetime or annual health care maximum benefits, and switching from traditional indemnity plans to health management organizations. Polaroid, for example, filed for bankruptcy protection in 2001, and sent retirees a letter notifying them that their health benefits were terminated, effective immediately. Courts routinely support the right of employers to reduce retiree health care coverage, even after an employee is retired and dependent on the coverage.

These trends likely will continue. In 2002, a study by Watson Wyatt Worldwide found that 17 percent of large employers eliminated their liabilities for retiree health care by requiring retirees to pay all the premiums. About 20 percent of large employers eliminated retirement health care payments for newly-hired employees. Those firms that continued to offer health care coverage to retirees reduced the coverage by requiring retirees to pay a larger share of the costs, according to the study. Another study in 2002, conducted by the Agency for Healthcare Research and Quality in 1997, found that 21.6 percent of private firms offered health insurance to retirees under 65 while in 2000 only 12 percent of firms did.

In short, the image of the employer as provider or paternal figure is steadily fading away. Few employers will continue to bear the uncertainty of future medical expenses. Employees more and more often are expected to make plans to provide for the bulk of these expenses themselves. Employers are likely to continue to help by setting up tax-advantaged savings accounts and other programs the government makes available, but employees will bear most of the cost and the uncertainty over future medical expense inflation.

Medicare covers only a portion of the medical expenses of older Americans, a far smaller portion than many pre-retirees realize. The cost of

Medicare to participants rises each year. In addition, because Medicare reimbursements to medical providers were reduced in recent years, there are fewer health care options open to retirees. In the years from 1997–2003, Health Maintenance Organizations (HMOs) covering more than four million retirees withdrew from the Medicare program. A number of new health care options were created under a 1997 Medicare reform law. But few medical care providers are offering the programs, because they do not believe they will be profitable. Some good news is that legislative changes in 2003 might reverse this trend.

Everyone Is an Investor

A retiree's standard of living often depends heavily on the ability to save and invest. Investment options are more complicated than in the past, and the results are uncertain. Financial deregulation produced many benefits for Americans. They are no longer saddled with the fixed-interest-rate savings accounts of the 1970s and earlier. The many options available today can substantially increase an individual's wealth and enhance retirement.

However, the new options also can mean more risk. Investors must understand more about investments and the various investment markets. They must develop an investment strategy and know when to follow it and when the strategy should be changed or they risk losing money or earning subpar returns. The average American must learn how to allocate a portfolio among stocks, bonds, and other assets in order to achieve the right mix of return and risk.

Compounding the situation is the likelihood that investment returns are likely to be lower in the next 20 years than they were in the last two decades. A retiree or conservative investor normally invests for income. In the early 1980s, a conservative investment in money market funds could earn 12 percent or more annually. Safe U.S. Treasury bonds also carried double-digit yields. But the yields on income investments declined significantly during the next 20 years. In 2003, most money market funds carried yields of 1 percent or less. Treasury bonds paid an interest rate of 3 to 5 percent. That's a big drop in income. During the late 1990s, I routinely heard from new subscribers to my newsletter, *Retirement Watch*, who had this problem. They invested in certificates of deposit or Treasury bonds years earlier. As these investments matured, the readers faced the prospect of having to reinvest the proceeds at interest rates that were about half of what they were used to receiving. Investors who count on safe investments for their retirement income either have to save more than the retirees of 20 years ago or select investments that pay higher yields but are riskier.

Stock market investors also are likely to face lower returns in the future. Stocks earned historically high returns from 1982 through 2000. The returns far exceeded the rate of growth in corporate profits. That's because the economy shifted from a period of high inflation, high interest rates, and low economic growth to one of low inflation, low interest rates, and high economic growth. During that transition, investors were willing to pay more for each dollar of corporate earnings. As a result, the price-earnings ratio of the Standard & Poor's 500 Index went from about seven in the late 1970s to over 30 by the end of the bull market in 2000.

But once the transition period is over, investors aren't willing to continue paying higher valuations for stocks. More than likely, in coming years stock prices will increase at about the same rate as corporate profits or perhaps a lower rate. That means investors can expect average annual stock returns of 6 percent to 12 percent in the future. Some forecasters believe that to make up for the excess returns of the bull market, returns for the following 20 years should be well below average, perhaps a 5 percent average annual return or less.

The Tax Surprise

Taxes on older Americans are high. It used to be a given that a person's tax rate would decline in retirement. Now, older Americans are the wealthiest generation and soon will be the largest generation. That's too tempting a target for the tax writers to resist. Older Americans now pay some of the highest marginal tax rates imposed, and they also must deal with some of the more complicated provisions in the tax code. Nowadays it is not unusual for someone to pay a higher tax rate in retirement than during his or her working years.

For example, Social Security benefits originally were tax free. Now a recipient might include up to 85 percent of Social Security benefits in gross income. Retirement benefits are supposed to get tax breaks, but the rules are complicated and a few small mistakes could result in thousands of dollars in higher taxes. In addition, the tax code contains a number of stealth taxes, such as the alternative minimum tax and the reduction in itemized expenses. These hidden taxes are more likely to hit older Americans. There still are tax breaks and other ways for older Americans to avoid these traps, but it takes a lot of work to learn them.

Fading Trust Funds

Social Security and Medicare are not in the best financial shape. Medicare paid out more than it took in from 1992 to 1998 and is projected to do so again beginning in 2010. Social Security will begin doing so around 2014, depending on which estimates are used. At some point, these programs are estimated to simply run out of money.

As the U.S. population gets older, there will be fewer workers to continue funding the benefits promised to older Americans. There soon will be fewer than two workers for each retiree. Payments to seniors already take up about 40 percent of the federal budget. Retirees should not expect increased benefits from these programs and should plan on the possibility of reduced benefits. Already, the average retirement age is scheduled to rise over the years. Future retirees must save more in order to offset the anticipated reduced benefits.

As the Baby Boomers age, they should expect circumstances that are dramatically different from those of the first generation of retirees. The senior years will be dramatically longer and more vibrant. That's the good news. The bad news is that the Boomers will have to save and invest to bear more of the expenses of those extra years. The Boomers also are unlikely to realize the buoyant investment returns or receive the postretirement tax breaks of their parents and grandparents to help with that burden. It is easy to see why many who have studied the trends believe that few Baby Boomers will have a period they can call the "golden years."

The New Retirement Opportunity

By now, you probably see why some observers paint a gloomy picture of retirement in the coming years. Those who don't address the trends and their effects will have retirements filled with worry and anxiety. Yet there is no reason for the majority of people to experience a retirement that is less satisfying than was experienced by the first generation of retirees. Most of us should be able to create the retirement we desire.

Retirement is an opportunity. It is an opportunity to do things you never could find the time for. It is a chance to plan how to spend your next 50 years. But to take advantage of the retirement opportunity, you have to plan and prepare. Most of all, you need to know the new rules of retirement planning.

We stand at the threshold of a transformation. The population is aging, and that is going to force us to reinvent retirement. We have seen the beginnings of this new retirement, but the real changes are coming in the next few years.

You should be prepared to save more than past retirees did and to take investing more seriously. You might not receive as much help from Social Security, Medicare, and your former employers as prior retirees did.

"Retirees" might not even retire, at least not until well past age 65. Retirement might come gradually. First there might be a reduction in hours worked or in the difficulty of the work. This may be followed by a gradual reduction in work-related activities until full retirement.

To take advantage of the new retirement opportunity, you have to adapt to the changes. Study the new face of retirement, plan, and prepare. Some very simple steps are to work past age 65, invest a bit differently, save more, and plan for health care expenses.

In this book, I'm going to show you how to incorporate the Age Wave into your planning and teach you the New Rules of Retirement. You'll recognize the likely effects of the Baby Boomers. But you don't have to hunker down and expect the worst. Instead, you should be prepared but also flexible enough that you can make changes if the effects of the Age Wave are either better or worse than anticipated. In the face of this tide, you can create and maintain the retirement you desire.

In the coming chapters, we'll explore the financial concerns of retirees and pre-retirees and how they are affected by the trends I've identified. We'll look at how to estimate retirement spending and how much money you should accumulate for retirement. I'll explain the health care options and how to pay for long-term care. You'll learn how to invest before and during retirement. I'll show you how to plan an estate, cut taxes, and provide for loved ones. We'll cover these topics and much more. I'm not going to give you the obvious advice, such as start early, invest the maximum in a 401(k) account, and invest for the long term. Think of this book as your instruction manual for the new world of retirement.

You can have the retirement you desire, but you must act now to stay ahead of the dramatic, rapid changes that are taking place. Even those who already are retired will be affected and must act. The time you lose may be your own. Those who don't learn about and understand the shifting world of retirement will have retirement years filled with worry and anxiety. Those who understand the new rules of retirement will make decisions with confidence and be able to take advantage of all their retirement opportunities.

CHAPTER 1

The Wave Is Coming

I t is coming. You cannot stop it. Neither can the government. It will transform virtually every American's retirement and lifestyle. We already have seen changes in health care, housing, the cost of retirement, the financial markets, pension programs, and much more. Because of key, unstoppable trends that already are in place, in the coming years changes in these and other areas affecting retirement will continue and accelerate. Even those who already are retired have felt the effects of these trends and will feel them in the future.

The trends are not bear markets, recessions, terrorism, war, or any of the other headline grabbers. The effects of those events on retirement will turn out to be relatively small and short-term. I'm not talking about a technology revolution, either. There are larger, more powerful trends at work, trends that are much stronger than any that have tested retirement plans so far.

These trends collectively can be called the Wave. They also are called the Retirement Wave or the Age Wave. The Wave can be summed up as: the aging of the large Baby Boom generation, longer life spans, and fewer offspring. Together, they amount to an aging population that has tremendous effects on the economy, the financial markets, and society. See Chart 1.1.

Where Will the Wave Take Us?

There's no doubt that demographic changes have an effect on the economy and society. Accurately forecasting the exact changes, however, can be difficult. Those who study the effects of population changes don't agree on the consequences of the Age Wave. In addition, there never has been an

CHART 1.1 Live Births

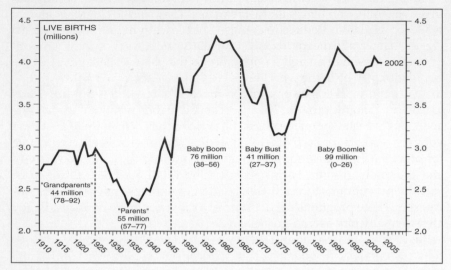

*Numbers in parentheses are the youngest and oldest ages of group members during 2002.
**Baby boomlet estimates for 2001 and 2002.
Source: National Center for Health Statistics. Reprinted with permission from Dr. Ed. Yardeni, *Consumer Handbook* (with Baby Boom Charts).

aging population of this size and scope. An additional complication is that retirement itself is a relatively new development. Forecasting the future of a new phenomenon would be difficult enough in itself. Mix in the effects of the Wave and the difficulty is greatly compounded.

Nevertheless, it is possible to sketch a general picture of the effects of an aging population on society and the economy. Certainly, there are many analysts who have put their forecasts on the record. Let's review the most prominent forecasts. Then, we'll consider what other events or trends should be considered before making a final prediction of the effects of the Age Wave.

Slower Economic Growth

An aging population usually means less robust economic growth. There are a host of reasons for this. One reason is that a higher percentage of the work force is past its peak productive years. With improvements in health care and lengthening life spans, we cannot be sure when the Boomers' productivity will peak. It is likely, however, that most Boomers will continue to work past their peak productive years. Because the Boomers will be a large portion of both the population and the work force, at some point productivity and economic growth are likely to fall as the Boomers age, unless there are offsetting factors.

Savings also are likely to decline as the Boomers age. This is because re-tirees generally don't increase their savings. They start to spend what they have accumulated. Reduced savings could lead to higher interest rates. Again, that usually means lower productivity and lower economic growth.

Another result of an aging population is that a lower percentage of the population will be in the work force. We will have fewer workers support-ing each non-worker. Fewer workers for each non-worker typically leads to slower economic growth. That is because a higher portion of the income and taxes of each worker supports the non-workers. When there are fewer younger workers for each older non-worker, there is less wealth available for other expenditures, some of which would lead to more productivity and economic growth. Social Security and Medicare are the two most prominent programs through which younger workers support older non-workers. These programs are not funded in advance by taxes. Instead, they are essentially pay as you go systems.

Taxes from those working during the Boomers' retirement years will fund payments to the Boomers. If there are fewer workers when payments to the Boomers are due, tax rates may have to be raised in order to foot the bill. Higher taxes cause lower fiscal efficiency and reduce economic growth.

Payments to the older non-workers possibly might be funded with debt instead of taxes. This increased debt would occur at a time when overall savings are likely to decline. A lower national savings rate coupled with higher debt could lead to higher interest rates or inflation—or both. The re-sult of either higher interest rates or inflation would be lower economic growth.

Whether taxes or debt (or a combination of the two) are used to fund the government payments to seniors, the transfer of economic resources from the working population to the large group of Boomer retirees is likely to re-sult in a decline in economic growth.

Higher Inflation

The United States has been blessed with declining inflation in the years since 1982. The dramatic decline in inflation began at a time when many were forecasting that high inflation was a permanent part of America's fu-ture. The disinflation also began when there were large federal budget deficits that many economists said precluded a decline in inflation. Those budget deficits eventually lessened, for at least a few years, but not until long after the disinflation took hold. See Chart 1.2.

There are several explanations for the decline in inflation. International monetary authorities became more educated about the dangers of inflation and how an increasing money supply leads to inflation. As a result, they became more vigilant about preventing inflation than they were prior to the 1970s. Also, the emergence of a truly global economy put a natural lid on prices as companies had to compete with goods and services from all

CHART 1.2 Age Wave and Inflation

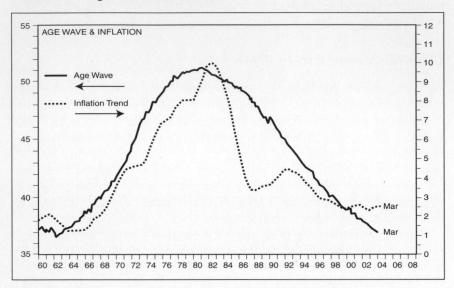

*Percent of labor force 16–34 years old.
**Five-year moving average of yearly percent change in CPI.
Source: U.S. Department of Labor, Bureau of Labor Statistics. Reprinted with permission from Dr. Ed. Yardeni, *Consumer Handbook* (with Baby Boom Charts).

over the world, not just from their own countries. Production in low-wage countries kept prices down worldwide. Technology, competition, and more efficient work methods also combined to increase productivity. This higher productivity allowed businesses to produce more goods and services at lower costs, which holds down prices and inflation.

Some analysts, however, point to demographics as a key to disinflation. They say that since World War II, there has been a close relationship between inflation and the percentage of younger employees. A low percentage of younger workers (those under age 34) is tied to lower inflation. But a high percentage of younger workers is associated with higher inflation. The theory is that younger workers are less productive, and lower productivity leads to higher inflation. As the Boomers entered their early adult years, inflation soared. As the Boomers matured, inflation declined. If the relationship holds, then as the Boomers retire and the work force again becomes younger, inflation should increase.

The tie between demographics and inflation could be coincidence. An alternate theory is that the age of the work force is similar to the age of the voting population. Older voters generally prefer low inflation and more conservative economic policies. Younger voters traditionally are less concerned with policies that keep inflation low. It could be that inflation rose and fell because of the demographics of the electorate.

The answer isn't clear. But it is possible that the aging of the retiree population and growing youth of the work force could lead to higher inflation in the coming decades.

Crumbling Real Estate Prices?

Owning a home has been the great American investment for decades. Housing prices exploded as the Baby Boomers entered their home-buying phase of life. The best financial advice for the early Boomers and their parents was: Buy the most expensive home you can afford and borrow all you can to finance it. People who followed that advice were rewarded throughout the 1960s and 1970s. The real estate boom paused in the late 1980s and early 1990s, then resumed. More recently, second homes and vacation homes joined the boom. Once again, that seems to be because of the Boomers. Many now have the money and time to enjoy second homes.

How will the next phase of the Boomers' life cycle affect real estate prices? The first generation of American retirees reached a point in life when many of them wanted less real estate to be responsible for and maintain. People get less active as they age, and some luxuries become burdens. Traditionally, as people age they sell large homes to move into smaller homes, condominiums, or some kind of senior housing coupled with medical assistance, such as assisted living or a nursing home. Many Boomers believe that a large portion of their retirement income will come from tapping their home equity through downsizing. They plan to sell their homes and use part of the equity to buy a smaller home and the rest to fund retirement.

The question many ask is "Who will buy the Boomers' homes?" If there are fewer people in the following generations, how could there possibly be enough buyers for the homes sold by the Boomers? Couple the smaller number of potential buyers with the possibility of higher taxes and lower economic growth, and the subsequent generations won't be able to pay the prices Boomers have come to expect for their homes.

Some economists have tried to forecast the effect of the Wave and the subsequent "Baby Bust" generation on home prices. In 1989 one study predicted that housing prices would begin falling by about 3 percent annually over the next 20 years. It predicted a real (after inflation) 47 percent decline in home prices by 2007. In 1993 a study sponsored by the National Institute on Aging reached similar conclusions. In that study, economist Daniel Mc-Fadden developed a model that identified 1980 as the peak for average U.S. home prices, adjusted for inflation. This model forecast that in 2020 home prices would be 19 percent below their 1995 levels, adjusted for inflation. By 2030 the decline should be 30 percent.

Others argue that even if there are enough younger people and immigrants to buy homes in the future, they will neither want nor be able to afford the homes the Boomers want to sell. Being older when they bought homes, the Boomers could afford large homes. In the 1990s, mini-mansions with two- and three-car garages were the home of choice in many suburban areas. Younger workers, possibly facing lower economic growth and higher tax rates, might not be able to afford such homes. With smaller families, they might not want the large homes.

A decline in housing prices could seriously undermine the financial health of the Boomers and the U.S. economy. Home equity is a major portion of the wealth of many Americans. For many older Americans, home equity is the only wealth they own or, at least, it is a substantial part of their net worth. For many people, home equity is a big part of their retirement plans. A number of those Boomers living in expensive urban areas plan to sell their homes at retirement and move into less expensive homes. They expect part of the sale proceeds to be available to help pay for retirement. Many others count on their home equity as an emergency reserve to be tapped in their later years or when needs arise. A home might be sold or mortgaged against to pay for nursing home care, for example.

If the aging Boomers sense that their homes won't be as valuable as anticipated, they are likely to reduce spending. That would reduce economic growth. The Boomers also might rush to sell their homes, hoping to salvage whatever value they can before the slide accelerates.

Home mortgages also are the largest part of the U.S. debt market. Major changes would be forced on the debt markets if demand for mortgages declines and people start prepaying mortgages in anticipation of housing price declines. Mortgage interest rates could drop dramatically. That would be good for those who want to borrow. But for older Americans who might use safe, interest-paying investments for their income, lower interest rates could be a disaster. If housing prices were to slide below the value of the outstanding debt, lenders would have to write off bad loans and take over ownership of homes for which there would be few buyers and steadily declining prices.

Homes and other real estate are an important part of the retirement nest eggs of many Americans. A decline in home prices or even a significant slowdown in appreciation could disrupt many financial plans.

The Great Financial Market Liquidation

The stock and bond markets in the United States began their greatest bull market in 1982. It continued through March 2000, with a few short interruptions along the way. The bull market coincided with the time that the Boomers became established in their homes and entered their peak earning years. Consequently, this is the time when one would expect this generation to increase its saving and investing.

It could be coincidence that stocks and bonds became attractive investments just at that time. Maybe the Boomers simply followed the markets and began investing heavily in stocks and bonds after those investments generated a few years of solid returns. Perhaps the Boomers would have invested heavily in real estate if inflation had remained a problem. Or it could be that the Boomers' life cycle caused them to buy more stocks and bonds during that period, and this flood of cash was a major cause of the bull market.

Whatever the cause of the bull market, what happens to stocks and bonds as the Boomers get older? In many instances, these investments were purchased to fund retirement. Presumably in retirement the investments will be sold to pay for living expenses. If so, over time the Boomers will be cashing in their investments. As with real estate, one has to wonder who will buy the Boomers' stocks. Further, the Boomers aren't the only ones in the markets. There are a number of employer-sponsored pension funds controlling trillions of dollars in stocks and bonds. As the work forces of these employers age, these funds will be taking in less money than they send out in benefits. That could mean they will sell stocks to make benefit payments.

Using demographic data, economists John Shoven and Sylvester Schieber prepared a forecast of stock market cash flows (Center for Economic Policy Research, Publication No. 363, September 1993). They found that cash should continue flowing into the markets until 2010. After that, they forecast that the markets will become stagnant. Finally, beginning in 2025 the value of America's pension plans should decline as they sell investments to pay benefits to the Boomers. The decline of pension fund values and stock market cash flow is estimated to accelerate through 2040.

If cash flow helps determine the prices of stocks, Boomers might need to revise their retirement plans. Most plans assume stocks will continue their historic average annual total return of 8 percent to 10 percent. Once cash flows into stocks flatten, stock prices also would stagnate. When big money begins to flow steadily out of pension funds, stock prices could steadily decline. The economists guess that stock prices could decline by 45 percent from this demographic effect. They point out that each generation at some point experiences a stock market decline of this extent, but government policies, rather than demographics, have been the culprit in the past.

Some forecasters think the decline due to the Boomers' cashing in could be worse. Their theory is that as the long-term price decline becomes apparent, many Boomers will sell quickly to avoid future price declines. They believe that eventually there will be an overwhelming rush to the exits rather than a steady decline in prices. In addition, the cash flow from demographics won't be the only problem weighing on the markets. If the other effects of the Wave also take hold, there would be serious economic problems in the United States and elsewhere, which also would spur investors to sell stocks.

Straining the Government

The demise of Social Security and Medicare has been forecast for some time. We are nearing the days of reckoning for these programs. Exact dates of their demise depend on the rates of economic growth and inflation. The stronger the economy, the more tax revenues that flow into these programs and the longer bankruptcy is delayed. Lower inflation reduces the growth of the benefits the programs pay each year, which also delays their demise. Most forecasts anticipate that Social Security will begin paying out more than it takes in around 2018. The program will run out of money around 2042. Medicare's collapse is forecast to occur much sooner. Its Hospital Insurance Trust Fund already is paying out more than it takes in. It might run out of money around 2019. You can get the latest official forecasts from the trustees of these two programs on their web sites at www.socialsecurity.gov and www.medicare.gov.

Social Security and Medicare might be only part of the problem. Much of the federal budget is allocated to older Americans. In 1965, according to the Congressional Budget Office, 16 percent of the budget was slated for the elderly. This rose to 24 percent by 1980 and 29 percent in 1990. By 2000, 35 percent of the budget was devoted to senior programs. Factor in Social Security benefits paid to retirees aged 62 to 64, plus pensions to civil service and military retirees, and 40 percent of the federal budget is going to senior Americans. The share of the budget allocated to programs for seniors will increase as the Boomers age. It will increase even more with the addition of new programs, such as prescription drug benefits for seniors.

If an older population leads to lower economic growth, then the government will have less tax revenue than is now forecast. That would leave the federal government with a choice to make: should it raise taxes on the younger generations, reduce benefits to older Americans, incur more debt, or reduce spending for all other parts of the budget (or some combination thereof)? Each of those actions could further reduce economic growth and tax revenue.

It is no wonder that there is a low level of confidence in Social Security. One survey found that more people under 30 believed in UFOs than believed they would collect anything from Social Security. Congress repeatedly has delayed addressing these problems. Ultimately changes will be made in both Social Security and Medicare. In the coming years, Americans can expect to see some reduction in Social Security and Medicare benefits. Most likely, the programs will be "means tested." Those seniors above a certain level of income will have their benefits reduced while those less well off will continue receiving benefits as promised. The eligibility age for these programs also might be raised. The extent of these changes will depend on how powerful the other possible effects of the Wave are— such as lower economic growth.

Nowhere to Hide?

In the 1970s when the U.S. economy was in sad shape, it was common for Americans to at least consider physically leaving the country for havens in other countries or shifting part of their assets overseas. There was a small but booming industry devoted to advising Americans how they could move some of their wealth out of the United States and invest in non-dollar-denominated assets. It seemed a prudent move. Other countries offered stronger currencies, lower inflation, more affordable lifestyles, and more stable societies. Some had lower tax rates. Japan's stock market was booming, while the U.S. market was stagnant. The interest in overseas havens decreased through the 1980s as the domestic financial picture improved. There was a brief uptick of interest in the early 1990s that was significant enough to cause Congress to pass a law that discouraged wealthy Americans from leaving the country for tax reasons.

But as a general rule, since the mid-1980s the U.S. has been the most financially desirable country in the world. Few want to leave, and many want to emigrate here. The dollar reigned as the world's strongest currency through 2002. Overseas, money consistently flowed into the U.S. financial markets through the 1980s and 1990s.

If the negative effects of the Wave are realized, Americans might once again consider seeking shelter overseas. Retirement in a foreign land might seem attractive. Even those who don't want to leave the country might consider placing some of their wealth outside the U.S. markets as they search for a way to avoid the steady declines in U.S. stocks and housing prices that some are forecasting.

Think again. If the U.S. has problems from an aging population, many developed foreign countries also will have severe problems. Japan probably is in the worst shape, with its population likely to age more rapidly than any other country's. Indeed, some analysts ascribe Japan's economic problems since 1989 to the fact that its Age Wave began then. They say that Japan is facing what the United States will experience beginning around 2010 to 2014. Most Western European countries also are aging faster than the United States.

Factors other than an aging population could well make the effects of the Wave worse in other developed countries. Together, they could contribute to economic disasters in those countries. Consider the following statistics:

- The other developed countries are aging faster than the United States. In addition to low birth rates, they have much lower immigration rates. While in the United States immigrants might help make up for a low birth rate, that is not likely to be the case in other developed countries. For example, by 2030, Italy will have three workers for every two retirees, under current forecasts. Other developed countries also will have much older populations than the United States.

- With the exceptions of Britain and Ireland, there is very little private sector retirement financing to provide a cushion for the coming retirees. In the European countries, retirement is paid for almost entirely by governments. For decades, the European system has been to impose high taxes on businesses and current workers in order to pay pensions to current retirees. In addition, there is virtually no advance funding of the government retirement programs in Europe. Workers are not expected or encouraged to set aside a portion of their income to help pay for their own retirement. One estimate reported in *Barron's* is that 84 percent of retirement benefits paid in the European Union are from unfunded government programs.

- Europe and Japan have been beset with stagnant economies and steadily shrinking tax bases for many years. As the Wave hits, unfunded government programs will need steady sources of increasing revenue. The revenue can come from a growing economy. Individuals and business making more money will pay more in taxes. A growing population and work force also could fund the programs. More people working means more people paying taxes.

  Unfortunately, those options don't appear to be available to much of the developed world. Heavily regulated economies are growing slowly, if at all. There seems to be no intention to deregulate the private sector or to privatize government-owned entities. Tax rates already are so high in most of the countries that additional taxes likely would further reduce economic growth and erode the tax base. Unemployment is generally high by U.S. standards. Government policy does little to encourage the unemployed to aggressively seek work and instead ensures that for an indefinite time the unemployed are well provided for.

- Retirement occurs earlier in much of Europe. In both Europe and Japan, early retirement is encouraged to make scarce jobs available for younger workers. A strong incentive for early retirement is a very generous pension at a relatively young age. Unlike in the United States, there aren't many financial penalties for taking early retirement. Japan's official retirement age is 55. In Germany, the average retirement age dropped below 60 in the 1990s. In France, 60 percent of the labor force aged 55 to 65 is not employed. Only recently have a few European governments realized that this situation is unsustainable. They have belatedly increased retirement ages and encouraged employees to invest in private pension plans.

Whatever problems the United States might face from the Wave, it is evident that you won't be able to escape them by seeking a haven in other developed countries.

You may, however, seek either a personal or financial haven in countries with younger populations and higher birth rates. Such countries are numerous in Latin America, Eastern Europe, the Middle East, and some parts of Asia. But you'll face trade-offs. These countries are less developed, and in many of them the pace of development is slow. Governments tend to be unstable, as do the investment markets and currencies. Many of these economies depend on the wealthier populations of the United States and Europe to buy their products. If the developed economies falter, these developing economies also most likely will suffer.

The Wave is not unique to this country. In fact, the United States is likely to experience some of the mildest consequences from the Wave of any of the developed nations. Possible exceptions are Britain and Canada.

Beware False Prophets

I keep a couple of books within easy reach on my shelves. One is *Facing Up* by Peter G. Peterson, Touchstone Books, published in 1993; the other is *Bankruptcy 1995* by Harry E. Figgie, Jr. with Gerald J. Swanson, Ph.D., Little Brown & Co., published in 1992. I keep the books handy, and I recommend them to you, not because I believe their arguments. Rather I refer to them, and call your attention to them, because they serve as reminders that long-term forecasts usually aren't terribly reliable. The factors that a forecaster identifies as the key trends might not influence the future nearly as much as expected. Other factors could intervene to alter the forecast. Or perhaps the correlation the researcher found between the factors and past trends was just a coincidence. There might not be a reason for the correlation to continue.

Each of these books argued that the United States was in sad financial shape in the early 1990s and the situation was about to get worse—much worse—very quickly. The key factor, according to the authors, was debt. High, relentlessly increasing debt was taking over the economy and government budgets. They were especially concerned about the federal budget deficit. The authors forecast severe consequences in just a few years if drastic steps, such as large tax increases and sharp spending reductions, were not taken quickly. Peterson subtitled his book *How to Rescue the Economy from Crushing Debt and Restore the American Dream*. On page 18 he summarized the "Reagan–Bush years" as follows:

> Our savings rate was going down, our capital investment was disappearing, our productivity was stagnant. To the degree we were achieving economic growth it was coming at the expense of the future—in the form of the most massively un-Republican bloating of government expenditures, deficits, and debt in American history.

Figgie and Swanson introduced us to the "hockey stick chart" or J-graph. This is a graph, usually of government debt, in which the debt level initially increases gradually much like the slightly-angled blade of a hockey stick. Then, compounding causes the line to shoot sharply upward, like the handle of the hockey stick. The authors' charts forecast that the federal budget deficit and debt levels would be rocketing up the handle by the late 1990s.

We know now that things turned out quite differently. At a minimum, the days of reckoning envisioned by these authors were delayed. Federal budget deficits rapidly turned into surpluses for a few years. The recession that began in 2001 and the stock market collapse of the early 2000s caused the federal budget to revert back to a deficit, which now is forecast to continue for at least 10 years. But, though the peak deficits will be higher in dollar terms than the previous record, they still are a lower percentage of the economy. In addition, a resumption of economic growth or some spending restraint or both would erase those deficits.

The federal budget deficit disappeared without any of the extreme actions recommended in these books. The growth rate of federal spending was restrained a bit. Thanks to technology, productivity in the private sector accelerated at record levels. Productivity, coupled with better management that was spurred by greater competition, allowed corporate profits to grow at record levels. Tax revenues, especially those for capital gains, soared beyond all projections. Policymakers quickly turned from how to handle "budget deficits as far as the eye could see" to dealing with unexpected surpluses. It now appears that some of the corporate profits and capital gains were the product of fraud and manipulation, but not enough to account for the bulk of the boom.

This doesn't mean the books were nonsense. Many of the facts reported in the books still are true. Health care spending by the federal government increases at a high rate, a rate that probably cannot be sustained indefinitely. Social Security still is likely to run out of money toward the middle of this century if changes are not made. Medicare probably will run out of money much sooner if experience matches current assumptions.

The point is that many variables make up the economy and the financial markets. Even when the trends that appear to be the fundamental forces remain the same, other factors could override them and make a forecast obsolete. Keep this experience in mind when considering how the Wave will affect your retirement. Readers who want additional examples of forecasts gone wrong should read *The Fortune Sellers* by William A. Sherden, John Wiley & Sons, 1997.

What Might Go Right

The worst consequences of the Age Wave simply might not occur, despite the amount of research and thought that has gone into the forecasts. Other factors could intervene to alter the effects of the Wave. Here are some possibilities:

- Technology could continue to improve productivity, allowing the economy to grow at a healthy rate despite an older population. Productivity grew at an unprecedented rate through the 1990s and even through and after the early 2000s recession, despite many forecasts that the productivity increases could last only a few years.
- Immigration could increase, bringing younger workers into the country and the workplace. The United States continues to be one of the most desirable countries in which to live. Many people from other countries clamor to enter the United States and participate in its economy. An increase in immigration easily could make up for the low birth rate of current Americans.
- The younger generations might save and invest more than prior generations. (That already seems to be the case.) This higher saving could offset the investment liquidation by Baby Boomers and pension funds.
- For a number of reasons, the older generations might not liquidate their stock portfolios as fast as some forecasters anticipate. If Baby Boomers work longer and accumulate larger nest eggs, they won't need to draw on their retirement plans until they are older. Investments might perform better than anticipated, which also might result in lower sales by the Boomers. There is reason to believe that many older people consider their portfolios primarily as an inheritance to be left to their children and grandchildren whenever possible.
- Older Americans probably will continue to work longer, at least on a part-time basis. That will keep tax revenue flowing into the general fund as well as into the Social Security and Medicare coffers of the federal budget. As mentioned previously, longer working lives also means that investment sales will take place later in life. It also is likely that older Baby Boomers will be more productive than were people of similar ages in prior generations as a result of better health care and better and more efficient use of technology. The decline in productivity that many forecasters anticipate may not occur, or might occur later than expected. (See the next chapter for details about Boomers extending their careers.)
- In response to forecasts of the worst consequences, Americans could change their spending, saving, and investing patterns in ways that avoid the big problems. Many forecasters assume that any anticipatory changes would make the situation worse, such as selling homes and stocks a few years before the huge price declines are anticipated. But Boomers might prepare for the Wave in ways that don't make things worse, hence, the purpose of this book.

Any one of the aforementioned preemptive measures could provide a significant, positive counter to the forecast consequences of the Wave. If the Boomers continue working beyond age 65, the effects would be dramatic. Government revenues, especially Social Security and Medicare taxes, would soar above current forecasts. The windfall would avoid or delay many of the worst effects of an older population. Portfolios would stay invested longer. The Boomers would retain their homes for years. They might even be active in the housing market. Those are just a few of the many possible outcomes.

The Wave already has affected your retirement and will affect it further —whatever your age. But don't structure your retirement around the worst-case forecasts. You and I don't know how all the possibilities will play out. It would be a mistake to bet on either the extremely optimistic or extremely pessimistic scenarios. Instead, plan on the most likely changes and also plan ways to protect yourself if things get worse. Also, look for opportunities to take advantage of better-than-expected developments. I'll show you how to implement these new rules for retirement in the chapters that follow.

Retirement Becomes a Process

Phillip L. Carret, who founded the Pioneer Mutual Fund in 1928, commuted from his home in Scarsdale, New York, to the Manhattan offices of Carret & Co. until his death in 1998 at age 101.

In Lakewood, Ohio, at the Bonnie Bell production plant, a seniors only department with an average age of 70 is on duty for each shift. In 2000, the *Wall Street Journal* profiled this crew of septuagenarians known as The Gray Team.

A 102-year-old doctor spends 40 hours each week editing a medical journal in Philadelphia while a 90-year-old doctor still makes rounds and performs surgery in Augusta, Georgia.

While serving on the Board of Trustees of my local government's employee pension fund, I see notices of employees retiring well into their 70s.

These cases no longer are unusual. More and more workplaces employ people who are past the "normal" retirement age of 65, and more people are interested in working past 65. In the years to come, the number of older workers will increase. This is a major change. For many years, the percentage of older Americans participating in the labor force steadily declined. The decline was most striking among men, because at the start of their careers most expected to be working until 65 or later. The "retire by 65" pitch was so effective that by 1985 only 30 percent of men over age 65 were in the labor force. But since the mid-1990s the participation rate of those who are age 65 and older has increased. Labor force participation by older Americans is at the highest rate since 1979. See Chart 2.1.

The Baby Boomers indicate they intend to continue this trend of staying in the workplace. A widely reported survey by Roper Starch for the AARP in 1999 found that 80 percent of Boomers planned to continue working ei-

CHART 2.1   Age Composition of Labor Force

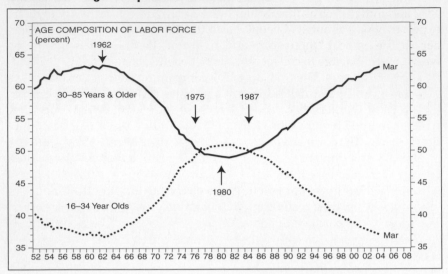

*Oldest and youngest Baby Boomers turned 16 in 1962 and 1980, respectively.
Source: U.S. Department of Labor, Bureau of Labor Statistics. Reprinted with permission from Dr. Ed. Yardeni, *Consumer Handbook* (with Baby Boom Charts).

ther full- or part-time after 65. An update of that survey in 2003 found that 45 percent of those over 50 said they plan to keep working into their 70s, and 27 percent expected to work up to 80. Another 18 percent of Boomers plan to work past 80. The Employee Benefits Research Institute's *2004 Retirement Confidence Survey* found that 68 percent of respondents expect to be earning money in retirement. That was higher than in past EBRI surveys. The U.S. Census Bureau expects the number of people in the work force over 65 to double over the next 30 years.

We should expect the Boomers to delay retirement. They delayed work, marriage, childbirth, and growing up in general. They have attempted to delay aging itself through exercise, diet, and a host of medical practices. Delaying retirement is the next logical step.

Why 65?

The concept of retiring at age 65 and not working again is obsolete for most people—and it should be. The now-classic concept of the carefree retirement beginning at age 65 worked well for the first real generation of American retirees. But it was an artificial concept and in the future won't serve many people well. More Americans realize there is no reason to stop being creative or productive at age 65, and there are many reasons to stay in the work force after 65.

Chancellor Otto von Bismarck of Germany created what probably was the first universal, government-provided retirement payments around 1890 and initiated 65 as the normal retirement age—when the average life expectancy was about 46. Legend has it that Bismarck first hit upon using age 70, the biblical "three score and 10 years." Because virtually no one would reach that age to collect retirement benefits, he reduced the eligibility age by five years. The first large U.S. companies to adopt pension plans took age 65 as the normal retirement age, apparently following Bismarck. But very few workers were covered by these early plans. Most Americans weren't covered by any retirement plan and didn't face a mandatory retirement age. They worked as long as they were physically able.

The U.S. government endorsed 65 as the official retirement age when it created Social Security. Even so, in 1950, 72 percent of 65-year-old men still were in the labor force. But when Americans began to adopt the idea of not working for life, they really took to the notion of retiring at 65 or earlier. The labor force participation rate of older Americans began to slide as Americans began to retire earlier and earlier. More and more workers were covered by pensions that paid fixed benefits for life, and Social Security benefits increased. Only 30 percent of 65-year-old men were in the labor force by 1985. Many companies imposed mandatory retirement ages, which weren't made illegal until 1986.

But the trend of earlier retirement now seems to have reversed. There are a number of reasons why Americans have been working past age 65 and plan to continue doing so in the coming decades:

- Age 65 is no longer old. The early post–World War II retirees lived only a few years after retiring. Not many lived more than five years after retiring. Given today's longer life spans, an equivalent retirement age is around 79. Americans not only are living longer, they are healthier as they age. For example, in the past decade the population of those over 65 increased by three million, but the number of disabled people over 65 dropped by 100,000. Many experts on aging believe that most people in their sixties still are at or near their peak productive powers. People recognize this change. One survey found that almost half of those aged 65 to 69 consider themselves to be middle-aged. Even a third of those in their seventies label themselves middle-aged.
- Mandatory retirement laws have been lifted. Americans cannot be denied jobs solely because they are too old, and they cannot be forced to leave a job because of age. There are exceptions for some professions and positions, but in general the labor market is open to older Americans.
- Social Security's normal retirement age is rising. A commission in the 1980s determined that Social Security would run out of money if changes were not made. One of those changes was to increase the normal retirement age from 65 to 67. The increase is being phased in. Full Social Security benefits don't kick in for those born from 1943 to 1954

until age 66. The minimum age for normal benefits is 67 for those born in 1960 and later. (For details, see Chapter 4.)

Social Security retirement benefits cannot be received before age 62. Those who begin receiving benefits between age 62 and normal retirement age receive a reduced benefit. For those born by 1936, the reduced benefit at 62 is 80 percent of the full benefit. But that will be scaled down to 70 percent for those born later, providing another incentive to work longer. Those who delay receiving benefits until after normal retirement age get an increased benefit. This increase for delaying benefits also will rise, creating even more of an incentive to delay receiving Social Security benefits. (See Chapter 4.)

The Benefits of Work

Changes in Social Security's normal retirement age undoubtedly have affected the age at which people consider retiring and will affect it more powerfully in the future. There are other factors, however, that also are causing people to choose to work longer.

- Work is more than a way to earn money for a number of people. That's why, according to at least one study, about one third of men who retired returned to work at some point. Most of them returned to work within the first year of retirement. Two-thirds of those returning to work took full-time jobs.

  Interviews with older workers reveal that having a job is a reason to get up in the morning and get dressed. Otherwise, some people fear they might remain in bed most of the day. Work puts structure in their lives. They don't know how they would fill up their days without the structure that a job imposes.

  Work also can create status and a sense of purpose. It is difficult to work every day from age 21 to 65 and then suddenly stop. Some people achieve a status or sense of purpose outside of work. They have hobbies, or belong to organizations, or they plan to take on new activities after retiring. They might go to school, get serious about a hobby, take care of grandchildren, or enjoy extensive travel. But many people don't develop those activities during their working years and don't have a plan before retirement to begin such activities. Most of their friends are at work. Work is not only what they do but, to some extent, it is what they are. Work can measure a person's progress: At the end of a workday, one can list what was accomplished.

  Going to work keeps people from becoming isolated. Interaction with a variety of other employees is important to one's physical and mental health. Work is a prime place to get that contact and interaction. At work, one usually is a member of a team. Someone leaving this environment for retirement could feel isolated and alone. The group interaction benefits of work are especially important to those who no longer have spouses and whose children are grown or have moved to other areas of the country. At the Bonnie Belle plant, most of The Gray Team no longer have spouses.

These nonmonetary benefits of work will continue for people who retire from one job to take another one.

- Recent medical research on aging, as well as anecdotal evidence from lives of the very old, reveal some keys to living a longer, healthier life. One of those keys is to stay mentally active. One should stay engaged in a number of activities, learn new things, and socialize. Many people find they are best able to do these things as part of the work force.

- Work ensures that income keeps flowing. It reduces the probability of outliving one's assets and sliding into poverty or dependence on family. Outliving their assets is one of the prime fears of older Americans. A simple estimate of the cost of retirement demonstrates why more people plan to work as long as they can. Suppose Max Profits plans to spend $40,000 annually in retirement. An investment fund of $800,000 is needed if Max plans to earn 5 percent interest and doesn't want to touch the investment principal. If Max is willing to dip into principal, will still earn 5 percent, and expects to live 30 years, then he needs a fund of about $615,000.

Of course, neither of these simple calculations allows for annual increases in income to keep up with inflation. For that, Max will need even more money. This simple calculation also doesn't include the possibility of extraordinary expenses, such as long-term health care, or leave a cushion in case Max earns less than the planned 5 percent.

Numerous studies indicate that the Baby Boomers have not saved enough for the retirement they expect. I won't rehash those gloomy reports here. In addition, this generation of retirees won't have the guaranteed pensions of their predecessors, and the financial health of both Social Security and Medicare is dubious.

Combine those factors with the increasing life expectancy of the Boomers, and it is easy to understand the reluctance to give up the opportunity to earn a paycheck. In the AARP survey, 23 percent stated that they plan to work in retirement because they will need the income. The survey might understate the true picture. It is likely that many pre-retirees aren't being honest with themselves, or at least with the survey takers. Another survey found that the amount of money saved will determine the Baby Boomers' retirement dates more than age will. That survey by the National Council on the Aging found that 69 percent of pre-retirees will place the primary emphasis on their finances rather than age in determining when to retire.

- Work might be too attractive to walk away from. As the 1990s closed and the 2000s began, many employers and industries became concerned about the number of experienced Baby Boomers scheduled to retire over the next decade or so. They worried about having enough skilled, experienced workers to fill their needs. If the Baby Boomers retire on schedule, this labor shortage will become acute. Some employers began adjusting work schedules and compensation to make it attractive for valued older workers to stay. The Baby Boomers might find this practice more common in the coming years. It costs a lot of money to search for, hire, and train new employees. If there is a labor shortage, those new employees are likely to leave for more attractive offers before the employer has recouped the initial costs. Employers know the cost of turnover and are likely to increase efforts to retain experienced current employees, regardless of age.

■ Work doesn't have to be for money. Volunteer work can provide structure, interaction, and a meaningful purpose to each day. Older Americans who do not have financial worries might very well volunteer their time or work for relatively low pay for nonprofit organizations.

Phased Retirement Is Here

For these and probably other reasons, the Baby Boomers will retire later than the preceding generation. Many probably won't retire at all, at least not before their health requires it. We still use the word retirement to describe that phase of life that begins sometime after age 60. Yet, retirement in the future will be different. Leaving a long-time employer and settling down to a few years of travel, relaxation, or just sitting around won't be the retirement game plan for many Baby Boomers.

Here is a more typical "retirement." A Baby Boomer in his or her late fifties or sixties will leave an employer after working for that employer for 10 years or more. That employer will be one of four or five during the Boomer's career. The next six months to one year will consist of relaxing and enjoying life. The Boomer might travel, take up a long-planned hobby, or just spend more time on the activities that used to occupy only weekends and vacations. Then the Boomer will search for a more meaningful use for some of his or her time.

The next phase of life might consist of full-time work in the same occupation the Boomer previously had or in a related field. But it is just as likely to be something completely different. In most cases, it will be a lower-paid position with fewer responsibilities and fewer hours. This job will continue for a few years. Then, the Boomer might shift to another position after deciding the current position is no longer fun or interesting. The Boomer might move on to another completely unrelated position that involves learning something new. Over time, the Boomer might ratchet down to part-time work, perhaps even minimum wage work, just to stay active and earn a little extra money. Eventually, the Boomer might stop working altogether or decide to spend the time on volunteer activities for a charity or his community.

That is just one scenario. There will be many others. An executive who loves golfing might take a job at his local clubhouse. Another executive might become a consultant, or take a job with a smaller business that needs an experienced hand, or even take a much lower-paying job to help run a charitable organization. Some hope to work at the same jobs for the same companies while working fewer hours. Those who study retirement refer to all these possibilities as bridge jobs.

Many Baby Boomers say that they plan to start businesses in retirement. One might start a small, part-time business that is not much more than an attempt to make money at a hobby. Another might have the ambition to build an operation with dozens or hundreds of employees. As stated earlier in this book, there are likely to be as many retirements as there are retirees.

Retirement, or at least the first retirement, might not occur when expected or at the retiree's discretion. More and more often, people are retiring because of decisions by their employers. An employer might eliminate part of its business or sell it to a firm that doesn't need all the current employees. An economic downturn may cause an employer to eliminate a number of positions. The elimination might be done via offers of early retirement packages or through layoffs. An illness or injury also might force a Baby Boomer out of the work force or prompt a decision that it is time for a change of pace.

The point is that there won't be a definite line between work and retirement, and there won't be a standard retirement age. People are more likely to retire in phases or stages. For some, at least one of the stages of retirement will be imposed on them by an employer or a health issue, rather than by choice.

We still don't have a name for this new time of life. Some use third age or third-stage adulthood. Others divide retirement itself into stages and say we should identify retirees by the stage they are in. (Some say there are two stages to retirement, others say three.) The National Endowment for Financial Education has suggested alternative terms instead of retirement, such as independence planning, freedom of choice, or downshifting. Redirection is another suggested term, as are my time, regeneration, aging opportunity, and the opportunity years. Some call it a second adolescence.

I don't find any of the terms entirely satisfactory. I think downshifting comes close to what many Baby Boomers envision for what used to be called the retirement years, and aging opportunity or the opportunity years express the potential of the new retirement. I suspect, though, that many Boomers also will do something different after age 65 but at the same pace as before, at least for a number of years. Perhaps redirection will best describe their activities. Some, of course, will seek the traditional retirement and stick with it.

Perhaps we'll derive names for the different phases or types of retirement and be able to identify a person's stage of life that way. Another description I like is the freedom years. While many older Boomers will believe they still have to work, they are likely to work at something they find enjoyable and at hours they find comfortable. Others will have the freedom to work or not to work. Current estimates are that about one third of Boomers won't have the financial freedom to avoid work or be selective about the work they take while the others will have some ability to be selective. For now, lacking a consensus or fully descriptive substitute, I'll continue to use the word retirement.

The New Retirement and You

You can choose whichever retirement you desire, if you start planning early enough. If you have the means and it is to your liking, you can opt for the traditional retirement of living off your investments and whatever other sources of income you have while filling your time with leisure activities. Or you can opt for the many other possibilities—or a combination of them.

Regardless of the retirement you choose, you need to know that many Baby Boomers will not participate in the traditional retirement. You need to track what the Boomers do, because it will affect the economy, the markets, and your retirement. The effects of the Wave have to be incorporated into retirement planning. Keep in mind, though, that those effects might not be what some people expect.

In the last chapter, we reviewed the dire forecasts that many say will be the consequences of an aging population and the retirement of the Boomers. We also reviewed reasons why events might not unfold according to these forecasts. The Boomers already are behaving contrary to some of the assumptions in these forecasts, and I anticipate that they will continue to chart a course that is different from that of prior generations. Recall, too, that other factors, such as immigration, also could intervene to alter the forecasts.

The aging Baby Boomers already have changed retirement, and they will change it more as the years roll on. But the changes needn't be dire, and there is no reason to panic. Keep in mind that retirement is a relatively new development. As recently as the turn of the twentieth century, few Americans lived past age 50. Only the very wealthy actually retired. We all are learning new things about retirement every day. You need to plan for retirement, and that plan needs to include the possible effects of the Wave on the many aspects of your retirement. But keep your plan flexible, and remember that the most extreme possible effects of an event rarely happen. Instead, count on change. All retirement plans are educated guesswork, as are the forecasts about the effects of the Wave. Your plan will require constant adjustments as we learn more and circumstances change. Even after you are retired, the plan will have to be modified to keep up with changes, so don't view yourself as being locked in to an inflexible retirement plan.

Now let's get to work. We know that the rules of retirement have changed and will continue to do so. We know that the Wave is going to affect many facets of your retirement. Let's look in detail at the key parts of retirement finances and the decisions that should be made now in order to enhance the retirement years.

3

How Much Will You Need?

We didn't realize how much everything would cost, that's the mistake we made."

I was talking to a woman who from all outward appearances was half of a very content, comfortably retired couple. They owned a large lakefront house (with an indoor swimming pool) in a secured golf course community in central Virginia. They also owned a condo in Florida where they spent winters near their grandchildren.

They were not hurting for money, but after about five years of retirement, this couple became concerned that they had underestimated the cost of retirement. They were worried that if changes weren't made they might outlive their income and assets. Not wanting to reduce their spending yet, he did some consulting, and she found part-time work as well.

Not having enough retirement income and outliving their assets are perhaps the biggest fears of most Americans who are in or near retirement. Even wealthy Americans worry that inflation will erode their standard of living during retirement, according to surveys. When I discuss retirement with people, the initial question is almost always "how should I determine the amount of money that I will need to live in retirement?" I've met multi-millionaires who were genuinely concerned that they wouldn't be able to maintain their preferred lifestyles after retiring.

Pre-retirees are becoming more aware that their money may need to last decades. Recent surveys show that after the bear market of 2000 through 2002, people are postponing retirement. More people are basing their retirement dates not on their ages but on the size of their portfolios. It is difficult to make retirement plans, even something as simple as setting a retirement date, without estimating the cost of retirement and how long financial assets are likely to last.

Unfortunately, this is an area in which retirees and pre-retirees receive poor advice or, quite often, no advice. Most of the advice on how much to save for retirement is nothing more than very simple rules of thumb. Part of the reason for the simple, general rules is that we don't have much experience with extended retirements.

Longer retirements and greater self-reliance mean that we must dispense with rules of thumb and devise a more accurate estimate of retirement spending and capital needs. Ask retirees what their biggest retirement planning mistake was, and a high percentage will say that they didn't do a good enough job of estimating retirement spending. Ask financial professionals, and they'll say that most people don't have a good handle on how much the retirement they desire will cost. Another reason to estimate retirement spending is that surveys show that people who estimate their expenses and capital needs, even if they make poor estimates, save more and are better prepared for retirement than those who do not make estimates.

There is not one right way to estimate retirement capital needs, but a good method of estimating should include several steps. First, estimate your spending for the first year of retirement (or the current year for those who are already retired). Second, subtract non-investment sources of income, such as Social Security. Third, estimate the average annual return on investments. Finally, use these numbers to estimate the amount of money that will be needed to meet future spending needs.

In this chapter I will show different ways to estimate the amount of money that should be accumulated for retirement. We will begin with a simple approach I call the quick-and-dirty method. This approach is for those who are young or who want a fast ballpark estimate as a general guideline. I'll explain, however, why it is not a great way to estimate needs for those approaching retirement. Then I'll show some better ways to estimate retirement spending needs.

Underestimating Your Needs

Here is a frequently-touted method for estimating how much money must be accumulated for retirement. Suppose our friend Max Profits expects to spend $40,000 annually in the first year of retirement, but this time he expects a total annual return of 7 percent on his investments. He'll need a $571,429 portfolio in order to draw off $40,000 annually in income ($40,000 divided by .07). That's a simple calculation that produces a retirement savings goal in a few minutes. It gives, however, a very incomplete answer. Someone less than five years away from retirement (and preferably within 10 years) needs a more accurate estimate.

One factor not considered in this estimate is inflation. The cost of living is likely to rise each year, and Max needs to factor this into his plan. After estimating the cost in today's dollars for the first year of retirement, Max should estimate the average annual inflation rate expected between now and the first year of retirement. Then he can look at Table 3.1 to determine how much the desired lifestyle will cost in the first year of retirement. For example, if Max will retire in 10 years and expects inflation to average 3 percent, he should multiply the first year's spending determined in today's dollars by 1.3. This will give Max the future cost of the first year of

TABLE 3.1   Dollars Needed to Retain Purchasing Power

Years	3%	4%	5%
		Inflation Rate	
1	1.0	1.0	1.1
2	1.1	1.1	1.1
3	1.1	1.1	1.2
4	1.1	1.2	1.2
5	1.2	1.2	1.3
6	1.2	1.3	1.3
7	1.2	1.3	1.4
8	1.3	1.4	1.5
9	1.3	1.4	1.6
10	1.3	1.5	1.6
11	1.4	1.5	1.7
12	1.4	1.6	1.8
13	1.5	1.7	1.9
14	1.5	1.7	2.0
15	1.6	1.8	2.1
16	1.6	1.9	2.2
17	1.7	1.9	2.3
18	1.7	2.0	2.4
19	1.8	2.1	2.5
20	1.8	2.2	2.7
21	1.9	2.3	2.8
22	1.9	2.4	2.9
23	2.0	2.5	3.1
24	2.0	2.6	3.1
25	2.1	2.7	3.4
26	2.2	2.8	3.6
27	2.2	2.9	3.7
28	2.3	3.0	3.9
29	2.4	3.1	4.1
30	2.4	3.2	4.3

retirement. Max can divide that amount by the expected investment return to estimate the size of the portfolio he'll need.

That is a much better estimate. However, there still is at least one more step that needs to be taken to get a reasonable estimate of retirement spending and capital needs.

Inflation is likely to continue during retirement. If Max's first year retirement spending is $40,000 and inflation continues, Max will need to spend more than $40,000 in each subsequent year to maintain that standard of living. That means Max must reinvest a portion of the investment return each year to ensure that the portfolio and its income will maintain their purchasing power. If Max expects 3 percent annual inflation, then he needs to reinvest three percentage points of the annual investment return. Max can spend only 4 percent of that 7 percent annual return. That brings the annual spendable income from the portfolio down to only $22,857. To meet his goals, Max needs to either increase the investment return to 10 percent or increase the retirement fund to $1,000,000. If Max's investments will earn less than 7 percent, he will need an even bigger nest egg.

Even after that step, there still are key elements missing from the estimate. The method assumes Max receives nothing from Social Security. Although Social Security has its problems and changes are likely to be made, Max is still likely to get $10,000 or more annually from Social Security, perhaps more, for many years. Factor in Social Security and Max will need to save less than this simple method indicates. Max also should be sure not to overlook any other income sources.

The quick-and-dirty method also assumes the investment principal never is touched. Most retirees don't want to dip into non-interest capital in the early years of retirement. But there's no reason to assume that the principal won't be touched in the later years. The only time to assume that none of the principal will be spent in retirement is when a primary goal is to pass the entire principal intact to a spouse, the next generation, or to charity. Otherwise, the quick-and-dirty method sets the savings goal too high. Trying to meet that goal might cause unnecessary deprivation in the preretirement years and into retirement. It also can cause constant worry about how long the money will last. Thus, the quick-and-dirty method should be viewed as a high estimate of the amount that should be saved to meet retirement needs.

The Most Important Step

A good estimate of retirement capital requirements begins with an estimate of monthly or annual spending in the first year in retirement. After that, the length of retirement must be estimated. Then the spending estimate should be adjusted for inflation over the length of retirement. Finally, an estimated investment return is used to estimate how much money should be accumulated at the start of retirement.

These are the essential steps to any estimate of retirement income needs. There are different ways, however, to execute these steps. We'll review some of the different ways throughout the rest of this chapter. Someone with the time and inclination can use all the methods and see how they yield different results. There is no right or wrong method, though each method has advantages and disadvantages, and they will give different answers. Select the method that best suits your resources and needs.

Whichever method is used, the critical first step in each method is the estimate of retirement spending. This estimate needs to be as complete and accurate as possible. Each subsequent step of whichever method is used builds on this estimate. A poor estimate here will be compounded into a big error as the rest of the calculations are made.

Unfortunately, much of the standard advice about estimating retirement spending leads people astray. Because of the inaccuracies, many people will establish a savings goal that is significantly either more or less than actually will be needed. A goal that is too high means over-saving and deprivation during the working years. It also causes worry about meeting an unrealistic goal. If the goal is less than the actual needs, the result is obvious. There won't be enough money to finance the desired lifestyle throughout retirement.

It is critical to begin the retirement plan with a solid estimate of your retirement spending. Let's discuss how to do that.

The Classic Advice

Those who have been exposed to any retirement planning advice have heard the classic and most common formula: Assume that retirement spending will be a percentage that is something less than 100 percent of preretirement income. The percentage recommended usually is 65 percent to 85 percent. I've reviewed a sheaf of retirement planning guides from financial services firms, and it is a rare guide that doesn't pick a number within this range.

The advice is quick, easy, and has a reasonable theory behind it. The theory is that not as much money will be spent in retirement as was spent during the working years. In retirement there won't be Social Security taxes or commuting expenses. There also isn't likely to be the need for as many new suits or other work clothes. Of course, 401(k) contributions won't be made. Perhaps lunches will be eaten at restaurants less often. Other expenses also might decline or disappear.

Unfortunately, this simple rule looks at only part of the picture. Upon examination, the simple rule not only is confusing but also is wrong for many people.

The first question many people have, of course, is which percentage of preretirement income should be used? Is it 65 percent? 70 percent? 80 percent? Or is it something else? How is the correct percentage selected? How does one tell if the average is not the right percentage to use? Most guides either don't give advice on how to select the right percentage of preretirement income to use or, if they recommend a specific percentage, explain how it was determined.

Some research sheds further light on this issue. Since 1988, Georgia State University, in a project funded by Aon Consulting, has used government data and other sources to determine the percentage of preretirement income that people actually spend in retirement to maintain their standard of living. This percentage is known as the replacement ratio. The study adjusts preretirement income for postretirement changes such as taxes on wages and income, savings, and expenditures related to age and work.

The Aon/Georgia State study regularly finds that the replacement ratio depends on income. The higher one's preretirement income, the higher will be the replacement ratio that is needed in retirement. For example, on average, a couple with preretirement income of $150,000 will need about 85 percent of that income in retirement. A couple with $50,000 in preretirement income will need only 74 percent of that income in retirement. The replacement ratio, however, rises again for lower-incomes. A couple with $30,000 of preretirement income, for example, needs 78 percent of that income in retirement.

The study also found that the cost of retirement rose during the 1990s. At all income levels from 1997 to 2001, the percentage of preretirement income that was needed in retirement rose. The full study is available on the Aon web site at www.aon.com. Enter "retirement" in the search function. In the results, look for the article "Benchmarking Retirement Income Needs."

This study gives a benchmark to consider in retirement planning. It can be especially helpful to those who want to use the quick-and-dirty method to get a fast estimate of retirement needs. Keep in mind, however, that the study gives only benchmarks. They are extrapolated from government data and some generalizations are made about how spending changes in retirement. This information might not be accurate for a particular individual.

The benchmarks from the study or the usual general rule can be helpful for the government or for employers trying to set the level of retirement benefits. Individuals should be wary of using these numbers in their own retirement planning without further analysis. Each person's retirement spending is unique. In fact, many retirees find that, contrary to the traditional assumption, their expenses don't decline in retirement, at least not in the first years of retirement.

It's true that certain expenses will be eliminated after retirement, but other expenses might take their place. After retirement, the time that used to be spent working has to be filled. It might be filled with no-cost activities such as watching television, playing cards, walking, visiting nearby friends, or sitting in the park. It also might be filled with hobbies or activities that cost money. These include golf, travel, eating out more often, or going to more movies and shows. The retiree might become a volunteer, which might require employment-type expenses such as commuting, lunches, and clothing. Another popular retirement activity is spoiling the grandchildren.

In addition, medical expenses are likely to consume a bigger percentage of income as the years roll on. With parents living longer and children needing more financial help, more retirees end up helping both parents and children at the same time. For many retirees, living expenses are the same or even higher in retirement than during their working years.

Another reason not to use the classic general rule is that the replacement ratios change over time. The Aon study found that the replacement ratio at each income level was higher for those who retired in 2001 than for those who retired in 1997. Perhaps after the economic expansion of the 1990s, new retirees had more money than their predecessors did, so they spent it. Or maybe the cost of retirement rose. Whatever the reason, someone who planned retirement using the replacement ratios from the 1997 study wouldn't have planned for the right level of retirement spending by 2001.

The point is that numbers from the studies and those given in traditional retirement advice are just averages and estimates. Spending by individual retiree varies.

Your Starting Point

The real question is: How much are you likely to spend in retirement? I recommend throwing out the general rules. Don't use a rule of thumb about replacement ratios. Don't look at annual retirement spending as a lump sum. Instead, draw up a budget for the lifestyle you want. Get a detailed list of possible monthly expenses and decide how much money is likely to be spent on each item in today's dollars. How much do you want to travel? Play golf? Give to the grandchildren? Dine in restaurants? These are all retirement expenses that are likely to be higher than before retirement. Don't forget to include taxes—all kinds of taxes. One of the myths about retirement is that tax rates will decline. That is rarely the case these days, as we'll discover in Chapter 10.

Health care is a wild card in any retirement budget. The average retiree spends anywhere from $2,500 to $6,000 annually on out-of-pocket medical expenses, depending on whose estimates are used. The estimates include all costs, such as Medicare and insurance premiums, deductibles, copayments, and non-covered expenses. But it is just an average. A particular retiree might spend more or less, depending on health, family history, and insurance coverage. The amount also is likely to increase above the average as the retiree ages. Study the medical expense coverage options carefully before estimating retirement expenditures.

Don't overlook infrequent expenses. These include home maintenance and improvements, appliance replacement, automobiles, travel, and help for family members. For these expenses, divide the estimated annual spending by 12 and put a monthly amount in the budget. This is what accountants call a sinking fund. Suppose you plan to buy a new car every four years at a cost of $30,000. At 3 percent inflation, the cost after the first four years is about $34,000. You could set aside $708 per month in the budget to ensure having accumulated $34,000 after four years. A more sophisticated approach is to assume some interest will be earned on the sinking fund. At 3 percent annual interest, the monthly amount to set aside would be about $668.

For each expense item, list its cost today. At this point, don't try to determine what the cost will be at retirement. Once all the amounts are determined, add them to get monthly and annual estimates of the cost of the first year of retirement.

All these factors need to be considered to develop a solid estimate of the cost of the first year of retirement. It is more work than the traditional and simple methods, but the consequences of using the wrong estimate make the additional steps worthwhile. An alternative to doing the calculations by hand is to use some of the computer software or online calculators discussed later in this chapter. The technology will automatically account for the irregular expenses that occur only every few years, so you won't have to factor them into the monthly or annual budget.

How Much Will You Need?

At this point we have the most important data in retirement planning, a solid estimate of the real retirement spending for the first year of retirement in today's dollars. As we've seen already, there are several ways this data can be used to make a reasonable estimate of retirement capital needs. We'll learn additional methods of completing the retirement plan in the rest of this chapter. In addition, we'll learn how to customize or modify the information to make even more reliable estimates of retirement needs.

The retirement spending estimate can be taken back to the beginning of this chapter and applied to the quick-and-dirty method of retirement planning. However, there are more sophisticated ways the data can be used. Some of these methods involve completing one or more worksheets along with annuity factor tables that help derive the present and future values of different amounts to account for investment returns and inflation.

These worksheet methods are available free from most mutual funds, brokers, and other financial services firms. Employers that sponsor 401(k) plans also usually make these available. Ask whoever does the employee education for your plan. Some worksheets assume that everyone lives to the same age. Others let the user estimate the length of retirement. Some make uniform assumptions about inflation and investment returns while others provide some flexibility. I've seen some worksheets with only six steps and others with three times that many.

Obviously some of the worksheets try to be more accurate, while others try to keep things simple so that people won't fail to complete the process. The simplest worksheet is the Ballpark Estimate from the American Savings Education Council. An online version can be accessed and printed from their web site, www.asec.org/ballpark. (A paper copy also is available by sending a self-addressed, stamped envelope with $1.07 postage to American Savings Education Council, 212 K St., N.W., Washington, D.C. 20037.)

The basic data used to complete one worksheet often can be easily transferred to another worksheet. Most people who are planning their retirement would benefit from completing several different worksheets and comparing the results. Most of these worksheets will estimate how large the investment portfolio should be on the first day of retirement to meet the spending goals. Most also will compute how much money should be saved and invested each month to accumulate that sum.

On to the Web

There is no longer a reason to do all the calculations by hand. Most financial service firms have a version of their retirement planning worksheets on their web sites. These web calculators will do all the computations required to complete a worksheet. In some cases, the web calculator is more streamlined than the paper version, primarily to minimize frustration for those with slower Internet connections. The best web-based retirement calculators probably are those from the three major no-load mutual fund firms: Vanguard, Fidelity, and T. Rowe Price. They generally have the more robust features.

Many other web sites also have retirement calculators that use the same methodology as the paper versions. The sophistication of these calculators varies. A typical simple calculator can be found at www.usatoday.com. A more sophisticated one is at www.usnews.com. The U.S. News calculator can show the effects of future changes in taxes and Medicare, which aren't available in most of the simpler tools.

Software that Helps

With today's technology, a fairly accurate estimate of retirement capital needs can be developed quickly once an estimate of retirement spending is developed. By turning to web sites and software, the calculations are performed easily, and with a level of sophistication and accuracy that are not found in the simple methods. Some key issues that are ignored or glossed over in the simple methods can be addressed using technology. To get similar sophistication using paper and a calculator would require a large number of calculations and the risk of error would be high.

Issues Resolved Using Technology

Here are examples of the issues that can be addressed when technology is used to develop a retirement plan.

Customized inflation. One of the biggest mistakes in retirement planning is failing to fully factor inflation into the plan. Over 20 or more years of retirement, inflation can make a comfortable income uncomfortably tight or even inadequate. A good retirement planning model, whether it is a simple one or a sophisticated tool using technology, will take inflation into account.

The most common approach is to apply a flat inflation rate to estimated annual spending. Prices of different goods and services, however, do not increase at the same rate. For example, in the 20 years ending in early 2002, prices of televisions declined 60 percent, long distance telephone call costs declined 34 percent, gasoline prices fell 7.4 percent, and audio equipment prices declined 27 percent. During that time, average prices as reflected in the consumer price index rose 88 percent, or 3.2 percent annually.

Take a look at the nine items with the highest percentage price increases over those 20 years. Tobacco products rose 448 percent; tuition and fees for the first through twelfth grades rose 342 percent; college tuition and fees rose 318 percent; hospital and related services increased 312 percent; prescription drugs and other medical expenses rose 263 percent; educational books and supplies were up 255 percent; motor vehicle insurance increased 219 percent; dental services rose 205 percent; and the cost of oranges rose 202 percent. The three educational categories don't apply to retirees at all, unless they are assisting with their grandchildren's education. The medical and dental categories, however, will take up a higher percentage of the average retiree's budget than of the typical pre-retiree's spending.

That's why a better approach to estimating inflation is to assign a separate inflation rate to each budget item. That gives a much better estimate of the inflation the individual is likely to experience during retirement. The recent inflation rates for different items can be obtained from the Bureau of Labor Statistics of the U.S. Department of Labor web site, www.bls.gov/cpi/home.htm.

Some computer software allows different inflation rates to be assigned to each item in the retirement budget. The difference between this approach and using one national rate for each spending item won't mean much in the first few years of retirement. After 10 or more years of retirement, however, the compounded difference could be significant.

Irregular expenses. Earlier I explained how to use a sinking fund to factor into the monthly budget expenses that are not incurred each month or even each year. An alternative is to use one of the software programs that allow more precise treatment. These programs ask for an estimate of the year when these expenses will be incurred. For example, a program might ask how often a car will be purchased and what the cost in today's dollars is likely to be. This information is included in the estimated income and spending for that year. Unlike the simple methods, the more sophisticated software calculates the spending of each year separately instead of assuming uniform spending each year. This can make for a more accurate projection of total retirement spending.

Mature-years spending. Simple retirement models assume the same amount is spent each year all through retirement. The truth is that most people slow down as they age. Sometime between ages 75 and 85 many people choose to travel less, golf less, and dine out less. In general, they spend less in many areas than when they were younger. The simple models cannot adjust for this, but some software is written to handle the change. Without factoring the mature-years spending change into a retirement plan, estimated spending could significantly exceed actual spending. In addition, for married couples, spending usually is reduced after one spouse passes away. Again, failure to adjust for this could lead to an overestimate of retirement capital needs. These changes are reflected in some of the computer models and can be made in a sophisticated paper estimate, while the simple models ignore them.

Changing assumptions. Ideally, more than one estimate of retirement spending and capital needs is made. A number of assumptions go into the calculation. Estimates include inflation, investment returns, and the actual spending on each item. Because of the number of assumptions, it is a good idea to do several projections, changing one of the assumptions each time. What happens to the plan if investment returns are less than expected? What happens if inflation is higher? Very small changes in these assumptions can significantly change the results, especially if there still are years to go before retirement and two decades or more to spend in retirement. This is another reason to consider using software or web site calculators to do the projections. These tools make it easy to change assumptions and compare retirement capital needs over several different economic scenarios.

Working the Data

One way to factor all these items into a retirement spending projection is to use a computer spreadsheet program such as Microsoft Excel instead of a prewritten software package. Setting up and compiling the spreadsheet is a fair amount of work, but the final product makes it easy to change assumptions and see the results. A spreadsheet that already is set up to project retirement spending this way can be found on the web site available to the subscribers of my newsletter, *Bob Carlson's Retirement Watch* (www.RetirementWatch.com).

Fortunately, for those of you who don't want to do all the work, there are some software packages and web sites that will make some or all of these finer adjustments for you. Quicken from Intuit and Microsoft Money have good retirement planning modules. The cost of each is low, and the modules are better than the free calculators available on the web. These two software packages are revised approximately every year. At this writing, they don't allow you to estimate a separate inflation rate for each item or account for a spending slowdown sometime during retirement. They do, however, handle irregular expenses well and let assumptions such as inflation and investment returns be changed quickly and easily.

A more sophisticated retirement planning tool is available from the mutual fund company T. Rowe Price. Its Retirement Analyzer allows separate inflation rates for different spending items and also will make many of the other adjustments needed to refine the retirement spending estimate and make it more accurate. The calculator is available in several forms. A paper version and web site version are free. There also is a stand-alone version available for $9.95. The stand-alone version is more robust than either of the other versions, allowing more flexibility and changes in more of the assumptions.

A professional financial planning software program that provides a great deal of flexibility and accuracy is Easy Money from MoneyTree Software. It allows for a separate inflation rate to be assigned to each item, for irregular expenses, and for a spending slowdown in later years. For married couples, it also adjusts spending after the death of one spouse. Individuals probably won't want to purchase it because the cost is prohibitive—$750 or more. There also are several related programs that can be bundled with it, driving up the cost further. Current information about the program is available at www.moneytree.com. An alternative is to hire a financial planner who uses the software. In addition, MoneyTree has a condensed version called Silver Financial Planner available for $395. This program gives you many but not all of the features of the regular version.

Most people will find that the web sites or paper products from Vanguard, Fidelity, and T. Rowe Price will meet their needs. For a more robust plan or to change more variables, you may wish to consider some of the more pricey software programs. Finally, consider working with a fee-only or fee-based financial planner who will help develop a solid retirement spending estimate.

Uncertainty and Monte Carlo

There is one common feature to all the retirement planning methods discussed so far. They assume that a steady rate of return is earned on the investments. If a 7 percent investment return is estimated, the method will assume that exactly 7 percent is earned each and every year.

Anyone who has been in or watched the markets for awhile knows that isn't the way markets work. Investment returns are likely to be variable. A 15 percent gain one year might be followed by a 5 percent gain the following year, a 12 percent loss the third year, a 20 percent gain the fourth year, and so on. Over time, these variable returns might amount to a 7 percent average annual return.

Most of the time, the difference between the assumption of steady returns and the reality of variable returns won't make a meaningful difference. There are times, however, when it can make a big difference. It is most likely to make a meaningful difference when the markets enter a strong bearish phase at the start of retirement. (The period from 2000 to 2002 was such a time.) The portfolio's value could fall dramatically during those years. Instead of spending income the first few years, the new retiree will be spending principal. That leaves less principal to generate gains when the markets eventually resume a bullish phase. The result in this scenario is that the wealth won't last as long as initially forecast unless spending is changed.

To deal with this potential problem, the financial community developed a new method to make estimates in retirement plans. The traditional method of assuming a constant rate of return is known as a linear or deterministic model. The newer method is a probabilistic model. The plan produced by a deterministic model shows the specific amount of money projected to be available each year of retirement. The probabilistic method concludes by showing the probability or likelihood that a particular plan of spending, saving, and investing will lead to a successful retirement. Probabilistic models weren't available only a few years ago. The computing power required was too expensive and slow. The declining cost and increased power of technology makes this newer approach available to anyone with a newer personal computer or access to a web site.

The most common probabilistic model is known as the Monte Carlo simulation. It actually was developed by nuclear scientists at the Los Alamos Laboratory to design atom bombs. Instead of assuming one average annual return, the Monte Carlo simulation calculates the results of a plan under a wide range of possible investment scenarios or outcomes. Some Monte Carlo simulations use many combinations of actual historic returns from the investment markets. Other simulations use random, computer-generated returns (within parameters set by the programmer). The Monte Carlo simulations for financial plans usually calculate 500 possible outcomes. That means for a 30-year retirement plan, the program will calculate investment returns over 500 different 30-year periods. The program determines the percentage of times that the investment capital lasts the entire 30-year period or longer, and that is the probability that the plan will be successful. For example, the report might say that there is an 85 percent probability that the assets will last through the retirement period. Most financial advisers recommend developing a plan with a 90 percent or greater probability of success.

The Financial Engines web site at www.financialengines.com probably was the first vehicle to make Monte Carlo simulation generally available. Now simulations are on the web sites of Vanguard, Fidelity, and T. Rowe Price. Many financial planners also use software that includes the Monte Carlo simulation method. The Easy Money software mentioned earlier includes a Monte Carlo simulation feature.

While the Monte Carlo simulation can be more informative than a simple deterministic model, it has its own drawbacks. A number of assumptions are built into each program. These assumptions include the average annual returns for each investment asset over time and the correlations among the different investments. Correlation is the extent to which the investments rise and fall together. Sometimes these assumptions are explicitly revealed; sometimes the program documentation is not clear about the assumptions. These assumptions could be unrealistic, wrong, or ones with which the user simply disagrees. An incorrect assumption would make the Monte Carlo simulation as unrealistic as the traditional deterministic method.

A large number of iterations is necessary for the simulation to be useful. A program or web site that doesn't want to incur the cost of a high number of simulations does a disservice to its users. In a public opinion poll, the number of people questioned determines the probability of error. Likewise, the number of simulations determines the probability of error in the program. Unfortunately, Monte Carlo simulation programs typically don't reveal their probability of error.

Of course, the probabilities are a lot like insurance. Suppose you look at the statistics and decide that there is a low probability of your house burning down this year. So, you don't buy homeowner's insurance. That probability doesn't do you much good if in fact your home does catch fire this year. Likewise, a 98 percent probability of success from a Monte Carlo simulation looks good. But the plan is not a good one if the actual results fall into the 2 percent of outcomes when the plan fails.

The Monte Carlo simulation also assumes that the retirement plan will be followed. In the real world, however, a multiyear bear market often causes investors to reduce their stock holdings. That reduces their ability to participate in the succeeding bull market. But that possible change in behavior is not factored into the probability of success calculated by the simulation program.

Of course, the simulation is only as good as the data on which it is based. That is why the most important part of retirement planning is to develop a realistic estimate of retirement spending, saving, and investing. Nothing else matters if those estimates aren't done well.

The Monte Carlo simulation is a useful tool in the retirement planning toolbox. Don't think, however, that because it uses high-level mathematics and computer power that the result is hard science. There are many assumptions and variables in the simulation. Solid judgment and key decisions are at least as important as computer power.

A Successful Retirement

The key to successful retirement planning is a good estimate of retirement spending. Everything else relies on it. Whichever method is used to estimate retirement income needs, keep the following principles in mind.

How to Forecast Successfully

Use your own spending.   Don't use rules of thumb or rely on surveys of other retirees. Decide what you want to do in retirement. Draw up a budget of how much that would cost today. This annual retirement spending might equal or exceed spending during the working years.

Count on inflation.   Even low inflation has a strong effect over 10 years or more. A 3 percent annual inflation rate cuts purchasing power in half over 24 years and by close to 20 percent after five years. Even a low 2 percent inflation rate cuts the standard of living by 20 percent after 10 years. For example, after 10 years of only 2 percent inflation, almost $12,200 is needed to buy what $10,000 used to buy (a 22 percent increase). After 15 years, almost $13,500 is needed. If inflation doubles to 4 percent, almost $15,000 is needed after 10 years and $18,000 after 15 years. Here's another way to look at it. A dollar in 1982 had the purchasing power of about 59 cents in 2002. A 1967 dollar equaled about 19 cents in 2002. It won't happen overnight, but it is painful over time. See Chart 3.1.

A key issue is which inflation rate to use.   People who were planning retirement in the early 1980s would use a 4 percent to 5 percent annual rate. The average annual inflation rate from 1962 to 1982 was 5.9 percent. That turned out to be much too high for the following 20 years, when inflation rose only 3.2 percent annually. Overestimating inflation causes a pre-retiree to save more money than required. Those planning retirement today might be tempted to use a 1 percent to 2 percent rate, based on recent history, but this would be risky. If inflation rates rise in the future, they won't have saved enough for retirement. Ideally, a separate inflation rate is assigned to each item of proposed retirement spending. The usefulness of that method, however, still depends on being able to estimate future inflation accurately.

Don't underestimate longevity. People who retire today have life expectancies that were only dreamed of during their youth. A common retirement planning mistake is to underestimate life expectancy and spend

CHART 3.1   How Inflation Erodes Fixed Income

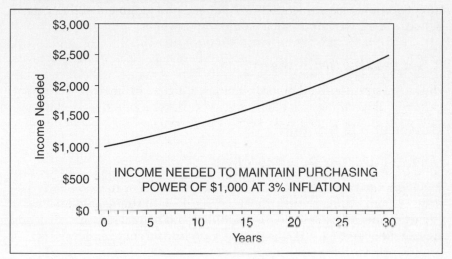

money accordingly. Most people should count on a retirement of at least 20 years and assume that at least one spouse will live longer than that, unless there are medical or family reasons that limit life expectancy. Many advisors say that the safest advice is to assume that at least one spouse will live at least 15 percent longer than the current life expectancy for his or her age. That means that many people should plan on 30 or more years of retirement.

Don't overlook all possible income sources.   The tools available from the financial services companies tend to overstate the amount of investment assets needed. Don't forget other income sources such as Social Security, home equity, a reverse mortgage, and so forth. Inheritances also might be part of the equation. Remember that in the later years, retirees should feel free to spend the principal investment, unless leaving money to loved ones or charity is a primary goal.

Make more than one estimate.   The primary projection will depend on the best estimates of inflation, investment returns, and other factors. Additional projections also should be made that will show the results if one or more of those assumptions change. Consider making alternate projections with higher and lower inflation and investment returns. The point is to see how long-term changes in the assumptions change the results. That makes it easier to adjust the plan over the years when it looks as if actual results will differ from the original assumptions.

Check the numbers regularly.   Things will change. A retirement plan should be revisited every few years. As one nears or is in retirement, the plan should be revised perhaps as often as annually. That will avoid big problems down the road. Small adjustments in spending or investing can be made early, which will avoid large changes later. Think of a retirement plan as a process that has to be fine-tuned regularly.

When estimated retirement needs don't match the available resources, it's time to make adjustments. Spending can be reduced, or it might be possible to increase investment income by investing a little less conservatively.

How Much Is Enough?

"How much is enough?" is partly a practical question and partly a philosophical one. So far, I've addressed it as a practical question. But let's look at it philosophically for a moment. How much do you really need to reach your goals? If you can't reach all the goals, which goals are the important ones?

Surveys regularly indicate that people could be very happy if they had twice as much money as they actually do have. People at every level of wealth believe they need more money to be happy and to fulfill their goals—it's a natural, very human response. As income grows, things that once were luxuries become necessities and are taken for granted. Then we train our sights on what might be available if we had even more money, and shoot for those things. But life is full of choices, and there are precious few of us who can afford everything we would like.

True wealth produces freedom. I've seen too many people who let their things own them, rather than owning their things. A big house or multiple houses, nice cars, golf club memberships, entertaining, and travel all cost money. They're great as long as the money to support them is available. But not everyone is comfortable with that much overhead or with the investment risks needed to support this kind of spending. In those cases, the people don't own the things, the things own the people. Nice things shouldn't increase one's level of stress. If the pressure of paying for things causes someone to be unhappy or to snap at loved ones, that person probably can't afford those things.

In later chapters, I will demonstrate how to invest to increase returns, reduce taxes and other expenses, and take other steps to make wealth last longer. These steps will enhance retirement. The first step, however, is to make a good estimate of retirement spending and capital needs and develop a plan to accumulate that amount. Not many people begin retirement with all the money they need to pay for their desired retirement. However, that doesn't mean they will outlive their assets or end up living with their children. It just means they have to make some adjustments as they go along. A key to successful retirement is knowing when adjustments need to be made and making adjustments that you can live with. Unsuccessful retirements generally occur when no early planning is done, the retiree lives however he or she desires, and later adjustments are forced by circumstances.

Maximizing Social Security Benefits

Social Security's problems are well documented, and surveys show that many people who are not yet retired do not expect to receive much from Social Security. For many retirees, however, Social Security is a key source of income, and it probably will continue to be for many years, despite all the negative headlines. For lower-income workers, Social Security benefits replace up to 90 percent of their pretax working years' income. Even for many well-off retirees, Social Security benefits provide a cushion that equals 10 percent to 15 percent of preretirement income. For the average retiree who begins receiving benefits at age 65, Social Security provides about 41 percent of preretirement income.

Social Security is a valuable asset for many retirees. Few people, however, know as much as they should about Social Security, and many aspects of the program are not automatic. Each beneficiary decides when retirement benefits begin, and that choice affects the amount that is received. The choices made can affect one's spouse and other family members. Recipients also can influence how much of the benefits are taxed and whether any of the benefits are lost because the recipient continues to earn income from working. To maximize Social Security benefits, some key decisions have to be made.

Will Social Security Disappear?

Social Security makes news once a year when the program's trustees submit their annual report on the financial condition of the program. It makes the news at other times when one group of politicians accuses another of invading the Social Security trust fund to pay for additional government spending or tax cuts. (The accusations ignore the inconvenient fact that Social Security does not have a "trust fund" in any sense of the term.)

The 2004 report from the Social Security trustees estimates that in 2018 the program will begin to pay out more in benefits than it receives in taxes. It is projected to run out of money in 2042.

These annual estimates have convinced many people under age 40 that they will never receive anything from Social Security. Many people over age 40 worry that their benefits will be reduced at some point. What is overlooked is that almost every year the date for Social Security's insolvency is pushed farther into the future. In addition, the system estimates that it can pay about 70 percent of promised benefits indefinitely. Trimming benefits for the highest income beneficiaries or increasing the normal retirement age could greatly lengthen the life of the system.

Social Security should receive a major overhaul, though, because its current setup is unsustainable. Even without major changes, however, just a few, relatively small changes will ensure that almost everyone reading this book will receive significant payments from Social Security. For example, means-testing could be applied so that full benefits are not paid to higher income individuals. Or the retirement age could be extended. The economic assumptions behind the program also tend to be conservative. If over time the economy is a little stronger than the forecasts or inflation is a bit lower, the system will take much longer to run out of money.

Social Security will change over the years. It has to change or die. Whatever the changes, however, for most people it will remain one meaningful leg of the three- or four-legged stool of retirement income. (Pensions, personal savings, and employment are the other possible sources.) For lower-income workers, Social Security will replace a high percentage of their preretirement salary. The replacement ratio for these workers can be as high as 90 percent of pretax income for someone earning the minimum wage. As income rises, Social Security replaces less of the preretirement income. Keep in mind that the after-tax replacement ratio is higher than the pretax ratio. That is because at lower incomes Social Security benefits are not subject to income taxes. Also, unlike wages, Social Security benefits are not reduced by payroll taxes. There is a maximum monthly benefit that is indexed for inflation, which was $2,111 in 2004 for someone retiring at age 70. There also is a maximum family benefit, which can further reduce benefits when both spouses receive benefits.

Social Security benefits are an asset. As with other assets, Social Security benefits can be managed to maximize their value. That's because the program provides options that can increase or reduce benefits. Benefits also might be subject to income taxes. In the following sections we'll examine the key issues affecting Social Security benefits and develop methods for making the best choices.

Some Social Security Basics

Social Security benefits are far-ranging and complicated. Though the retirement benefits are the best-known, there are other benefits available under the program. We'll review some of the most basic benefits. To get comprehensive details, go to the Social Security Administration web site at www.ssa.gov or read the Social Security Handbook (free from your local Social Security office) or call the Social Security hotline (800-772-1213).

Social Security retirement benefits are earned after an individual earns 40 work credits. Each quarter (three months) that income subject to Social Security tax is earned counts as a work credit. Therefore, 40 quarters of work entitle an individual to benefits. Once payment of benefits begins, they are indexed to inflation. The level of retirement benefits is based on earnings during the 35 years in which the worker earned the most. Lower-income workers receive a higher percentage of their preretirement income, and the percentage declines as income rises. Estimated replacement ratios are in Chart 4.1A and B.

The Social Security Administration now sends everyone a statement of estimated benefits a few months before his or her birthday every year. The statement estimates the monthly benefits that will be received if benefits begin at three different ages: 62, full retirement, and 70. The statement also estimates the non-retirement benefits that might be available. Perhaps the most important part of the statement is the salary history. If the earnings history is wrong, then the eventual benefits paid will be wrong. Any errors must be corrected within three years of the year in question.

Many people do not realize that only a little over 60 percent of Social Security benefits paid are retirement benefits. There are other types of benefits. One of the other benefits is disability. To qualify for disability benefits under Social Security, the worker must be completely disabled and unable to engage in any kind of employment. If a worker dies, the spouse or children might be eligible to receive survivor benefits. Children under age 18 (19 if a full-time high school student) generally are eligible for a monthly survivor benefit of up to 50 percent of the deceased's benefits. A surviving spouse also might be eligible for survivor benefits, depending on the spouse's age and whether or not there are minor children. A divorced spouse also might be eligible to receive benefits. We'll discuss spousal benefits later in this chapter.

The major Social Security benefit, however, is the retirement benefit. Major changes in retirement benefits began in 2002 and will continue.

The Full Retirement Benefit or Normal Retirement Benefit is the benchmark or baseline benefit. The calculation of the benefit is complicated, but beneficiaries need to know only a few things. As we discussed, the formula pays higher relative benefits to lower income workers and less of a benefit to those with higher incomes. As a result, lower income people

CHART 4.1 A AND B   The Extent to Which Social Security Replaces Workers' Preretirement Earnings

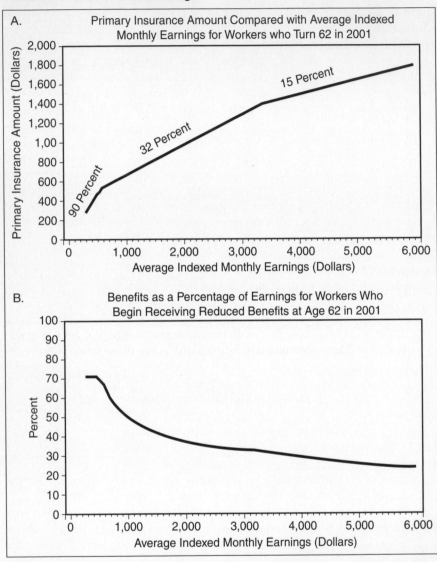

A.   Primary Insurance Amount Compared with Average Indexed Monthly Earnings for Workers who Turn 62 in 2001

(Chart A: line graph with y-axis "Primary Insurance Amount (Dollars)" from 0 to 2,000 and x-axis "Average Indexed Monthly Earnings (Dollars)" from 0 to 6,000; line segments labeled "90 Percent", "32 Percent", and "15 Percent")

B.   Benefits as a Percentage of Earnings for Workers Who Begin Receiving Reduced Benefits at Age 62 in 2001

(Chart B: line graph with y-axis "Percent" from 0 to 100 and x-axis "Average Indexed Monthly Earnings (Dollars)" from 0 to 6,000)

need to save less money during their working years, because Social Security will replace more of their working income than it will for higher income taxpayers.

The formula also uses the highest earning years to determine the full benefit. The maximum income credited in the calculations is the maximum Social Security wage base, which was $87,900 for 2004 and is indexed for inflation. Earnings above that amount won't affect benefits. For example, suppose Max Profits would like to stop working at age 60 but doesn't plan to begin Social Security benefits until 65 because of the early retirement reduction. Because Max already has a 35-year history of earned income and that income was above the wage base, working from 60 to 65 probably wouldn't increase his Normal Retirement Age benefit by much, if at all. Likewise, if Max's earnings were below the wage base but he doesn't expect a meaningful increase in wages between 60 and 65, working the additional years are unlikely to affect his Normal Retirement Age benefit. In either case, continuing to work won't increase Max's Normal Retirement Age benefits.

The Full Benefit is paid if payments are elected to begin at Full Retirement Age. Traditionally, Full Retirement Age was 65. The reforms enacted in the 1980s to make the program last longer changed the Full Retirement Age. The reforms also changed the computation of benefits that begin either before or after Full Retirement Age. Those born in 1936 were the last to be eligible for both a Full Retirement Age of 65 and the traditional credits for delaying receipt of benefits. Those born before 1938 have a Full Retirement Age of 65, but they get higher credits for delaying receipt of benefits past 65. The Full Retirement Age increases on a sliding scale until those born in 1960 or later have a Full Retirement Age of 67. Table 4.1 shows the Full Retirement Age and differentials for different ages.

There were two other significant changes in the 1986 reforms. Those who begin receiving benefits before Full Retirement Age will get lower relative benefits than previous early retirees did. Also, those who delay benefits until age 70 will, in some years, get higher benefits than in prior years. The reduction in benefits for early retirement is a little complicated. The beneficiary loses 5/9 percent of the full benefit for each month of the first 36 months before Full Retirement Age, and 5/12 percent of the full benefit for each additional month before Full Retirement Age that benefits begin. The table shows the reduced benefit for taking benefits at 62 for each age group.

Recipients get an incentive for delaying retirement benefits. Under the old law, benefits increased by 6 percent for each year the initial benefit payment was delayed. The maximum benefit, payable at age 70 or later, was 130 percent of the normal benefit. The credit for delaying benefits for those born after 1936 rises until it reaches 8 percent for each year of delay for those born after 1942. For those born more recently, the maximum benefit as a percentage of full benefits that is payable at age 70 first rises but then declines.

When to Take Benefits

The key decision for a retiree is when to begin receiving Social Security retirement benefits. The benefits can start at age 62 or later. Should a beneficiary take benefits as soon as possible (age 62)? At the Full Retirement Age?

TABLE 4.1 Full Retirement Age Schedule

Year of Birth	Full Retirement Age (FRA)	% of FRA Benefits at Age 62	Annual Credit for Delayed Retirement	% of FRA Benefits at Age 70
1936 and before	65	80%	6%	130%
1937	65	80%	6.5%	132.5%
1938	65 & 2 mos.	79⅙%	6.5%	131.42%
1939	65 & 4 mos.	78⅓%	7%	132.66%
1940	65 & 6 mos.	77½%	7%	131.5%
1941	65 & 8 mos.	76⅔%	7.5%	132.5%
1942	65 & 10 mos.	75⅚%	7.5%	131.25%
1943–1954	66	75%	8%	132%
1955	66 & 2 mos.	74⅙%	8%	130.66%
1956	66 & 4 mos.	73⅓%	8%	129.33%
1957	66 & 6 mos.	72½%	8%	128%
1958	66 & 8 mos.	71⅔%	8%	126.66%
1959	66 & 10 mos.	70⅚%	8%	125.33%
1960 and later	67	70%	8%	124%

Or should he or she wait for the maximum payout at age 70? Those who need the income and who have stopped working have no decision to make. They begin receiving benefits as soon as allowed because they need the income. Many people, however, have a choice. These people need a logical way to make the decision.

The first step should be to calculate the break-even point. When benefits are taken before Full Retirement Age, a reduced payment is received. That's the disadvantage. The advantage of taking benefits early is that the cash flow begins earlier. The break-even point is the year it takes for the total benefits received after waiting for full retirement to equal the total benefits that would be received if benefits were begun early. Here's an example of how to calculate the break-even point.

Suppose Max Profits is trying to decide between full benefits at age 65 or a higher benefit at 70. His normal benefit at 65 would be $1,400 per month, and waiting until age 70 would result in $1,820 monthly or 130 percent of the normal benefit. That extra benefit is $420 per month. By beginning to receive benefits at 65, the lower benefits are received for an extra 60 months.

Max needs to multiply the normal retirement benefit by the number of months it would be received. That's $1,400 times 60 for a total early payment of $84,000. Divide that by the additional monthly benefit that would be received by waiting until age 70, which is $420. The result is 200. That is the number of months it will take for the higher lifetime payments Max would receive for waiting until age 70 to catch up with the lifetime payments that would be received if Max started benefits at 65. Divide by 12, and that comes to 16 and two-thirds years. Max has to live until almost age 87 to make the delay in benefits pay off. That exceeds the average life expectancy of both men and women for this age group, so Max has to live beyond life expectancy for delaying benefits to pay off. If Max dies before age 86 and eight months, Max and his family have lost money.

What about taking benefits at age 62? Suppose Max turned 62 in 2002. His benefits would be 77.5 percent of his normal retirement benefits of $1,400. (The reduction is even higher for those born later.) That means Max would receive $1,085 monthly beginning at age 62. Full Retirement Age for Max is 65 and six months. By taking benefits at 62, he will receive the benefits for an extra 42 months. That means total benefits received by Full Retirement Age would be $45,570. Divide that amount by the $315 additional benefit Max would receive by waiting until Full Retirement Age. Max finds that it will take 144 and two-thirds months to make up for waiting until normal retirement age. That means Max will have to live until about age 78 to break even for waiting until normal retirement age. Only if he lives longer than this would he benefit.

This result should be expected. After the 1980s changes, the reduced benefit for beginning payments before Full Retirement Age was designed to be breakeven for those who live to normal life expectancy. In short, if someone lives to average life expectancy for his or her age group, the lifetime benefits received should be the same whether benefits are begun early or at Full Retirement Age. Early benefits and late benefits now are supposed to be calculated so that it makes no difference to those who live to life expectancy for their year of birth.

The break-even point is only a simple calculation. There are other factors to consider. The retirement benefit is indexed for inflation. The simple calculation doesn't reflect the annual increase in benefits due to inflation. At recent low inflation levels that is not a significant factor. If Max makes the added computation of factoring in inflation, the break-even point will be pushed a little further into the future in each case.

Another factor is that some or all of the benefits received early could be invested. If someone can choose to delay benefits, then obviously he or she doesn't need the benefits to pay expenses. If the benefits are not delayed, then all or some of the benefits could be invested. (Or the benefits could be spent and investment accounts could compound untouched instead of being used to pay for spending needs.) The investment earnings would push the break-even point further. The better the investments do, the further the break-even point is pushed.

Federal income taxes are another reason to delay benefits. Social Security benefits used to be free of federal income taxes. Some benefits became taxable in the 1980s and more became taxable after 1993. We'll discuss the details of income taxes on Social Security benefits later in this chapter. Those with significant other income might want to delay receiving benefits while they plan ways to structure income to reduce income taxes on the benefits or at least to delay the extra taxes as long as possible.

Whether or not a person continues working also should affect the decision. The additional earned income could cause a recipient to lose part of the benefits. Beginning in 2002, outside income will not reduce Social Security benefits for those who are age 65 and older. But those between the ages of 62 and 65 could lose benefits if they work. We'll examine the details later in this chapter.

There also are the intangible factors to consider. For example, family history might indicate that a beneficiary is likely to live beyond the age group's life expectancy. If that happens, delaying benefits pays off. On the other hand, if an individual is not in good health or does not have a family history of longevity, he or she might opt to receive benefits as early as possible.

Most Take It Early

Many people opt to take Social Security early because the benefits are a certainty, while the payoff from waiting is uncertain. About 52 percent begin their benefits at 62. Less than 2 percent begin benefits at age 70. About 30 percent begin benefits at 65, and the rest start their benefits at some other age between 62 and 70. About 70 percent take their benefits before age 65. That means a little over 20 million beneficiaries receive retirement benefits with a reduction for early retirement, while about 7.75 million receive benefits with no early retirement reduction.

For many people who took benefits by 2002, they probably made the better decision, especially after the time value of money is taken into account. The scheduled increases in Full Retirement Age and adjustments in the computations for early and late receipt of benefits make the choice a bit different for those born after 1936. The adjustments are designed so if one lives to average life expectancy there should be no lifetime difference in the cash received whether one takes benefits at age 62 or at the Full Retirement Age. Those born in 1943 and later also should receive the same lifetime cash whether they begin benefits at Full Retirement Age or at 70. Because women on average live longer than men and longer than the average of both sexes for their age group, women might want to wait to receive benefits until at least age 65. That's because benefit payments are calculated using the average life expectancy for both sexes. Because blacks, especially black men, tend to have lower life expectancies than do others in their age group, they might want to opt for the earliest benefits. Others might want to balance personal health or family history to decide whether they want to gamble on living longer than the average life expectancy or not.

Those calculations, however, do not take into account the time value of money and also do not reflect the other factors. It is likely that many people will continue taking their benefits before Full Retirement Age, and that probably is the better option for most of them. Those who die at or before life expectancy make the right move by taking benefits early. Those who anticipate living beyond the life expectancy of their peers, however, would benefit by waiting to receive benefits.

The Social Security web site (www.ssa.gov) can provide more estimates of benefits under different scenarios. It has a calculator that allows changes in assumptions about future earnings and other factors, which produces a more accurate estimate of what the benefits would be at different ages.

Benefits and Your Spouse

Social Security benefits also are payable to a spouse, and the amount the spouse might receive is a factor some people consider in their planning. More than one quarter of Social Security benefits, in fact, are paid to survivors and family members.

A spouse who earned wages qualifies for his or her own Social Security retirement benefits. A spouse also is eligible for a retirement benefit that is 50 percent of his or her spouse's benefit. In addition, a surviving spouse is entitled to receive 100 percent of his or her deceased spouse's retirement benefit. When the spouse is eligible for more than one of these benefits, he or she will be paid no more than the highest benefit. For example, if the wife's own earned benefit is less than 50 percent of the husband's, then the wife will receive her own benefit plus an additional spousal benefit that brings her total benefits up to 50 percent of her husband's benefit.

Let's look at an example. Suppose Max and Rosie Profits each work until eligible for full retirement benefits. Max is entitled to a monthly benefit of $1,000 and Rosie is eligible for $300 monthly. Because Rosie's earned benefit is less than 50 percent of Max's benefit, she can receive an additional $200 as Max's spouse, bringing her total to $500. Suppose Max dies first. Then Rosie can shift to the $1,000 per month she is entitled to as Max's widow. If Rosie dies first he continues to receive his $1,000 benefit.

There's one more trick to these calculations. Suppose the wife is eligible for her own earned retirement benefit. Suppose also that she begins the reduced benefit at age 62 while her husband still is working. When the husband begins taking retirement benefits, the wife's total benefits will not equal 50 percent of her husband's payments. That's because the wife's early resumption of benefits will continue to be factored in. She cannot begin her benefits early and still get the full 50 percent of her husband's benefits.

The effect on a spouse is something to keep in mind in deciding when to receive benefits. For example, a husband might decide that he has no reason to expect any special longevity and is inclined to begin benefits at age 62. The decision might change, however, if he considers his wife. As a woman, she is statistically likely to live beyond her husband's total lifespan. If her retirement benefits are lower than her husband's or she qualifies only for the 50 percent spousal benefit, she will upgrade to her husband's benefit after his death and receive that for the rest of her life. After considering this, the husband might be inclined to delay his benefits so that his wife will receive higher benefits after he passes away than she would if he were to begin benefits early.

If there are minor children surviving, they also might be entitled to benefits. In that case, keep in mind that the total benefits paid to a family based on a deceased's working history is limited to between 150 percent and 188 percent of the worker's benefit, depending on the circumstances.

Are You Earning Too Much?

Social Security always has had a limit on outside or earned income of beneficiaries. One of the goals of Social Security when it was created during the Depression was to ease older people out of the work force so that more jobs would be available to younger people. To meet that goal, Social Security benefits were reduced for those who earned income from employment or a business while receiving retirement benefits. This generally is known as the earned income limit or earnings test.

The nature of the labor force and economy has changed over time. Congress recognized that in 1997 and changed the earnings test.

There never has been an earned income limit for those aged 70 and over who receive Social Security benefits. Beginning in 2002, there also is no earned income limit on those aged 65 and over. Those from age 62 up to 65 do, however, face a limit on their earned income while receiving Social Security benefits.

For those 62 through 64, one dollar in benefits will be lost for every two dollars of employment earnings above the limit. The limit for 2004 was $11,640 or $970 per month. (The limit is indexed for inflation each year.) For example, in 2004, someone who is 63, receives Social Security benefits, and earns $20,000 from a job will lose $4,180 in benefits. Each dollar earned above $11,280 costs 50 cents in benefits.

In the year a beneficiary reaches 65, benefits are reduced for excess earnings in the months before the sixty-fifth birthday. The earned income limit in 2004 was $2,590 per month or $31,080 annually. One dollar in benefits is lost for every three dollars of earnings above the limit. At age 65 and after, there is no limit on earnings.

Keeping Your Benefits

Losing some of Social Security benefits because of employment is bad. But it is worse to use some of the many bogus schemes that are being promoted as ways of getting around the earned income limit. Beneficiaries who use one of those methods and get caught will have to refund the benefits plus pay interest and penalties. So stick with methods that definitely work. Let's look at the methods that work and some variations of them that do not work.

Deferred income.   This is probably the best way for working seniors to beat the earned income limit. The strategy is to work today but not receive the income that is above the limit until sometime after age 65, when the earnings limit doesn't apply. That lets the senior keep the full Social Security check plus the earnings up to the limit.

Earnings are included in income for Social Security earnings test purposes when the right to receive the payment is fixed, even if the payment won't be received until later. In other words, to effectively defer income there must be some substantial risk of forfeiture of the income. Or, to put it another way, the right to receive the income cannot be fully vested.

Some tax qualified employer pension plans work for this, others don't. Any salary deferred into a 401(k) plan is vested. So the earnings limit cannot be avoided by contributing part of one's salary into the 401(k) plan. But some other employer plans might work. If the employer makes contributions to a plan but the benefits are not vested until some future time, then those earnings should not be counted against the Social Security earnings limit.

Another option is the nonqualified deferred compensation plan. These are plans that don't meet the tax code's pension plan requirements. They are not tax-exempt, but they also are not subject to limits on contributions, minimum payouts after age 70½, and other disadvantages. A worker and employer enter into a contract under which the worker foregoes some current income, and the employer agrees to pay that amount plus interest at some time in the future.

There are a number of IRS rulings that explain what a substantial risk of forfeiture is under these plans. To have that risk of forfeiture, the employer cannot put the money in a trust for the worker or buy an annuity in the employee's name. The employee must take the risk that if the employer goes bankrupt, the worker will be just another general creditor and might lose all or part of the deferred income. If the employer is financially solid, the employee might consider this approach. One of these plans should not be established without the help of a good tax lawyer. They don't work in every situation, and attention to the details is required.

Your corporation.   Self-employed individuals might use a corporation to avoid the earnings limit. The key is that regular corporate dividends and S corporation distributions do not count towards the Social Security earned income limit, but salary and bonuses do. Technically, an owner-employee can keep the salary below the earnings limit and take other money from the corporation as dividends and distributions.

But be very careful with this strategy. The IRS and Social Security Administration don't like it and have successfully charged people with fraud when the salary is unreasonably low. It is important not to receive a normal salary until the year Social Security benefits begin, then cut that salary below the earnings limit the first year benefits begin. That's clearly an artificial salary and it won't stand up. The recipient has to establish that the low salary is reasonable. The salary should be cut more than a year before receiving benefits and it should be established in the corporate minutes why that salary is reasonable. Dividends and distributions should not be increased by the amount of the salary reduction. Give careful consideration to additional steps such as transferring voting control of the corporate stock to someone else (perhaps a family member) and having an independent board of directors and officers set the salary.

The key is that the salary paid must be reasonable for the work done. If reasonableness cannot be established, the Social Security Administration will say that it was set artificially low to avoid the earnings limit. This technique is very difficult to implement safely.

Exempt income.   A better approach is to maximize tax-free compensation, such as health insurance and other tax-free benefits. This works whether the beneficiary owns the business or is merely an employee. Tax-free compensation is not counted as wages for purposes of the Social Security earnings limit. Take maximum advantage of benefit programs so that more compensation is received as tax-free benefits.

Special income.   Some income is taxable under the income tax rules but won't reduce Social Security benefits. Only earned income reduces Social Security benefits. Earned income is money that is received from the performance of personal services.

Rental income is a type of income that doesn't reduce Social Security benefits. Some work is required to manage rental properties and generate rental income, but that isn't earned income for Social Security benefit purposes. Other types of income that won't reduce benefits are pension and IRA distributions, jury duty pay, worker's compensation, unemployment compensation, lottery and prize winnings, and employer reimbursements for travel or moving expenses. To learn the classification of a specific type of income, get a copy of the Social Security Handbook (free from your local Social Security office) or call the Social Security hotline (800-772-1213). Many answers also are available at www.ssa.gov.

Taxes on Benefits

Most people think that marginal tax rates (the rate on the last dollar of income earned) as high as 90 percent no longer exist in the United States. It's true that for the bulk of people those high rates ended with the 1981 and 1986 tax laws. For some retirees, however, high marginal tax rates still exist thanks to the tax on Social Security benefits. Marginal tax rates of 70 percent to 90 percent (in some cases even higher) are imposed on some beneficiaries after state taxes are included.

Originally Social Security benefits were free of income taxes. That went out the door in 1986, when some benefits first were taxed. Taxes were increased on higher income beneficiaries in 1993.

In 1986, taxpayers with adjusted gross incomes above $32,000 began to have up to 50 percent of their benefits included in gross income. In the 1993 tax law, those with an adjusted gross income exceeding $44,000 began to have up to 85 percent of their benefits taxed. The details of computing the tax are complicated, and can be found in IRS Publication 915 (call 800-TAX-FORM).

Suppose Max Profits has adjusted gross income of $31,999. He gets a distribution from a mutual fund that pushes AGI to $32,100. The distribution is taxable. In addition, it triggers taxes on some Social Security benefits that were tax free. Once Max's income exceeds $32,000, each additional dollar of income means more than one dollar is included in gross income—the dollar earned plus up to 50 cents of Social Security benefits. Once Max's adjusted gross income exceeds $44,000, each additional dollar of income could cause up to 85 cents of Social Security benefits to be added to income.

In most states there also are state income taxes on the benefits. That's why those in high tax states, such as California, who have an AGI above $44,000 can have the marginal tax rate on each additional dollar earned reach 90 percent.

Originally said to target only the wealthiest Social Security recipients, the tax on Social Security benefits is imposed on a large number of retirees, and the number is rising rapidly. In 2001, 10.7 million individual income tax returns reported taxable Social Security benefits. That is an increase from 9.5 million in 1999 and 8.9 million in 1998. The total taxable Social Security benefits in 2001 were $93.5 billion, up from $75.08 billion in 1999. The numbers will increase each year because Social Security benefits are indexed for inflation but the threshold at which benefits are taxed is fixed.

Strategies that Work

Fortunately, there are steps that can reduce the taxes on Social Security benefits, but first, let's throw out a couple of strategies that won't work. Having the higher-income spouse delay Social Security benefits so that only the lower-earning spouse receives them doesn't work. The combined joint income of the two spouses is used to determine the amount of benefits included in income. The tax is not computed separately based on the income of each spouse. Married, filing separately also won't help. In fact, it will make the tax worse, because the benefits will be taxed when adjusted gross income of each spouse is above $0.

If adjusted gross income is significantly above the threshold at which benefits are taxed, there probably is not much that can be done to reduce benefits. Taxpayers who are near the threshold for taxing benefits, however, should consider some strategies that can reduce the amount of Social Security benefits taxed.

Tax deferral is an easy way to reduce the taxes on benefits. Those who are earning taxable income that exceeds their spending needs could benefit by deferring some of that income. There are a number of possible tax-deferral strategies.

Don't take distributions from IRAs, pension accounts, or annuities until the money is needed to pay expenses Once past age 70½, this strategy no longer is viable with qualified retirement plans, including IRAs, because of the required minimum distribution rules. Before that age, consider minimizing retirement plan distributions to avoid taxes on Social Security benefits. For more details on required minimum distributions and when to take more than the required distributions, see Chapter 11.

Investments in taxable accounts can be changed to reduce taxable income. Investments, such as mutual funds, can be held for long periods to minimize capital gains. Mutual funds with high annual distributions can be replaced with others that generally have low annual distributions. That way, there is income only when shares are sold instead of when the funds distribute income and gains. Capital gains taxes might be incurred the first year this strategy is implemented when shares of the original funds are sold to buy new ones. After that, the move could save taxes.

Taxable accounts also can be used to purchase fixed or variable annuities. Income and gains in the annuities won't be taxed until distributed as they are earned each year. Annuities are not subject to the required minimum distribution rules, so money can be left in the annuities until it is needed.

There are additional costs associated with annuities, and some flexibility is lost. For more information on annuities and when to buy them, see Chapter 13.

Shifting income to other family members is a good way to reduce income taxes and also a good estate planning strategy. When assets exceed what is needed for the rest of one's life, it can be a good idea to give assets to other family members either directly or through trusts. That gets the property out of the estate and also gets the income off the tax return. For more details about estate planning, see Chapter 12.

Tax-exempt interest can reduce taxes on Social Security benefits in an indirect way. When computing the amount of benefits included in gross income, tax-exempt interest is added to regular adjusted gross income. Therefore, taxes on benefits aren't avoided by shifting all taxable investment assets into tax-exempt bonds. The exempt bonds, however, generally earn lower nominal interest rates than do taxable bonds. That means the modified adjusted gross income used to figure the taxable benefits will be less when money is invested in tax-exempt bonds instead of taxable bonds. Those who earn a lot of interest income should give careful consideration to using tax-exempt bonds.

Several deductions can reduce the taxes on Social Security benefits. Look for opportunities to take these deductions. Itemized deductions (mortgage interest, medical expenses, real estate taxes, and state income taxes) do not reduce the tax on benefits.

Deductions for capital losses reduce the tax on benefits. Capital losses shelter capital gains dollar for dollar. When losses exceed gains for the year, up to $3,000 of capital losses can be deducted against other income. Excess losses can be carried forward to future years until they are fully used. Each year, look for opportunities to sell investments with paper losses to offset capital gains for the year. Even those who don't have any gains for the year can use up to $3,000 of the losses to reduce other types of income. Any unused losses can be carried forward to future years to offset gains or other income.

An asset with paper losses can be sold to reduce taxes even if its long-term prospects are attractive. To use the loss and still be able to invest in the asset for the long term, the wash sale rules must be avoided. The asset can be sold and the loss recognized. Then wait at least 31 days to repurchase the asset. As long as more than 30 days pass before repurchasing the investment, the loss can be deducted. Or another asset can be purchased immediately after the sale if that investment is not "substantially identical" to the one that was sold. If a mutual fund is sold, a different fund with a similar investment style can be purchased immediately. Then the investor is not out of the market but still benefits from taking the tax loss. Be sure to check sales charges and redemption fees before making the tax sales.

Business loss deductions also can reduce taxes on Social Security benefits. The amount of deductible losses is not limited. Some retirees find it beneficial to turn a hobby into a business that generates a tax loss at least in some years. The losses can be deductible if a profit is made in at least three out of any five consecutive years. The losses also can be deducted if the operation never earns a profit but is managed in a professional manner with the intention of making a profit.

Taxpayers who receive Social Security benefits need to be vigilant about the possibility of taxes being imposed on the benefits. Additional capital gains or distributions from a retirement account could trigger extra taxes.

The New Rules of Investing

Retirees and those planning for retirement sometimes get the worst investment advice. Some variation of the strategies developed for pension funds and the wealthy often get filtered and passed down to individual investors. These variations tend to be unsuitable. Evidence of the poor advice the average investor receives—or at least follows—is documented in a study conducted by Dalbar Inc., a mutual fund research firm in Boston. The firm uses reported cash flows in and out of mutual funds to estimate the returns actual investors earned and to compare those with actual market returns. The results are distressing if you are an average investor saving for retirement or already in retirement. From 1984 through 2002 (the latest data available in 2004), stock investors earned an average annual total return of 2.6 percent. By comparison, simply buying and holding an S&P 500 index fund during this period would have generated an average annual return of 12 percent. Bond investors actually did better, with an average annual return of 4.2 percent, but that still trailed the 5.5 percent return that would have been earned simply by buying and holding Treasury bills.

There are other studies showing that investment returns for individuals lag behind what they could and should be earning. One can quibble with the methodology of the studies and how close the estimated returns are to actual returns. But it seems clear that individual investors' returns are not as high as they could be.

The 7 Percent Club

Because of less-than-optimum investment strategies, most investors apparently are members of what I call the 7 Percent Club. An experienced money manager I know says that in over 25 years of meeting with clients and prospective clients, he routinely asks people about their prior investments. He estimates that most earned about 7 percent annually during a time when the stock market was appreciating by about 16 percent annually. Investors wasted a lot of money on tax shelters, limited partnerships, market timing, and all the other fads of the past few decades. Many bought the latest hot investments at their price peaks. Some were scared out of stock investments by the many "professional bears" who get a lot of media attention but rarely were right. The people this money manager talks to either are above average investors or don't report their investment experience accurately, because 7 percent annual returns exceed those found in the studies that reviewed actual results.

The main reasons for this poor performance generally are market timing and fad following, which are the same thing for most individual investors. The average investor apparently follows current market trends and headlines when making investment decisions. As a result, most investors buy high and sell low. They buy what has done the best recently, usually just as those assets are peaking in price. Then they hold these assets until they decline in price. The result is poor returns.

There is no reason for retirees and pre-retirees to earn low investment returns. To earn higher returns, investors first need to review the strategies commonly followed by individuals and to understand the shortcomings of those strategies. Then, a more appropriate and profitable investment plan can be developed. Developing an investment plan before making any investments is a key to success. Most investors suffer either because they don't have investment plans or they follow plans based on bad advice.

The investment advice given to retirees and pre-retirees usually falls into one of three categories. We'll look at them in detail, then develop a fourth, more profitable approach.

The Classic Advice

The investment advice for retirees used to be simple. As retirement approaches, the portfolio should be shifted from riskier investments—such as stocks—into safer, income-producing investments—such as annuities, bonds, certificates of deposit, and money market funds. The theory behind this advice also was simple. A retiree needs regular income to pay expenses. A retiree also does not want the principal of the portfolio to fluctuate as much as stocks do. That's why, according to this advice, a retiree wants a portfolio that pays income and maintains a reasonably stable value.

The strategy made some sense when the average retirement lasted about five years, as it did for those who were in the first generation of retirees. Also, for those retirees an investment portfolio was a mere supplement to Social Security and employer pensions.

Things are different now. Retirement can last 20 or 30 years—and even longer for some. That fact makes following this classic advice a very dangerous thing indeed.

The key problem is inflation (see Chart 3.1). Even a low inflation rate will eat away at the purchasing power of income each year. Over 10, 20, or 30 years the compounding of that inflation will dramatically reduce the income's purchasing power. The purchasing power of the principal also will decline. To maintain purchasing power in the face of inflation, both the income and principal have to increase by at least the inflation rate each year. To maintain the purchasing power of $40,000 when inflation is only 2 percent annually, after 15 years more than $53,000 of income is needed. That result cannot be achieved under the classic retiree's investment strategy. With fixed income and stable value investments, income cannot be increased over time. The classic investment strategy works only when the retiree spends less than the annual income and reinvests the rest.

The classic strategy was especially punishing to those who started following it after 1982, because the period from 1982 to 2002 revealed a special problem that sprang from two factors. One factor is that most income investments eventually mature. That means the investment principal is returned and must be reinvested to generate future income. This is true of bonds and certificates of deposit, though generally not of annuities.

The second factor was the steady decline of interest rates after 1982. An investor could purchase safe investments that would yield more than 10 percent in the early 1980s. When the investments matured years later, the principal could not be reinvested to yield 10 percent without taking significantly more risk. Reinvesting the principal in the same type of investment would earn a steadily lower yield over the period. When originally invested, $100,000 could earn an annual income of $10,000. Years later, that $100,000 could earn $5,000 or less annually. See Chart 5.1.

Investors suffered a double loss during this period. First they suffered from the reduced purchasing power of their income due to inflation. Then

CHART 5.1   Interest Rates

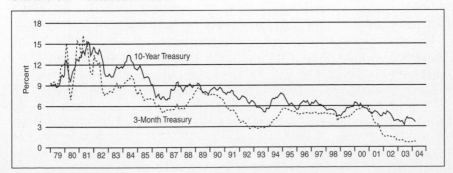

they suffered a loss in the actual dollars received after the investment matured and the principal had to be reinvested.

The good news for investors who consider the classic strategy now is that interest rates aren't going to fall over the next 20 years as much as they did over the last 20. Investors who follow this classic strategy in the future aren't going to suffer as much from declining interest rates. A smaller loss from declining rates still is possible, and might even be likely depending on the point during the interest rate cycle the investments are made. Whatever happens with interest rates, the purchasing power loss will be incurred as long as there is inflation.

There is another potential source of loss from this strategy. Suppose interest rates rise over time instead of falling. Any rise in rates is likely to be due to inflation. The market value of existing bonds declines when interest rates rise, because the interest earned by the existing bonds becomes less valuable. That is not a problem if the bond is held to maturity. But if the bond is sold before maturity, a loss would be incurred. If bond investments are made through mutual funds, the investment will not mature and the loss of principal likely will be permanent.

In a time of rising interest rates, the decline in principal value can be avoided by investing only in short-term investments such as money market funds, short-term bonds, and short-term certificates of deposit. These investments generally pay lower yields than those of longer-term investments. The investor must decide whether to accept lower current yields in exchange for greater safety of principal. A benefit of short-term income investments in a time of rising interest rates is that as the principal matures it can be reinvested to earn a higher yield than the original investment.

Money market funds probably are the safest investment in a time of rising inflation and rising interest rates. Because money market funds buy debt that matures in one year or less, the principal won't be affected much by rising interest rates. As the debt matures, the fund can constantly reinvest the principal to earn higher income in the newest debt being issued.

The classic investment advice for retirees makes sense now in only a few circumstances. The classic strategy can be used if retirement is expected to last five years or less so that the effects of inflation and changing interest rates would not be severe. The strategy also can work if the income from the portfolio exceeds the amount that must be spent, so that the excess can be reinvested. If inflation is 3 percent annually, an amount equal to 3 percent of the portfolio must be reinvested to maintain the purchasing power of the principal and the income. If the portfolio yields 5 percent when inflation is 3 percent, up to 2 percent can be spent and the rest must be reinvested. The classic strategy also can work when there are other sources of income that will help overcome the loss of purchasing power over time.

Stocks for the Long Term

More recently, retirees and pre-retirees were given the opposite advice. In the extreme version, retirees were advised to invest all their wealth in stocks. The reasoning is that stocks appreciate over the long term more than any other investment and almost never lose value over any long-term period. Stocks also are the only investment that consistently beat inflation. For example, $10,000 invested in the Standard & Poor's 500 stock index on January 31, 1973 would have increased to $291,238 by March 2001. The same amount invested in a portfolio of government bonds through the Lehman Brothers Long-term Government Bond Index would have increased to only $124,976.

The only sure way to retain purchasing power in the face of inflation is to own stocks. In addition, since stocks will appreciate more than inflation over time, there is a very good chance the real purchasing power of the wealth will increase. Even after taking money for annual expenses and leaving some of the returns in the portfolio to compensate for inflation, stock returns could be high enough to make the portfolio increase over the years.

In this strategy, the retiree doesn't spend only the income that is distributed. An all-stock portfolio will have both income (from dividends) and appreciation (capital gains). When spending needs exceed the dividends and other distributions, some stock or mutual fund shares should be sold to cover the spending. Or a broker or mutual fund company that holds the portfolio can be instructed to send a check for a fixed amount each month or quarter. The company automatically will sell shares from the account to the extent necessary to make the payment. Each year or so, the amount distributed can be increased to cover inflation. This is known as a check-a-month or automatic withdrawal program and is available from most brokers and mutual funds.

American Century, a large mutual fund firm, gives an example of such a program using its American Century Growth fund. Suppose an investor put $100,000 in the fund at the end of 1971 and a check-a-month program began the next year. The program paid $500 monthly the first year and increased the payout each year by 7.18 percent. All distributions were reinvested. By the end of 1998, the monthly payments would have climbed to $3,033. In addition, the value of the account would have grown to $4.4 million. Under this example, the retiree received both higher income and a greater net worth over time.

This is perhaps the strongest case for the all-stock portfolio. The American Century Growth fund was one of the great funds of the 1970s and 1980s, when it scored phenomenal returns. Yet, there are drawbacks to the plan that should keep many people from implementing it.

The biggest drawback is that the stock market does not rise steadily each year. Instead it rises for a few years then declines for a few years.

Many people would be comfortable with this program if they could be sure that their portfolios would rise for the first few years after retirement begins. That would build up a cushion for the inevitable market decline. Otherwise, large stock market losses could cause a high portion of a portfolio to evaporate quickly. The Nasdaq's worst annual loss was just under 40 percent in 2000. From its peak in March 2000 to the fall of 2001, the Nasdaq lost over 60 percent of its value. The decline continued into 2002, until the Nasdaq eventually lost over 80 percent of its peak value. Its next two worst calendar years were a 30 percent drop in 1973 followed by a loss of over 30 percent the following year. The Dow Jones Industrial Average's worst year was a 27.6 percent loss in 1974, preceded by its third-worst year with a loss of about 15 percent in 1973 (which was duplicated in 2002).

Not many investors could stick with this program in the face of such serious market losses, especially if the losses are incurred early in retirement. In fact, most probably would do the worst possible thing at that point. They would sell their stocks and invest in more conservative assets. That would ensure that they would never make up the losses.

The American Century Growth fund example actually begins at one of the worst possible times to adopt such a program, just before the severe bear market of 1973 and 1974. The holdings in the American Century Growth fund would have declined from $100,000 in 1972 to $64,065 at the end of 1974. It wouldn't be until 1976 that the portfolio's value would exceed the initial investment.

The results would not be as dramatic if a stock index fund or other mutual fund were used. American Century Growth is an aggressive fund that lost a lot of value in bear markets but substantially outperformed the average fund and the market indexes during the early part of the bull market that began in 1982. There also were periods, especially in the 1990s, when American Century Growth lagged both the index and the average fund because of its ever-growing size and aggressive growth style. Investors would have been tempted to switch funds during one of these periods, perhaps incurring substantial capital gains taxes that would reduce the size of their portfolios. Few other funds, however, would have recovered their bear market losses as quickly as American Century Growth did.

The all-stock portfolio can work for retirees and pre-retirees. For it to work, the retiree needs both the resources and the fortitude to continue the program during a steep market decline, especially one that occurs during the early years of retirement. In fact, it is likely to be 10 years or more before one can be reasonably secure that a market decline won't result in spending principal at some point. The portfolio also must be invested to earn high growth over several decades. The growth will have to make up for inflation, spending, and the inevitable market declines.

The investor also must be fortunate enough to select a top mutual fund or portfolio of stocks. American Century Growth was one of the top-returning funds for the period. The results would not have been nearly so attractive if the investor selected an average or a below average fund. Finally, the rate at which money will be distributed from the portfolio must be set at a level that can be sustained for decades. Details about the level at which to establish the distributions are found in Chapter 6.

The biggest obstacles to this program are the wrong investments, the investor's emotions, and the cyclical behavior of the markets.

The Modern Buy-and-Hold

The third category of likely investment advice is some variation of what is known as modern portfolio theory and the capital asset pricing model, or CAPM. These actually are two separate theories, but generally are lumped together. Many investment professionals follow this approach using a computer program called a portfolio optimizer. Most often, this approach is known simply as buying and holding a diversified portfolio.

This investment approach began as an academic idea in the early 1950s. The idea was not practical at the time, but as computer power grew it became inexpensive and easy for many people to implement the strategy using a portfolio optimizer. Today, investors can use some version of a portfolio optimizer free at many web sites. The originators of this approach were awarded the Nobel Prize in Economic Science for their intellectual contributions.

The basic idea behind this investment approach is that a mix of diversified investments will yield close to the same long-term return as a portfolio of only the highest-return investment. For example, over time a portfolio composed of different types of stocks (large and small companies, U.S. and foreign) plus bonds and perhaps some other investments will generate about the same long-term total return as a portfolio of all U.S. stocks. In addition and most importantly, the diversified portfolio will have less risk (defined as volatility) than the all-stock portfolio.

Diversification works when the different assets in the portfolio do not rise and fall in lockstep. In other words, their returns should have a low correlation. Bonds generally rise or hold their value when stocks are falling, and vice versa. Likewise, small company stocks and large company stocks often are in bull markets at different times, as are international stocks and U.S. stocks. The result is that there are always parts of the diversified portfolio that are rising while others are falling or holding their value. If over long periods of time each or at least most of the assets appreciate from their initial value, the entire portfolio will appreciate. Because the assets aren't likely to all decline at the same time (i.e., they have a low correlation with each other), the portfolio is likely to decline less in a bear market than an all-stock portfolio will.

The optimizer is a computer program that uses the historic returns and correlations of different assets to determine the right mix for the diversified portfolio. The investor determines the desired long-term rate of return and the amount of permissible volatility. The computer determines the appropriate mix of assets that can achieve the desired risk and return based on history. One of the principles underlying CAPM is that few if any investors will be able to determine which investment assets will rise and fall at different times. Therefore, the best an investor can do is to determine the appropriate long-term mix of assets and hold that mix indefinitely.

Most pension funds and other institutional investors use some form of CAPM. It also is used by many financial planners, brokers, and other investment advisers to construct portfolios for their clients. Investment advice from a web site sponsored by a broker or mutual fund likely will use an optimizer to determine the recommended portfolio.

Despite its widespread use, there are some disadvantages to the long-term buy-and-hold strategy of CAPM that make it inappropriate for many retirees and pre-retirees. Investment risk under CAPM is defined as the standard deviation, or volatility, of investment returns. That means the risk of a portfolio or asset is considered to be the amount by which its price fluctuates over a period of time, usually annually. It doesn't matter if the fluctuation is upward or downward or how long each up or down trend lasts. For most investors, however, risk is something else. Risk ultimately is the possibility that the portfolio won't achieve the investor's goals, such as paying for retirement and leaving assets for heirs or charity. By this definition, an asset could have low volatility and still be very risky to an investor. Or an investment could have very high short-term volatility and still not carry much long-term risk of not meeting the investor's goals. An investor using CAPM is using a model that defines risk as something other than what the investor considers to be risk.

Another disadvantage of CAPM, and one that the recent bear market highlighted, is that it focuses only on the very long term and only on one rate of return over that long period. This might be fine for a pension fund that essentially has an indefinite life. Most pension funds can withstand years or even decades when the portfolio's returns are below expectations. In time, the investment returns will return to the long-term average and the fund will meet its goals. Individual investors don't have the luxury of an infinite life. They should be concerned with returns over perhaps the next 10 years, not the last 80 years. Ten years of below-average returns—which has happened every generation or so—could be too much for the individual to overcome and could lead to a reduced standard of living.

A related disadvantage is that historic returns often are used in the portfolio optimizer. CAPM assumes that the past pattern of investment returns will be the future pattern. We actually have verifiable, reliable investment returns for U.S. stocks only for a relatively short period of time. For other investments, we have even a smaller database of returns. Most statisticians would state that the amount of historic returns we have for our investments is not long enough to draw conclusions or to reliably forecast future returns. This is especially true for relatively new asset classes, such as emerging market stocks. In addition, the economies and markets constantly are changing. There is no reason to assume that economic and investment scenarios of the past will be repeated in the future.

Likewise, most CAPM models use historic correlations between investments. The correlation between different investments, however, seems to change over time. A portfolio that is properly diversified at one time will act like an undiversified portfolio at another time.

The use of historic returns and correlations probably results in great errors in portfolios. It is a good thing for many investors that the computer power to use portfolio optimization software wasn't available in the late 1970s and early 1980s. If it were, many portfolios in the 1980s probably would have been invested heavily in real estate, international stocks, and gold and barely invested in U.S. stocks and bonds.

Most advocates of CAPM also advocate using only index funds or similar investments in a portfolio. The theory is that the markets are perfectly efficient. Few investment managers outperform an index over a long time without taking significantly more risk, and those managers probably succeeded more because of luck than skill. CAPM also holds that an investor cannot identify in advance those investment managers who are likely to beat an index over a long term. Therefore, investors should avoid active managers and simply invest in a market index.

One way to overcome some of the disadvantages of CAPM is to use the portfolio optimizer only to determine the probability of success. Traditionally, the optimizer is used to produce one recommended portfolio that is considered the efficient one for the investor. Advances in computers, however, allow a more robust use of the model. Using a sophisticated tool known as the Monte Carlo simulation method (described in Chapter 3), the model can use either actual past returns or randomly-generated returns to show the results over hundreds of possible scenarios for the future. The result is the probability the portfolio will achieve its goals.

Combining the portfolio optimizer with the Monte Carlo method does not produce one portfolio with the conclusion that it will achieve a stated return and volatility over time. Instead, a recommended portfolio is produced with the conclusion that it is likely to meet the investor's goals with a stated probability. The result might be that the portfolio has a 95 percent probability of success. That means that, using either historic returns or randomly generated returns, the portfolio achieves its goals in 95 percent of scenarios. That way, the investor knows that despite the use of computers the portfolio construction is not an exact science. He knows that, given the historical returns, there is a 5 percent chance the goals won't be met with that portfolio. The investor then has to decide if that is a high enough probability and he wants to take the chance that his immediate future won't be like the 5 percent of scenarios in which the goals won't be met.

Some users of the portfolio optimizer overcome other disadvantages by modifying it. Instead of using historic returns, they make forecasts of future returns and correlations. These forecasts, of course, could be wrong. In fact, they are likely to be wrong to some extent. An educated, informed judgment of future returns by an experienced professional, however, could be closer to the mark than mechanically following historical returns.

In addition, the effectiveness of the optimizer can be improved by limiting the time frame to 10 years or less. Most pension funds review the portfolio optimizer inputs and results every four or five years and adjust their portfolios accordingly. Those who use forecasts instead of historical returns will make ten-year or shorter forecasts instead of using long-term historic numbers. That way, they don't attempt the difficult forecasts of one year or less. Yet, they can make an assumption, for example, that if stocks returned higher than historic average returns over the last ten years, they are likely to return less than the historic average over the next ten years.

There are other ways investors overcome the disadvantages of CAPM. Unfortunately, it is difficult for the individual investor to use these modified methods. The computer programs available to individual investors generally use historic returns and lock in other assumptions that cannot be changed by the user. Most financial firms and professionals that develop portfolios for individual investors also do not use these modified methods with a portfolio optimizer. Even these modifications do not overcome all the shortcomings of CAPM.

A Better Way to Build a Portfolio

A few of us were critical of the conventional investment strategies for years. The number of critics steadily increased after the stock market indexes peaked in March 2000. Conferences for pension fund investors since 2001 have emphasized alternatives to the conventional investment approaches. For example, Peter Bernstein, author of the book *Capital Ideas* (Free Press, 1993) and long-time advocate of CAPM and index funds, threw in the towel in late 2002 and early 2003. He recommended that pension funds and other institutional investors abandon CAPM and what is known as the fixed policy portfolio. Bernstein started advocating a far different approach to investing that involved hedging against different possible investment outcomes and hoping for a fairly modest long-term return with low volatility.

Those are a few signs of the unhappiness with the traditional approaches to investing. I have advocated and used a nontraditional approach for years. Only recently did I learn that it is largely supported by an academic theory developed in the 1990s known as Rational Beliefs. I believe this approach recognizes and corrects many of the problems in the other strategies and is superior for retirees and those saving for retirement.

The key difference in Rational Beliefs is that it recognizes and explains valuation cycles and makes managing valuation cycles the cornerstone of investing. The different investment markets have cycles, and these cycles occur because of extreme changes in valuations. The markets are not perfectly efficient, and many of them aren't even generally efficient.

A valuation cycle works like this. An investment gradually will become wildly popular. Its price will increase gradually at first. As investors see consistent returns, more purchase the investment. The profits attract more investors who push the price still higher until it is soaring. The rising prices also push the valuation higher. Valuation is measured differently for different investments, but the investment moves from undervalued to fairly valued and finally to overvalued. Eventually, some investors become concerned about the high valuation and begin to sell the investment. There are few investors who haven't already purchased it and can be brought into the market. The price begins to fall, and the cycle reverses. Often, some unexpected events trigger or accelerate the change. In any case, the price steadily declines as more and more investors seek other opportunities.

Efficient market theory and CAPM teach that all investors are both rational and right all the time. Rational Beliefs states that all investors are rational but not necessarily right or in agreement. Each investor has his own theory about the current investment cycle, how long it will last, and what the next move in the cycle will be. Some investors are always bearish; some are always bullish; most investors swing between the two and determine the cycles. Each investor will select investments based on his or her current outlook and the resulting expected risk-adjusted returns. While investors will process the same information, they will not interpret it the same way. The valuation cycle that exists at any time is determined by the ratio between optimists and pessimists in the population and also by their relative intensity.

Among a population there tend to be a correlation of beliefs and also a persistence of beliefs. These are two important points in explaining cycles. A sizeable part of the population tends to adopt the same view most of the time, and once formed those views tend to persist for extended periods of time. The persistence explains long, or secular, bull and bear markets. Swings between optimism and pessimism by relatively small segments of the population can cause short-term rallies in a long-term bear market, for example, but the opinion of the majority determines the long-term trend. Outlooks and beliefs of the majority change slowly. Once investors fall in love with stocks, it takes a great deal of disappointment for them to fall out of love with stocks. Once investors have been burned in a severe bear market, it takes most of them a long time to forget that and become optimistic about stocks again. (Some analysts use similar theories to explain political cycles.)

I won't go into the more technical explanations Rational Beliefs theorists use to explain the valuation cycle. What is important for the individual investor is to recognize that valuation cycles exist for all investments, and that the cycles are the biggest risk to the individual investor. The key to successful investing is not trying to earn the normal or most efficient long-term return, as CAPM teaches. That long-term return is merely an average arrived at over many decades. The key for the individual is that there will be overvaluation and undervaluation cycles that make up the long term. Each of these cycles is likely to last for ten to 20 years or even longer. Since most individuals cannot count on being around for the long term, identifying the cycles is important.

We know that there will be long bull and bear markets. We also have a good estimate of what the long-term return from stocks will be, and that this return will exceed what is available from other investments. What we don't know in advance is when a new long-term trend will begin or how long it will last. Because of the cycles, simply buying stocks in an index fund for the long run is not rational for the individual investor. There are better and safer ways to manage a portfolio.

An investor, especially a retiree or pre-retiree, should be concerned about investment returns, especially from stocks, for the next ten years or so, not the average return over the past 70 years or more. The investor should search for structural changes in the markets, the economy, or both, and invest the portfolio accordingly.

There also are shorter valuation cycles within the long-term valuation cycles. A rational investor can try to identify the long-term valuation cycles and ride out any short-term changes within those long-term cycles. Or the investor can also try to identify the intermediate cycles (of from one to five years) and capture the profit opportunities within those cycles.

Another conclusion that can be drawn from Rational Beliefs is that the consensus at the extremes of the valuation cycle usually is wrong. Investors as a group are most bullish near a market top and are most bearish near a market bottom. This really is just common sense. The valuation cycle could not be pushed to an extreme without having most investors believing the same things. While it is comforting to invest in line with the way most people are thinking, it is not likely to be profitable at the valuation extremes.

Investing with the majority, however, can be profitable when valuations are not yet at an extreme. Remember that the valuation cycle is caused by the vast majority of investors moving from one extreme toward the other. That process can take years, and the shift is likely to continue pushing the markets in one direction for some time.

It is important in identifying valuation cycles that one not focus on the short-term and the latest news. The short-term news is known as market noise and will not improve returns. A good practice is that of bond fund manager Bill Gross and his team at PIMCO. Gross advocates looking at the likely scenario for the next three to five years and ignoring short-term fluctuations in between. Focus on the major trends that seem likely in the markets and economy for that intermediate term and adjust the portfolio accordingly.

Though few are familiar with the details of the academic literature, Rational Beliefs and the valuation cycle inform the investment practices of value-style investment managers, especially those in the stock market. Valuation cycles also have been the basis of my investment recommendations for years. Let's look at how the investor who is in or preparing for retirement can use this information.

The Better Investment Pyramid

I have long advocated an investment pyramid approach to building a portfolio. This investment pyramid is an effective tool whether an investor is in retirement or planning for retirement. This pyramid is divided into three levels. Every investor does not need all three levels. Only the levels that are appropriate for that investor need to be included. I'll explain the different levels of the pyramid and how investors can decide which levels of the pyramid are appropriate for them.

The Core or Foundation Portfolio

The large bottom section of the investment pyramid is the Core or Foundation. For most investors, I believe this should be the largest portion of the total investment portfolio or at least half of the portfolio. The Core Portfolio is a fixed, diversified, and balanced portfolio that is held for the long term with few changes. But it is not built using the same approach as a capital asset pricing model portfolio.

The Core Portfolio is diversified among different types of assets that are expected to do well over the next ten years or so. It does not try to include all types of assets and investment styles. I recommend that it consist primarily of mutual funds and that those funds be managed with a value approach. I do not recommend growth stock funds or index funds in the Core Portfolio. These managers will be watching the valuation cycle and managing their portion of the portfolio according to the cycle. They will sell the overvalued assets in their class and buy only those selling at discounts or at least lower valuations.

The Core Portfolio is constructed with the idea that the primary goal of every investor is to avoid large, permanent losses. Even the more aggressive investors should want to avoid large losses. Other investment approaches, such as buy-and-hold strategies, accept large losses over different time periods. Large losses matter to investors who are retired or planning for retirement. Large losses, even if temporary, can cause at the least a great deal of uncertainty and anxiety. If not temporary, large losses require changes in spending plans. Short-term losses are inevitable in the investment markets. But capital preservation over the intermediate and long term is a goal of every portfolio. The aim of the Core Portfolio should be steady, solid returns, and there always should be a margin of safety in the portfolio.

Let's examine in more detail why value investment managers should be in the Core Portfolio, using U.S. stocks as an example.

Value stocks tend to decline less than the market indexes in a bear market and even can appreciate when the market indexes are declining (as happened in 2000 and 2001). Value stock funds also tend to appreciate when the market indexes essentially are flat. Growth stocks usually perform best only in the early and late stages of a bull market. More importantly, growth stock funds tend to lose a lot of their gains in bear markets. There is an ongoing debate over whether value stocks or growth stocks perform best over the long term. Much depends on the starting and ending points one selects for the analysis. But my analysis is that because they avoid large losses and have steadier returns, value stock funds are the best for the long term, especially for an individual investor who cannot afford a permanent decline in capital.

Efficient market theorists recommend index funds. The reason is that only a minority of active managers beat the indexes, and it is difficult to determine in advance who those managers will be. My point is that retirees and pre-retirees shouldn't be concerned primarily with meeting or beating a market index. It doesn't do the individual investor much good to meet an index's returns or beat it by a small amount when the index is down 20 percent or more. Most individual investors should be concerned with avoiding large losses and earning steady, solid returns with a margin of safety.

Index funds became especially dangerous for retirees and pre-retirees starting in the late 1980s. That is because the market indexes changed. When a mutual fund tracks a market index, it has to pay a royalty to the index compiler for use of the index. As more and more investors, especially large institutional investors, adopted index funds, compiling indexes became a lucrative business. Index creators began competing to have the best performing index in the bull market. As a result, the indexes changed more frequently through the 1990s than they did in previous years. In addition, to boost returns the indexes became less representative of the overall stock market and became more growth-stock oriented than in the past. The result is that indexes now carry more risk and volatility than they did, though they are likely to outperform nearly all mutual funds in bull markets.

In addition, the major indexes are capitalization weighted. That means the larger a firm's relative market value, the greater its weighting in the computation of the index value. Because of this, index returns and fluctuations are dominated by the performance of 50 or fewer large stocks. The behavior of smaller stocks, while in the index, hardly changes the index. Though the indexes purport to track hundreds or even thousands of stocks, a small number of large companies determine most of the results.

Value in Action

Let's take a look at how value stock funds handled the 2000–2002 bear market. In fact, let's start with 1998. Value stocks actually had a rough time in the last years of the bull market, because investors almost exclusively purchased growth stocks, particularly technology company stocks. Once growth stocks fell sharply, value stocks began rising. It was only during the period from June through October 2002, when almost all stocks declined, that the bear market finally took a toll on value stock funds.

The box that follows shows how some of my favorite value stock funds performed during the last phase of the bull market and during the bear market compared to the Vanguard 500 Index. You can see that all of the value funds earned solid returns during the last leg of the bull market, though they lagged behind the market index. Each of them also did significantly better than the index during the bear market. The returns among the value funds differed greatly during this period. If I cut off the second period at May 31, 2002, the value funds would have looked even more attractive. The period from June through October 2002 was when all stocks and mutual funds sharply declined, including the value funds. The 1998–2002 period essentially is a full market cycle. The market index basically ended the period where it started, yet the value funds had strong total returns.

Fund	1998–2000*	2000–2002*	1998–2002
Dodge & Cox Stock	27.03%	13.46	44.13%
American Century Equity Income	11.81%	30.06	45.41%
Torray	31.65%	-14.81	12.16%
Third Avenue Value	37.73%	-10.36	23.46%
S&P 500	59.22%	-39.08	-3.00%

*Total returns January 1, 1998–March 31, 2000; April 1, 2000–December 31, 2002.

Simple Core Portfolios

An alternative to setting up a Core Portfolio is to simply purchase a balanced mutual fund that invests in different assets. Balanced funds usually invest in stocks and bonds, though some add other assets. Some balanced funds keep a fixed allocation between stocks and bonds. Other funds will change the allocation based on market conditions. The balanced fund is an especially good choice for the small investor, the new investor, or the investor who doesn't want to spend much time managing a portfolio. My recommended balanced funds are Dodge & Cox Balanced, Vanguard Wellesley Income, Vanguard Wellington, and Oakmark Equity & Income.

A Few Tweaks

Once the Core Portfolio is established, it is held for the long term. The individual mutual funds are monitored to be sure they are doing what was expected. A fund is replaced when it changes managers, gets too big to invest effectively, changes strategy, or for other reasons seems unable to duplicate its past performance. A fund is not sold, however, because it is in one of those temporary periods when it does not perform well relative to an index. Periods of unsatisfactory performance are common to all investment managers and mutual funds. Temporary bad performance is not a reason to sell a mutual fund from a long-term Core Portfolio.

The Core Portfolio will stray from its original allocation because of market actions. Stocks might appreciate, for example, while bonds decline or stagnate. Because of this, at least once a year the Core Portfolio is rebalanced to the original intended allocation. The regular rebalancing is very important. It is a way to ensure that investments are bought low and sold high. In a rebalancing, holdings of investments that have done well in the past year are reduced and holdings of the poor performers are increased. Rebalancing is essential to reducing long-term risk and increasing returns.

Beyond that, the Core Portfolio allocation should be reexamined regularly to determine if any long-term changes in the investment markets warrant changes in the portfolio. These changes should be rare, because only long-term changes that are likely to last for ten years or so should be considered. Shorter-term changes are not part of this portfolio.

Some investors might not want to look beyond the Core Portfolio. They don't want to do any more work than this portfolio requires and are content with its long-term performance. There's nothing wrong with that. The portfolio is designed to achieve solid long-term returns and to avoid big losses in bear markets. Investors who are willing to spend more time on their portfolios and who seek higher returns with potentially higher risk should consider the next levels of the pyramid.

Managing the Valuation Cycles

The next level of the pyramid is what I call the Managed Portfolio. This part of the portfolio fully aligns with the research in Rational Beliefs investing, and it is where investment returns can be meaningfully increased while risk is reduced.

The Managed Portfolio essentially begins with the same allocation as the Core Portfolio. Then, different assets are overweighted or underweighted based on the investment outlook for the next one to five years and on the valuation cycle. Investments that are not even in the Core Portfolio will find their way into the Managed Portfolio when they seem to be undervalued and have low risk.

This portfolio does not involve market timing and is not a frequently traded portfolio, though it does involve more changes than are made in the Core Portfolio. The intent is not to try to capture short-term trends in the markets or to respond to the latest headlines and market noise. Instead, the strategy for this portfolio is to sell assets that are overvalued and buy assets that are undervalued or that are likely to benefit from what looks like the next phase of the valuation cycle.

The valuation cycle exists not only for all types of investments, but also for sectors of the stock market and other markets. For example, large capitalization and small capitalization stocks have separate valuation cycles. So do growth stocks and value stocks. We know that there will be extreme bull and bear markets for each asset. We also know that some investments will be in their bull markets while others are in bear markets, because sectors of the stock market fluctuate at different times.

This is similar to the philosophy expounded by Bill Gross of the PIMCO Funds, as discussed earlier. Gross is the long-time manager of PIMCO Total Return, the largest and perhaps most successful bond fund. During the 2000–2002 equity bear market, PIMCO Total Return surpassed popular equity funds to become the largest mutual fund. Gross believes, as I do, that maximum profits are earned by capturing the intermediate trends of the investments markets. An intermediate trend as defined by Gross is one that lasts for three to five years. I prefer looking at a one- to three-year cycle. During the intermediate trends, some investments will earn more than their long-term averages and others will earn less than their averages. An investor who can capture some of the good intermediate trends and avoid some of the bad trends will increase long-term returns with less risk.

While the Managed Portfolio should earn above-average returns, the idea is not to seek the next hot investment or mutual fund. Instead, the approach should be to reduce risk by limiting exposure to investments that seem overvalued and at risk of tumbling. Eliminating the high-risk assets and seeking those with lower risk automatically avoids the likely big losers. It also positions the portfolio in the assets that are likely to do well over the next few years. The strategy reduces the risk and volatility of the portfolio. Reducing risk and losses in this way increases returns in the long run.

It is not easy to spot turns in a valuation cycle, whether one is trying to call the long-term cycle or the intermediate turns. For example, in the early- and mid-1990s in my role as a public pension fund trustee, I frequently heard arguments that stocks were overvalued, the bull market was over, and a long bear market was due to begin. This advice was a few years early, and following it at that time would have been expensive. In addition, there are times when an asset appears to be undervalued, yet it continues to decline.

To reduce the risk of loss from mistakes, I recommend a couple of additional strategies in building the Managed Portfolio.

One strategy is the automatic sell signal or stop loss. Most investors should try to limit losses from any investment in the Managed Portfolio to

5 percent to 7 percent. When buying an investment, at least a volatile investment, it is a good idea to set a sell signal. If the investment, despite what appears to be a low valuation, continues to decline below the sell price, the investor should admit a mistake, sell the investment, and reassess the situation.

Also, in the Managed Portfolio, I rarely recommend putting 50 percent or more of the portfolio in one fund or asset class. Use diversification and balance to limit the effects of mistakes. The most attractive asset will get the largest portion of the Managed Portfolio, but other investments also will be included in the portfolio.

For those who are willing to do the additional analysis and trading, the Managed Portfolio can increase returns and reduce risk.

For Aggressive Investors

The final section of the pyramid is the Aggressive Portfolio. This is the top portion of the pyramid, and so it should be the smallest portion of the portfolio for most investors. The Aggressive Portfolio is traded on a shorter-term basis. Many investors, especially retired investors, will not have an aggressive portion in their total portfolios. They don't want to spend the time required to monitor their portfolios, or they don't want to take the risk involved with aggressive investments.

There are many aggressive strategies available to investors. Those who are interested in adding an aggressive portion to their portfolios should study the alternatives. Some are available through newsletters or web sites. Others are available by having that portion of the portfolio managed by an investment firm. Sometimes an aggressive strategy involves purchasing and holding specific investments. For example, an aggressive strategy is to invest in small nonpublic companies through a private equity fund. Those investments can pay off handsomely, but they also carry high risk and can produce significant losses.

Investors who are interested should find an aggressive approach that is compatible with their investment philosophy and the risks they are willing to take. They should not choose a strategy they do not understand, even if someone else will be executing it for them. Also, because of the higher risk and volatility inherent in an aggressive strategy, the expected return from the strategy should exceed the return of the S&P 500 by several percentage points.

I recommend that most investors start out by building a Core Portfolio. Once they are comfortable with the Managed Portfolio concept, about half the total portfolio can be moved into a Managed Portfolio as market opportunities appear. Finally, investors who are interested in an aggressive strategy can move a portion of the Managed Portfolio into the aggressive portion when an appropriate strategy is found.

The Safety Fund

For many retirees and near-retirees, a major concern is the effect a serious or sustained market decline would have on their portfolios. Too often, a 20 percent or greater decline in stocks—which happens with some regularity—causes investors to alter their long-term allocations. They decide that they are not willing to take as much risk as they thought. That usually is the worst time to make such a move.

One way to avoid that risk is to create a safety fund that is separate from the portfolio pyramid just described. The safety fund should be established before any other investments.

The first step in the safety fund is to estimate annual living expenses for each of the next few years. Be sure to include inflation and one-time expenses such as new cars or home repairs. Second, determine how much of these expenses will be paid by Social Security and other sources of income. Third, estimate how much money will be needed from the portfolio to pay for the rest of the expenses each year.

Now, take an amount equal to the next year's expenses that will have to come from the portfolio and put that amount in a money market fund or similar safe, liquid investment. This way, the investor knows that no matter what happens, the next year is taken care of.

Next, the investor should determine how many years of wealth protection are desired. Two to five years are the best range to consider. Take an amount equal to the expenses that must come out of the portfolio over that period and invest it in bonds. Don't use long-term bonds. Their values are too volatile as interest rates change. Buy intermediate bonds. The Vanguard Total Bond Index fund is a good choice for this investment. A portion of this portfolio can be invested in high yield bonds for those who don't mind severe fluctuations in value from time to time. But the bulk of this fund should be in intermediate term bonds. The bonds won't fluctuate too much in value over time and will earn higher yields than money market funds. If interest rates decline, capital gains will be earned from the bonds.

The rest of the portfolio then is invested according to the investment pyramid described in this chapter. This safety fund provides a cushion and the flexibility to let you ride out most bear markets without having to sell longer-term investments near the bottom of the price range.

How Much Can You Spend?

Running out of assets and income is perhaps the biggest financial fear of most Americans. No one wants to run out of money before running out of breath. Much of retirement planning is designed to avoid just that. That's why the traditional retirement planning process involves estimating retirement spending and matching it with expected sources of income. If the two don't match, adjustments are made to the plan. Spending can be reduced, or perhaps income can be increased. The previous five chapters explained much of that process.

If Chapter 3 was intimidating, seemed like too much work, or depended on too many assumptions, don't worry. There is a way to jump straight to the bottom line. With a lot less work, we can estimate how much can be spent safely each year in retirement or how much must be accumulated for the desired retirement. This method also serves as a check against the results of the traditional process.

This method involves answering the question: What is the maximum amount that can be withdrawn from your portfolio each year without prematurely depleting the portfolio? In other words, how much can be spent each year without taking the risk of running out of money?

In this chapter, I'll explain a method that virtually guarantees that your wealth will last through a worst-case scenario or how much needs to be accumulated for a best-case retirement.

The Weakest Link in Most Plans

The shortcoming of the method used to develop most retirement plans is the assumption that the investment portfolio will earn an average annual return. The planner begins by estimating the average annual return the portfolio will earn over the long term, then assumes that return will be earned by the portfolio each and every year.

Unfortunately, that's not the way the world works. Even if the average annual return estimated for the retirement period turns out to be exactly right, this method still can drastically overestimate the amount of money that can be spent each year. That's because while the stock market has an average annual return of 8 percent to 10 percent, it doesn't earn 10 percent each and every year. In some years, stocks return 20 percent or more. Other years, they decline 20 percent or more. In fact, over the long term the Dow Jones Industrial Average has lost more than 10 percent about 21 percent of the time and has gained more than 10 percent about 49 percent of the time. About 15 percent of the time it has lost more than 16 percent, and about 35 percent of the time it has gained more than 16 percent.

The difference between actual returns and average annual returns can be significant—especially if someone is in the early years of retirement or is near retirement and the actual returns differ significantly from the average annual returns.

The retiree will begin spending part of the portfolio immediately after retiring. If investment returns in the early years of retirement are so low that the portfolio declines, the retiree will be spending principal in addition to suffering the investment losses. It will take a while for the portfolio to make up both the losses and the spending to get back on the forecasted track. If losses in the early years of retirement are severe, the portfolio might never recover.

Look at the actual period from 1968 to 1998. The average annual return for the S&P 500 during this period was 11.7 percent, well above the historical average. The early part of this period, however, was especially tough for investors. The stock market had several sharp declines, and bond prices also suffered during this period because of inflation. The Dow average actually broke above 1000 for the first time in 1966 but didn't get above 1000 to stay until 1982.

A retiree who had $250,000 at the start of this period and who knew the average annual return going forward would be 11.7 percent would have forecast a rosy retirement. He would calculate that 8.5 percent of the portfolio could be withdrawn the first year and that amount could be increased by 3 percent each year without running out of money for the entire 20 years.

The actual returns, however, created a completely different financial result. The average annual return for the period was the result of post-1981 returns that were well above average. Unfortunately, this retiree's portfolio would not last until 1981 to reap those high returns. Because of the sharp stock market losses in the early years, the retiree would run out of money by 1981 if he withdrew 8.5 percent of the portfolio the first year and increased that by 3 percent each subsequent year. A much more attractive result emerges if the stock market returns were reversed, with the high returns in the early years of retirement and the low returns at the end. In that case, the retiree has more money after 20 years than was anticipated using the average annual return. See Chart 6.1.

In the previous chapter, we saw the shortcomings of an all-stock or all-bond portfolio. A more diversified portfolio is needed to increase financial security in retirement. A retiree needs sources of both income and growth in a portfolio. There also should be assets in the portfolio that perform well at different times (called negative correlation by investment professionals). A diversified portfolio and its average annual return, however, are not the final answer to a secure retirement.

From the example above, it is clear that using the average annual return of a diversified portfolio to plan retirement spending still does not generate confidence that the portfolio won't be exhausted before the end of a 20 or 30 year retirement. To have confidence in the amount that can be withdrawn safely from a portfolio, fluctuating annual returns must be considered. Using the Monte Carlo simulation method discussed in Chapter 3 can increase the confidence level, but it still leaves a lot of uncertainty. To have

CHART 6.1   How Much Can You Withdraw from Your Retirement Portfolio: 1968–1998?—The Pitfalls of Projecting Average Returns

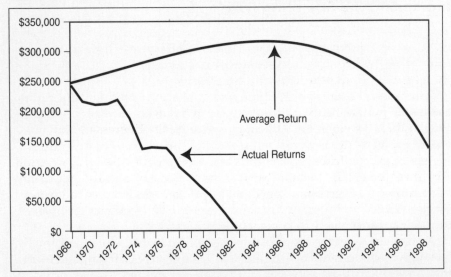

Assumptions: Initial withdrawal amount increases by 3 percent each year for inflation. Withdrawals are made at the start of each year. Taxes and minimum required distributions from tax-deferred accounts are not considered in this illustration. Performance is based on historical returns for these periods of the S&P 500 Stock Index (60 percent of the portfolio), U.S. Intermediate Government Bond Index (30 percent), and 30-day Treasury bills (10 percent). *Source:* T. Rowe Price Associates. Performance data supplied by Ibbotson Associates.

high confidence that a withdrawal rate is safe, the early years of retirement must be assumed to be similar to the worst years the investment markets experienced in the past.

Fortunately, much of the work already has been done and published in different studies. Assuming the worst case of very bad historic returns at the start of retirement, the research found that to ensure a portfolio lasts 30 years, the first-year withdrawal rate should be no higher than 4.1 percent of the portfolio's value. After the first year, withdrawals can increase by 3 percent each year to compensate for inflation. The withdrawals are before taxes. The taxes on income and capital gains must be paid from the withdrawals, so the retiree actually will be spending something less than 4.1 percent. A few studies that use different portfolio allocations estimate the first-year withdrawal rate closer to 5 percent.

Those who are deciding how much to save for retirement can turn the calculation around. First, decide how much will be spent in the first year of retirement and subtract noninvestment sources of income, such as Social Security. Let's say the result is $40,000 of first-year spending to be financed by investments. Divide that by 4.1 percent, and the result is $975,610. That is the portfolio that has to be accumulated to safely withdraw $40,000 annually in today's dollars and have the portfolio last through a 30-year retirement.

Increasing the Spending Rate

That 4 percent to 5 percent withdrawal rate seems rather low to many people and could crimp the retirement plans of many Americans. There are some points to consider and possible modifications that could allow a safe increase in the withdrawal rate.

Remember the 4.1 percent withdrawal rate is the maximum allowed to ensure the portfolio survives when the early years of retirement resemble 1966 to 1972, the worst investment period since the Depression. Inflation was high and rising, as were interest rates. Oil price volatility was disrupting the economy. Taxes were high. The government was increasing military involvement in Vietnam while simultaneously rapidly increasing other forms of government spending. The dollar was in a free fall in currency markets, and gold prices were soaring. The stock market indexes dropped approximately 50 percent over two years.

A prospective retiree could reasonably conclude that while there might be tough economic and investment times in the early years of retirement, they aren't likely to be as bad as that period. For example, while the stock market indexes declined sharply from 2000 to 2002, bond prices and shares of real estate investment trusts appreciated nicely. A diversified portfolio would have survived this period better than the earlier one. With this assumption, a new retiree with a diversified portfolio might decide not to so severely restrict spending to 4.1 percent of the portfolio in the early years of retirement until it is clear that something approaching the worst-case scenario is occurring.

A retiree also might take into account that spending tends to decrease in the later years. People tend to slow down sometime between ages 75 and 85, reducing travel and other activities that cost money. It is possible that major medical or long-term care expenses might crimp spending over the years, and we'll discuss ways to deal with those expenses in later chapters. To keep from depriving oneself in the early years of retirement, however, a retiree might want to spend more in the early years in the belief that spending will be reduced later.

Another factor to consider is that many expenses can be changed over time. A retiree might want to take a higher withdrawal rate for the first year or two. If the investment markets do not earn at least the average annual return in the early years, nonfixed expenses can be reduced without drastically reducing the standard of living. For example, some travel might be postponed or more meals might be eaten at home. Some other expenses can be eliminated or postponed.

Also, the studies published generally simplify matters by using S&P 500 stocks, a bond index, and Treasury bills in the portfolios. Long-term returns probably can be increased with the addition of other assets. Small company stocks should be part of a portfolio. International stocks also can be added to increase long-term returns. In the 1968 to 1982 period, when U.S. stocks were having a difficult time, many international stock indexes did much better. Purchasing international stocks also enabled U.S. investors to profit from the declining dollar. High-yield bonds and real estate or real estate investment trusts (REITs) also are good additions to many long-term portfolios.

In fact, REITs could greatly benefit a portfolio, and I have long favored them in long-term portfolios. In 2001, this move was endorsed by Ibbotson Associates, one of the leading firms in developing long-term asset allocation strategies. Ibbotson says its work shows that adding REITs to a portfolio gives a higher long-term return with less volatility. In addition, REITs do not have a high correlation with the stock market and many other traditional investment assets. That means REITs tend to move in the opposite direction of those assets. Indeed, when stock market indexes declined sharply in 2000 and 2001, REITs generated solid returns.

Old-fashioned fixed-payment annuities also might increase a portfolio's ability to survive, according to a study published in the December 2001 *Journal of Financial Planning*. The study examined four portfolio combinations, from conservative to aggressive. The conservative portfolio was 20 percent stocks, while the aggressive was 85 percent stocks. Using a Monte Carlo simulation, the study found that for each type of portfolio, putting 25 percent or 50 percent of the fund into a fixed annuity increased the odds of success. The greatest improvement was in the conservative portfolio. While the annuity also improved the odds of success for the aggressive portfolio, the existence of a lot of stocks in that portfolio already gave it over a 90 percent probability of survival. Adding the annuity increased the survival odds only a bit. The odds of survival for the conservative portfolio, however, were 32.6 percent with no annuity. They improved to 53.3 percent when 25 percent of the portfolio was moved into an annuity and to 81.3 percent when the portfolio was 50 percent in a fixed annuity.

An annuity offers advantages bonds don't have. The payout on an annuity is fixed once regular distributions are begun. As we've seen when discussing the all-bond portfolio in the previous chapter, bond yields can decline as interest rates decline, or the bond principal can decline as interest rates rise. A bond acts like an annuity only if interest rates are fairly stable for 30 years. More details about this study and about annuities are given in Chapter 13.

Rather than ensuring survival of the worst-case scenario, a retiree or pre-retiree might choose to take a little more risk. One way to do that and still receive a high level of comfort is by using a Monte Carlo simulation as described in Chapter 3.

The Endowment Formula

The Monte Carlo simulations still don't get the job done for most people. A retiree doesn't want to know that he has a 90 percent probability of not running out of money. He wants to know what is the most he can spend each year if he experiences the worst investment markets on record, especially at the start of retirement.

Perhaps the best way to plan retirement spending is to adopt strategies similar to those used by endowment funds and foundations, such as the Yale University Endowment Fund. A group of Yale's economics professors and its endowment officials developed the spending rule years ago. Under the rule, spending increases over time only as the markets allow. It also avoids overspending in good years and sharp spending reductions in bad years. In other words, the rule keeps market performance from dictating year to year spending. Yet, it also ensures that the endowment will last as long as the university needs it. Spending adjustments are made automatically, but gradually.

Here's one way to adapt the Yale spending rule for your own retirement fund. First, decide the target spending percentage of your portfolio. The studies mentioned here say that target should be 4 percent to 5 percent of the beginning value the first year of retirement, though I've given some reasons to justify going a little bit above that if you want. Let's say you pick 5 percent.

Then, divide your annual spending into two portions. The first portion is last year's spending plus whatever inflation was for the last year. Multiply this by 70 percent. The other portion is your target first-year distribution rate from the fund. Multiply this by 30 percent. Add the two numbers, and that is your distribution for the year.

Example: Suppose you have a $500,000 retirement fund, set a 5 percent spending rule, your spending was $25,000 last year, and inflation was 2 percent. Here's how you do the calculations.

Last year's spending plus inflation is $25,500. Multiplied by 70 percent, that is $17,850. Five percent of your fund is $25,000. Take 30 percent of that to get $7,500. Add the two results, and you will take $25,350 from the fund this year.

Now, suppose the portfolio declines to $480,000 for the next year, and inflation is 2 percent. One bucket of your spending will be $25,350 (last year's spending) increased by 2 percent, or $25,857. Take 70 percent of that to get $18,100. The other bucket is 5 percent of the fund's new value, or $24,000. Take 30 percent of that, or $7,200. Add the two and your spending is $25,300. You will have a small spending reduction to recognize the reduced value of your portfolio.

For comparison, under a fixed 5 percent plus inflation rule, you would have spent $25,500 the first year and $26,010 the second year.

The endowment spending rule is designed to make your fund last longer than under the strict percentage-plus-inflation rule, as an endowment fund is supposed to last forever. If your portfolio experiences a period of poor investment returns, distributions gradually will be reduced under this method, because 30 percent of the spending is based on the portfolio's value. Under the traditional spending formula, your distributions will increase each year regardless of what happens to your portfolio.

The endowment approach also means you are less likely to be deprived in good times, because if market returns exceed expectations, distributions will rise with the returns.

A benefit of this approach is that about 30 percent of many retirees' budgets tend to be flexible. You can defer purchases of new cars, clothing, and other things. Travel, recreation, and entertainment spending can be reduced. The exact amount of flexibility depends on each retiree's budget and spending patterns.

Because an individual's retirement fund doesn't have to last forever, unlike an endowment, you get additional flexibility. If bad markets cause spending to decline for several years in a row to the point that essential spending is being deferred, you can suspend the spending rule and dip into principal for necessary spending. The next year's spending would incorporate this, because 30 percent of the spending would be based on the fund's value.

No spending formula or plan is perfect. You want to develop a plan that is flexible, recognizes changed circumstances, takes emotions out of the process, and makes gradual changes. The Yale rule meets these goals. It also gives you an edge by increasing the likelihood that your fund will out-last the worst markets.

As I've pointed out, a great deal of research already exists to determine the maximum amount of a portfolio that can be spent safely each year. The studies consistently show that the viable withdrawal rate is between 4 per-cent and 5 percent of the portfolio's beginning value, with subsequent spending increased by inflation each year. A 6 percent withdrawal rate is considered aggressive for a portfolio that needs to last 20 years or longer. A 4 percent withdrawal rate is the safest rate; I have not seen a study that indicates spending should be less than 4.1 percent of the portfolio's value to ensure surviving the worst-case scenario.

A prospective retiree can use these results as a starting point. If the 4.1 percent spending rate is too low, a prospective retiree can adjust some of the variables, such as the investment allocation, later years spending, and other factors. Or a retiree can start with a first-year percentage rate distri-bution and use a formula such as the Yale spending rule to determine fu-ture distributions.

Make Your Own Health Care Reform

Paying for medical care during retirement used to be simple. Most retirees had medical care covered by former employers. By the 1980s, even 70 percent of early retirees still had employer-paid health care coverage. But rapidly rising health care costs—due to longer life spans, more sophisticated medical technology, and greater use of prescription drugs—caused employers to cut back on retiree health coverage. The reductions began in the mid-1980s and have accelerated in recent years.

A series of headlines says it all. "Health Benefits for Retirees Continue to Shrink, Study Says," reported the *Wall Street Journal* in 2002. The subheadline was "Outlook Is Even Bleaker for Workers Leaving Jobs Over the Next 20 Years." The *New York Times* reported "Health Plans Are Offering Fewer Choices and Higher Costs." Another headline from the *Wall Street Journal* said "Medicare Clients to Lose Coverage as Plans Bail Out." These are just a small sampling of the reports about declining employee and retiree medical expense coverage.

The stories fleshed out the unhappy details. Employers, including those that provide pensions, are not required to provide any retiree medical expense coverage. Retiree health care coverage of any amount now is provided by only about 27 percent of firms. Only 37 percent of early retirees and 26 percent of those over age 65 have some kind of health benefit through their former employers. Those that do offer coverage to retirees are cutting benefits, raising retiree contributions, or both. In 2001, 35 percent of firms either increased retirees' share of premiums or raised copayments and deductibles. Many companies report their intention to make such moves in the future.

Here are a few other facts from recent studies.

- Between 1998 and 2002 about four million Medicare members had to seek new coverage because their HMOs withdrew from Medicare participation. The HMOs said that Medicare reimbursements no longer were adequate. Other HMOs continued to participate but increased costs to members and reduced benefits. (The law was changed in 2003 to encourage HMOs to provide Medicare coverage again, so these trends are expected to reverse.)
- Bankrupt companies reduced or eliminated their retiree health benefits. These included Polaroid and several large steel companies. Some airlines probably will follow suit.
- Other employers are requiring retirees and employees to bear a greater share of the cost of medical expense coverage. In 2002 the average retiree personally paid about 68 percent of retirement medical costs, compared with 39 percent ten years before. A study by Watson Wyatt Worldwide in 2002 found that 17 percent of all large employers virtually eliminated retiree coverage by requiring retirees to pay the full premiums, and 20 percent of large firms eliminated retiree health coverage for new employees.
- A report in April 2002 said that seniors now carry a record amount of debt for that age group, and that half of those seniors filing for bankruptcy say medical expenses pushed them over the edge.
- A federal government report in 2001 estimated that a typical retired couple would spend almost $6,000 annually on Medicare premiums, Medigap coverage, and a long-term care policy. These expenses do not include out-of-pocket costs, prescription drugs, deductibles, and costs above policy limits. Older couples, married couples in which at least one spouse was in poor health, and those that purchased more generous policies all paid more than the average.
- In 2003 a 65-year-old living in a moderate medical cost area would need $47,000 in savings to pay only the premiums on Medicare Part B and the most comprehensive Medicare Supplement Insurance until age 80. In a more expensive state, the cost would be $82,000. That does not include the savings needed to pay for long-term care or for medical expenses that are not covered by Medicare and insurance policies.

There are other studies and statistics, but the point is clear. The cost of retiree medical expense coverage is shifting from former employers and the government to retirees. Some firms, especially some that filed for bankruptcy, are eliminating health care coverage even for those who are currently retired. No one should feel secure simply because an employer-provided retiree health care plan is in place. Courts consistently uphold the right of employers to reduce or eliminate the coverage at any time. If a former employer goes bankrupt, there is no one else available to pay for the coverage.

Don't Depend on Medicare

Things aren't much better for other types of retiree health care coverage. Medicare premiums rise each year. Premiums for Medicare supplement insurance, also known as Medigap policies, increase annually and usually at double digit rates. In recent years it has not been unusual for premiums on some Medigap policies to increase 40 percent or more in one year.

People are living longer, but many do so with chronic diseases or conditions. Many older Americans regularly take prescription medications to control diseases or conditions such as high blood pressure, diabetes, high cholesterol, heart disease, and others. These prescription drugs are doing wonderful things. The drugs can be expensive, however, and many health care plans, including traditional Medicare, provide limited coverage or increase premiums to pay for the medications. Congress added a prescription drug benefit to Medicare in a 2003 law and also made some other changes to the health care system that affect both seniors and non-seniors. It remains to be seen, of course, how this law will affect costs.

Many people retire before age 65. That means they aren't yet eligible for Medicare and probably aren't eligible for any employer-provided health care coverage. They are known as health care orphans.

Medicare is aggressively reducing its costs by reducing payments to doctors and hospitals. As a result, a significant number of doctors are refusing to take new Medicare patients. Medicare cut payments to doctors by 5.4 percent in 2002 and planned to reduce payments by a total of 17 percent from 2002 to 2005. The American Academy of Family Physicians reported in 2002 that 17 percent of family doctors are not taking new Medicare patients. Older Americans frequently have complained about difficulty in finding doctors and having to wait longer than other patients for non-emergency care. Those problems are bound to increase, especially for those living in rural areas.

Medical costs are pushing more older Americans into bankruptcy. In 2001, about 244 percent more Americans age 65 or older applied for bankruptcy than in 1991. That's a total of 82,000 older Americans in one year, according to the Consumer Bankruptcy Project of Harvard. Almost half of those filing for bankruptcy reported doing so primarily because of medical expenses.

Perhaps worst of all, retiree health care options change and few people really understand the options available to retirees. Surveys show that most Americans believe Medicare covers long-term care expenses, such as nursing homes. The truth is that Medicare pays for only 25 percent of nursing home expenses, and those payments largely are for short-term rehabilitation after an illness or injury. Residents and their families pay most long-term care expenses. Many nursing homes won't even accept some types of patients because Medicare reimbursement rates are too low to pay for the care. Long-term care is a unique topic, and I'll cover that in detail in Chapter 8.

Medicare also doesn't pay as many routine medical expenses as people believe. Research shows that Medicare pays only about half of the bills for most participants. Prescription drugs, for example, generally are covered under regular Medicare only if the drugs are administered during a hospital stay.

Depending on whose numbers are used, the average retiree is estimated to pay $3,000 to $6,000 annually for health care after adding all premiums, deductibles, copayments, and uncovered expenses. Many, of course, pay much more than this. Older Americans' out-of-pocket payments for health care rose 50 percent from 1999 to 2001, according to the Commonwealth Fund.

New forms of coverage under Medicare, in addition to traditional fee-for-service Medicare and (HMOs), were authorized in a 1997 law. But not all the options are available in all areas. In fact, private health care providers declined to offer many of the nontraditional options, because they concluded that the reimbursements from Medicare were not sufficient to make the offerings profitable. Congress raised the reimbursement rates effective in 2004 in an attempt to spur greater offerings of the new forms of coverage. In short, the system is getting more complicated, more costly, and covering less than it used to.

The Age Wave isn't going to make things any easier. As more people enter their later years, the demand probably will drive health care prices higher. Government, insurers, HMOs, and employers will continue to look for ways to cut their costs and make retirees responsible for more of their health care costs. While Social Security gets most of the headlines, Medicare is in worse financial shape.

For these reasons, medical expenses are a primary worry of most retirees and rightly so. Health care costs for retirees are rising faster than general price inflation, and coverage is being reduced. As one ages, medical expenses are likely to take an increasing share of annual spending. In this chapter, we'll review the medical expense coverage options available to retirees and how to select the best option.

Road Map to Retiree Health Care

Planning health care coverage for retirement requires several decisions. In many cases, the decisions must be revisited every few years. Because of the rapid changes in retiree medical coverage, even people who are satisfied with their coverage should re-evaluate the alternatives. Following are some decisions that might need to be made by the typical retiree.

- The bridge years must be covered. Most people have some kind of employer-provided or group health care coverage while they are employed. Medicare and other retiree coverage are available at age 65 or when Social Security benefits begin. Most Americans, however, retire before age 65. Many people retire in their fifties. For those early retirees, there is a period during which they are health care orphans.
- Once the bridge years are over, several options might be available. There might be employer-provided retiree coverage, though it is available to fewer and fewer people each year. Medicare is available, with several versions in at least some parts of the country. There also might be group coverage available through professional associations or similar organizations. Private individual coverage can be purchased, but it is likely to be expensive. The basic coverage won't pay for all medical expenses. The retiree can self-insure for all or part of the uncovered expenses. Or a Medicare supplement policy, also known as a Medigap policy, can be purchased.
- Prescription drug coverage might be available under an employer's retiree coverage or another plan, though the extent of coverage varies. Additional drug coverage is available in some Medicare supplement policies. Medicare will add an optional prescription drug coverage plan in 2006 and offers sponsored discount prescription drug discount cards in the interim. There are other discount cards and additional options for reducing the retiree's cost for prescription drugs.
- Finally, long-term health care such as nursing home care is a consideration. There are several options for covering this potential expense discussed in Chapter 8.

Health Care Limbo: Covering the Bridge Years

Most Americans retire before age 65. Some do so involuntary, because of corporate cutbacks or health problems. Others retire before 65 because they want to. Whatever the reason for leaving the work force, those who retire early need medical insurance.

Some large employers still offer health care coverage to former employees who are under age 65. When large corporations offer buyouts or dismiss large numbers of employees, continuing medical insurance typically is part of the package. Even among large companies, however, the number offering medical coverage is declining. Only 76 percent of large employers offered medical coverage to former employees under 65 in 1999, compared with 88 percent in 1991. The percentages are even lower outside the universe of large employers. In fact, few smaller employers offer medical insurance to retirees younger than 65; many don't offer retirees any medical expense coverage.

Because most employers subsidize coverage for current employees, the cost and even the availability of unsubsidized coverage is a shock to many new retirees. They don't realize how significant the cost is, how rapidly it can increase as one ages, and the items that won't be covered.

Buying a policy at any price can be difficult for a retiree who has a less-than-prime medical profile or who has a dangerous habit or two. Unlike the group policies offered through an employer, insurers tend to investigate closely before issuing an individual policy. The process, known as underwriting, involves getting details about an individual's medical history and other factors such as occupation and personal activities. All this information will be evaluated to determine the premium and policy terms. The policy might be declined, or it might be issued with restricted coverage. Existing medical conditions might not be covered at all or disallowed for an initial period of six months to two years.

Individuals in their late fifties or early sixties will generally pay premiums of $500 per month or more, depending on their age, health status, and residence. The best way to decrease the premiums is to raise the deductible and copayments. In other words, self-insure for the routine expenses and let insurance cover the higher costs. Changing residences also can change premiums. An individual with the same profile could reduce premiums by hundreds of dollars per month by moving to an area where health care costs are typically lower. Policies and premiums can be compared at Quotesmith.com.

There are estimates that about three million Americans between ages 50 and 65 carry no medical insurance. Some studies estimate that about 10 percent of those between ages 58 and 63 are uninsured. The numbers probably will increase, especially if the eligibility age for Medicare is increased to more than 65 in order to combat the program's financial problems.

Those considering early retirement should do extensive health insurance research early. There are many sources to consult to avoid paying too much for a policy with limited coverage. Here are the steps prospective retirees or new retirees need to take:

- Contact your employer. There is at least one option and possibly two options available through the retiree's former employer.

  The Consolidated Omnibus Budget Reconciliation Act of 1985 (COBRA) requires employers with 20 or more employees to offer medical expense coverage to former employees for up to 18 months. The employees have to pay for the coverage, plus an administrative cost of up to 2 percent, but this might be a good deal. Coverage is guaranteed. More importantly, an employer policy usually is a group plan, and insurers generally charge less for group premiums than for an older person's individual policy. Under a group policy, younger members subsidize or offset the costs of older members. Using the COBRA provision is a good short-term option for someone who retired unexpectedly or without anticipating the need to secure health insurance. It gives the retiree up to 18 months to find a longer-term solution.

The COBRA option, however, might turn out to be too expensive. If the employer has what employees consider a good health plan, then it probably has low deductibles and copayments and covers many expenses. The premiums are likely to be high. In 2000, the average employer health plan cost $400 per employee per month.

The second option is that the employer might offer some kind of continuing health care coverage to former employees, especially if the employer is large. Again, this kind of coverage is disappearing, but it is worth asking about.

- Check professional, trade, and other associations. Many professional and trade associations offer some kind of medical expense insurance plan. These are group plans, so the premiums potentially are lower than for an individual policy. Any retiree or prospective retiree who belongs to an association should check the offerings from such associations. Some nonbusiness organizations, such as college alumni organizations and service organizations, also offer policies to members. Anyone who belongs to a special interest organization should check available benefits. Veterans should inquire as to their eligibility for benefits.
- Contact local brokers and agents. There are many health insurance companies in the United States, and each insurance broker and agent works with only a few. Few health insurers work directly with individuals. That is why it is important to comparison shop among several brokers and agents.
- Ask national brokers and agents. They can be contacted through the Internet or toll-free telephone numbers. Quotesmith.com is a popular and comprehensive broker (800-556-9393). It is a good way to get a ballpark idea of what an individual policy will cost you. Another option is ehealthinsurance.com.
- Ask other retirees about their health coverage.
- Get advice from government agencies and the Internet. Local governments generally provide free counseling to older Americans through an Office on Aging or similar agency. On the Internet, www.healthfinder .gov offers a lot of free information on health care insurance and buying a policy. It is run by the U.S. Department of Health and Human Services. Also, take a look at www.healthinsuranceinfo.net, a venture of the Georgetown University Institute for Health Care Research and Policy and the Robert Wood Johnson Foundation. This site is a good place to find the rights and protections under each state's law.

At www.medicare.gov, the Centers for Medicare and Medicaid Services have a feature that compares the senior health care options in a user's geographic area. The site identifies the specific firms in the area that participate in Medicare and summarizes their offerings. It won't specify which providers offer plans to those too young for Medicare, but it is a fast and convenient way to get a snapshot of which providers offer plans in an area, the basic features of the plans, and the costs. Another feature estimates the annual out-of-pocket costs for someone of the user's age and general health status. A survey of member satisfaction with each plan also is available. This web site provides information on nursing homes and prescription drug discount plans in the area. The web site, however, is only a starting point. It does not indicate, for example, which doctors belong to an HMO. It also doesn't say which drugs are covered under plans with prescription drug coverage.

- Look in the local telephone book for health insurers listed there. A few will deal directly with individuals. Don't forget to look into health maintenance organizations (HMOs). Some have bad reputations, but others provide good care at competitive cost. Reports about an HMO's quality are available from the National Committee on Quality Assurance at www.ncqa.org.

- Start a business. Turning a hobby or new interest into a business allows you to become self-employed and eligible to join a professional association or one of the associations formed primarily to provide group health plans to individual business owners. If you join an association, however, carefully review the health insurance. Some associations are formed by insurers primarily to offer health insurance policies that avoid a lot of state regulations.

- Raise the deductible. The most certain way to reduce insurance premiums is to raise the deductible. Raise the deductible from the typical $250 to $1,000, and in many cases the premium will drop by around 50 percent. Self-insuring means the user pays many of the routine expenses and leaves insurance to cover the major problems.

- Consider short-term health insurance. This is a niche in the insurance industry offering health care coverage for up to 12 consecutive months. The coverage can be much cheaper under than most other plans, but there are reasons for the low cost. The policies usually have high deductibles. In addition, preexisting conditions generally are not covered. When the policy expires, longer-term insurance must be obtained. If a chronic disease or lingering injury is incurred while under a short-term policy, then when a longer-term policy is obtained the chronic problem likely won't be covered for the first six months or longer. That's why this insurance generally is sold only to young, unemployed people. A few states prohibit these types of policies.

- Many states have a guaranteed-issue law that requires health insurers to make coverage available to everyone regardless of medical history. The premiums might be high, and there might be a limited enrollment period during which anyone can enroll. Some states also offer special insurance pools for small business owners or for high-risk people who have trouble getting insurance.

- Some people return to work either full- or part-time primarily for the health insurance. Or, one spouse remains employed using employer health insurance that covers both spouses until they are both old enough for Medicare.

It might take some scratching, but an early retiree can find medical expense coverage during the health care limbo years.

Basic Senior Health Care

Once a person reaches age 65, more health care choices are available. The choices can differ significantly in price and coverage, so the options should be evaluated carefully before a decision is made.

An employer or union retiree health plan usually is the top choice if one is available. Though the number of these plans is declining, the plans that do exist usually offer the best coverage and price available. The plan might be integrated with Medicare. In that case, members have to sign up for Medicare and have it be the first payer of medical care. The employer or union plan then picks up some of the expenses not covered by Medicare.

Retirees should be aware that few employer or union retiree health plans are pre-funded. That means the costs are paid out of current cash flow each year. Also, employers generally can reduce retiree health benefits at any time. A retiree who is dependent on a former employer needs to monitor the financial condition of the plan's sponsor. In recent years, several major corporations have run into significant financial problems and reduced or eliminated retiree health coverage with little notice.

When an employer or union plan is not available or is unattractive, Medicare is the next option and is the one selected by most seniors. Medicare has two parts, Part A and Part B. Part A is hospital insurance, covering inpatient care, critical access hospitals, and skilled nursing facilities (nursing homes). Most people do not pay a monthly premium for this coverage. There are copayments and deductibles for the hospital care, and not all services are covered. Part B is medical insurance that covers doctor visits and other nonhospital care. For this coverage, a monthly premium is charged and the premium increases each year. The premium usually is deducted from Social Security checks. There also are copayments and deductibles for the services. Details about the coverage can be found in the free booklet *Medicare and You*, available by calling 800-MEDICARE or at www.medicare.gov.

There are different types of Medicare coverage, though not all are available in every area. The most frequently selected option is fee for service or indemnity Medicare, also known as original Medicare or traditional Medicare. The member goes to the doctor of his or her choice, if the doctor participates in Medicare. Then Medicare pays whatever part of the cost it covers. The member pays the rest. The doctors who participate in the program will submit a reimbursement request to a Medicare contractor and bill the member only after Medicare determines how much it will pay.

Members have a deductible and copayments for coverage under this option. The deductibles and copayments change each year, so refer to the booklet, *Medicare and You*.

Traditional Medicare gives the member the most options. The only restriction on which doctors can be visited and how often they can be visited is whether or not the doctor participates in the program. Because of 1997 reforms designed to reduce the cost of Medicare, this also is the most expensive form of Medicare for the members. In this program, members pay a relatively high monthly premium.

In addition, there are several types of plans known as Medicare + Choice (Medicare Plus Choice) plans. These are managed-care plans, the most well-known of which are HMOs. Other types that might be available are preferred provider organizations, provider-sponsored organizations, HMOs with point of service options, medical service accounts, and private fee for service. There is no reason for a Medicare member to know the details of each type. Not all types are available in each part of the country. Another type of alternative Medicare plan is called Medicare Advantage. This is an HMO plan that provides increased benefits in order to receive higher reimbursements under a 2003 law. Any Medicare member can find the types of managed care plans available in any part of the country by calling 800-MEDICARE, by consulting *Medicare and You*, or on the web site www.medicare.gov.

Managed care plans provide all the basic services of Medicare Part A. A plan also might offer additional services, such as prescription drug coverage, additional stays in the hospital, or vision coverage; it also might pay for all or part of a participant's Medicare premiums.

Potential disadvantages of these plans are that only certain doctors or hospitals are available (at least without incurring additional costs), access to specialists might be restricted, care received outside a service area might be an additional cost, and doctors can leave the plan at any time.

Another disadvantage is that the HMO can choose to leave Medicare and give members only about two months' notice to find new coverage. More cash will be flowing into the Medicare + Choice program under the 2003 prescription drug benefit law. Many HMOs had dropped out of Medicare or reduced benefits because Medicare reduced reimbursements. This new cash should cause HMOs to increase their benefits or return to the Medicare market in 2004 and later. Be alert for news that HMOs are becoming more attractive in your area.

There will be some changes to the traditional Medicare coverage that were included in the 2003 prescription drug benefit law. Beginning in January 2005, new enrollees to Medicare will be eligible for covered routine physicals and all enrollees will be covered for heart disease and diabetes screenings.

In addition, there will be some means-testing under Part B beginning January 2007. Currently, beneficiaries pay 25 percent of the outpatient care and doctor visits under Medicare Part B. This percentage will increase to 35 percent for seniors with incomes of more than $80,000 and further increase on a sliding scale until those with incomes over $200,000 will pay 80 percent of these expenses. The annual deductible for outpatient care has been fixed at $100 for years. It will rise to $110 in 2005 and increase annually after that.

If these sources of basic medical care coverage are not acceptable, there are a few other options. Military veterans should determine their veterans benefits. Low-income seniors should ask their states about assistance with the Medicaid premiums and other costs. Some seniors choose not to join any version of Medicare. They simply pay their expenses with their own resources and carry a catastrophic medical insurance policy for large expenses.

Finding the right medical plan can be a difficult process. The Medicare web site has a Medicare Personal Plan Finder. This feature tells which plans are available in a particular geographic area and offers some details about the plans. The feature also offers some information about the quality of each plan. Those who do not use the Internet can get the same information over the telephone by calling 800-MEDICARE.

Supplementing the Basics

Most seniors—about 85 percent—still enroll in original Medicare and purchase a Medicare supplement policy (Medigap policy) for additional coverage. Supplemental policies are purchased because Medicare pays only about half the medical expenses of participants. In the booklet *Medicare and You*, Medicare itself classifies original Medicare as having high out-of-pocket costs.

The out-of-pocket expenses include Medicare's premiums, deductibles, and copayments. In addition, Medicare doesn't cover a number of procedures and expenses. For example, in 2004 the Part B Medicare premium was $66.60 per month. The hospital deductible under Part A was $876 per benefit period. The hospital copayment under Part A was $219 per day for the sixty-first through ninetieth days of each benefit period. After the Part B deductible, participants also pay 20 percent of the Medicare-approved amount on each covered expense and 20 percent of all outpatient, physical, and speech-language therapy. Medicare doesn't cover any medical care received outside the United States. There are other possible out-of-pocket costs and uncovered treatments. Details and changes are at www.medicare.gov.

To help pay for uncovered expenses, participants can purchase a Medicare supplement policy. The Medigap policies used to be something of a scandal. There were numerous types of policies available, making it difficult for seniors to compare policies. In addition, unscrupulous insurance agents would sell numerous policies to the same individual, causing the person to pay a lot of money for duplicative coverage.

Federal law now standardizes the Medigap policies, which has added some consumer protection. It is now fairly easy to compare policies, and seniors are protected from purchasing duplicate policies and from other underhanded practices.

There are ten types of Medigap policies available. These types and their features are standardized by federal law. Plan A, the basic plan, covers the fewest items, while Plan J covers various types of services, copayments, and deductibles. The plans are summarized in Table 7.1. The most frequently purchased policy is reported to be Plan C.

The first step in considering a Medigap policy should be to narrow down the plans that will be considered. Obviously, the more a policy covers the more expensive it will be. Keep in mind, however, that each plan might not be available in every area. After narrowing the plan choices, get premium quotes from different insurers. Premiums can vary significantly among insurers, so price shopping is important.

TABLE 7.1   Standard Medigap Plan Benefits

	A	B	C	D	E	F	G	H	I	J
Part A hospital (days 61–90)	✓	✓	✓	✓	✓	✓	✓	✓	✓	✓
Lifetime reserve (days 91–150)	✓	✓	✓	✓	✓	✓	✓	✓	✓	
365 life hospital days	✓	✓	✓	✓	✓	✓	✓	✓	✓	✓
Parts A and B blood	✓	✓	✓	✓	✓	✓	✓	✓	✓	✓
Part B coinsurance 20%	✓	✓	✓	✓	✓	✓	✓	✓	✓	✓
Skilled nursing facility			✓	✓	✓	✓	✓	✓	✓	✓
Part A inpatient deductible		✓	✓	✓	✓	✓	✓	✓	✓	✓
Part B deductible ($100)			✓			✓				
Part B excess doctor charges						100	80		100	100
Foreign travel emergency			✓	✓	✓	✓	✓	✓	✓	✓
At-home recovery				✓			✓		✓	✓
Outpatient prescription drugs								Bas	Bas	Ext.
Preventive medical care					✓					
High premium	113	112	182	118	105	183	130	146	195	244
Low premium	355	660	828	590	806	840	679	146	142	190

Source for prices: quotesmith.com

Here are some points to consider when narrowing the plan choices:

- Plans F, G, I, and J pay the difference when a doctor does not accept Medicare's rates. But about 80 percent of doctors who participate in Medicare accept its rates, so this coverage might not be worth the cost.
- Prescription drugs are not covered under Medicare except during hospitalization until 2006, and then the coverage is optional. Plans H, I, and J do offer prescription drug coverage. But study the details before selecting a plan or policy. The policies with drug coverage tend to be expensive and have copayments. The policyholder might need to use several thousand dollars of prescription drugs annually to break even after the extra premiums and copayments are added. In addition, though a policy covers prescription drugs, it might not cover *all* prescriptions. Prospective policy owners should get details about the prescription coverage before making a decision, especially those who already take certain medications regularly. There also might be a waiting period during which there is no coverage for preexisting conditions.
- Prescription drug coverage, if it is available in a particular area, might not be affordable. Because seniors choose which coverage they want, there seems to be some of what insurers call adverse selection. Seniors who already use drugs regularly, or who believe they are likely to in the future, often opt for the prescription coverage. Relatively healthy seniors don't elect policies with drug coverage. The result is that insurers paid more in drug coverage than anticipated in recent years. That caused most insurers to either not offer prescription drug coverage or to raise premiums for the coverage by significant amounts.
- Those who don't travel much outside the United States probably won't benefit from a policy that covers foreign travel emergency coverage. Short-term policies can be purchased before each trip when overseas travel is anticipated.

The next step is price shopping. The last two rows of Table 7.1 show prices that were offered at the same time for a hypothetical retiree. Don't use these as benchmarks for your own cost. The premiums will vary considerably by place of residence, age, and other factors. The point of showing these two rows is to demonstrate how the premiums for the same or similar policies vary widely. It pays to shop around.

Current premiums are not the end of the selection process. Two more things to check are the history of premium increases for similar policies from a particular insurer over the last few years, and how that company determines its premiums.

Premiums for Medicare supplement insurance climbed sharply beginning in the late 1990s. Insurers regularly increased premiums 10 percent and more. For some policies, the premiums increased over 40 percent. The rate of increase depended on the location of the insured and the type of policy. The highest premium increases have been for policies covering prescription drugs.

Also, insurers have several different ways of determining premiums, and the method can affect the rate of future increases. An "issue age" premium generally does not change each year with the policyholder's age. Instead, premium changes are based on general increases in medical costs or the insurer's claims and investment experience. The base premium stays the same. Other insurers charge "attained age" premiums. These premiums increase each year as a policyholder ages, along with increases for medical costs and the insurer's experience. Attained age normally is cheaper in the first year, but will increase significantly as a policyholder ages. Another formula is the "no age rating" or "community rating" policy. Under this method, all policyholders are charged the same amount. Younger enrollees pay more than they would from other insurers, but older enrollees pay less. This type of policy tends to attract older individuals, which makes it likely that the insurer will incur higher claims than other insurers, and premiums might rise more each year.

Try to compare what the policies will cost in five or ten years, not just the first year cost. An attained age policy that is barely affordable the first year probably will be a burden in five or ten years.

For help with evaluating Medigap policies, each state has an Office on Aging, or its equivalent, that usually offers free counseling, seminars, and literature. From the federal Centers for Medicare and Medicaid (800-638-6833) the free publications *Medicare and You* and *Guide to Health Insurance for People with Medicare* are available and more information can be found on the web site, www.medicare.gov. Most state agencies that regulate health insurers publish a booklet listing the premiums charged on Medigap policies by different insurers in the state. A state's corporation commission or insurance department usually is the appropriate agency to contact. There also are insurance web sites that compare premiums, such as www.quotesmith.com.

Once premiums for the different policies are obtained and estimates are made of future premiums, reevaluate the decision to buy a Medicare supplement policy. One option is to buy only a basic Medigap policy or none at all. The money spent on premiums will be saved, and the individual will be self-insuring for the items that would have been covered by a policy. Here's how to make the final decision on whether or not to buy a Medigap policy.

Table 7.1 listing the different Medigap policies shows the expenses each policy will cover. Further details about how much of each of these items Medicare will and will not pay can be found in the Medicare booklets and on the web. Reviewing this information and using a general knowledge of medical costs in your area, you can estimate your likely out-of-pocket costs and compare these to the cost of a policy.

For example, during a hospital stay of more than 60 consecutive days in a benefit period, the insured must make coinsurance payments of $203 per day for the sixty-first through ninetieth days. Those coinsurance payments can total a maximum of $5,887. As the first row in Table 7.1 indicates, a Medigap policy will cover these coinsurance payments.

Work through the list of items covered by a policy and determine the maximum and likely out-of-pocket costs for each item. This review might lead you to conclude that some or all of the coverage under a policy is valuable. Or you might conclude that the coverage isn't cost efficient. Personal and family wealth also are factors. Someone who has the reserves to fund major medical expenses might be less inclined to purchase a Medigap policy than would someone whose standard of living (or their spouse's) might be adversely affected by large, uncovered medical expenses.

Comparing Programs and Policies

After reviewing all the policy information, use the following strategies to make the final choice.

Which doctors belong to the plan?   The best source for this, of course, is the doctor's office. Unlike printed directories of participating doctors, a physician's office will be able to say if the doctor is thinking of adding or dropping participation in some plans. Then, you can decide if keeping a particular doctor is more important than saving money.

Which prescription drugs are covered?   Too often, seniors sign up for plans only to learn later that the drugs they use aren't covered or won't be covered for the first year of participation.

What other services are covered?   Some people want vision, dental, and mental health in one plan. For others, this isn't important.

What preventive care is covered?   Health problems are best discovered and treated when found early, hence the importance of preventive exams and tests. Some plans won't pay for tests unless there are symptoms or a doctor's order. Others allow preventive tests only on a schedule based on age and health history. Ask about any limits on annual exams and preventive testing.

Is there a wellness or disease management program?   Patients who have or are at risk for chronic diseases get better control of the conditions and improve health by participating in special programs designed to educate them and closely follow their condition. Many plans offer reduced rates or special benefits for those who voluntarily enroll in these programs.

What are the typical costs likely to be?   Premiums, copayments, deductibles, prescription costs, and other expenses add up. Draw up a schedule of likely medical care during a typical year and see how much that would cost in the plans being considered.

What is the worst-case cost?   Most plans have a coverage limit, and all have deductibles and other out-of-pocket costs. Try to work through the limits and exclusions to determine what the cost of a major illness would be.

Paying for Prescriptions

When seniors and government officials complain about rising medical care expenses, they often are complaining about prescription drug costs. Prescription drugs are more numerous and more important to health care than ever before. Unlike the early days of Medicare, today drugs are the prime treatment for many diseases and conditions. Often, diseases are treated or controlled by taking medication for life. Drugs are a big reason why, despite a larger elderly population, a lower percentage of that population is disabled than in the past.

Consequently, medicine has become a bigger portion of health care spending, and that amount is rising at a high rate. In 2001 alone, spending on prescription drugs increased 17 percent. Governments and employers are trying to keep their costs in check by limiting what they will pay for medicine. Medicare pays only for drugs taken in a hospital. The result is that seniors pay most of this rapidly rising cost.

We've seen that prescription drug coverage is available under some Medigap policies and won't be available under Medicaid until 2006. However, even that coverage might be too limited and too expensive for most people. Statistics indicate that about 30 percent of people on Medicare do not have some kind of insurance coverage for prescription drugs (though the percentage varies from survey to survey).

Comparing Drug Purchasing Plans

In response, many discount drug-buying services have sprung up. There are so many of these services, however, that they can make buying medicine even more confusing for some seniors.

Medicare has its own discount drug-buying service that will exist from 2004 to 2006 under the 2003 prescription drug benefit law. In addition, pharmaceutical companies and drug store chains announced in early 2002 the creation of a number of discount prescription drug plans. These plans are in addition to a number of already existing prescription drug plans. Sorting through these hundreds of drug purchasing plans can become a full-time job!

These drug purchasing plans have some common features and important differences. Keep in mind that all these plans are unregulated, except for general laws that apply to all businesses. Any person or organization can set up a prescription purchase plan. Let's examine these plans in a question-and-answer format.

What types of plans are there?   Private firms and organizations that negotiate discounts with either drug stores or drug manufacturers offer the older drug discount plans. Membership often is open to anyone, though some restrict membership to seniors, lower income people, or those without other drug coverage. The AARP, for example, offers a plan, but it is exclusively mail order and only for AARP members. There are many others. Some plans charge an annual fee, some don't.

More recently, the larger pharmaceutical companies created their own discount plans. In addition, seven drug companies joined together to form one program, called Together Rx, to offer discounts on more than 150 medicines. Many chain drug stores offer their own discount cards. In March 2002 about 200 chain stores, working through the National Association of Chain Drug Stores and its Pharmacy Care Alliance, joined to announce the Pharmacy Care One Card, then merged that program with Together Rx.

Most of the drug company plans are open only to low-income people who do not have insurance coverage for medicine. Estimates are that about 30 percent of those on Medicare are eligible for those programs.

How do the plans work?   After joining and receiving a card, a member shows the card when making drug purchases and receives the appropriate discount. Members generally only have to be sure to use a pharmacy that participates in the discount plan. Some pharmacies will take all the discount cards a customer has and try to find the best deal on each prescription.

How much can be saved?   Here's where things get very complicated. The savings differ based on the drug, where it is purchased, and which plan is used. Many times the customer doesn't know the discount in advance, because discounts on each drug fluctuate under some plans. Generally there are higher percentage discounts for generic drugs than for brand names. Advertising for the plans often claims discounts of "up to 50 percent or more." Such discounts, however, often are available only for one drug. Discounts on most drugs average about 10 percent.

Here's one example, reported in the *Washington Post*, of how tricky the plans can be. In 2002, Peoples Prescription Plan charged an annual fee of $95.40 per household. The plan, however, was administered by AdvancePCS, which ran its own Advance PCS Prescription Plan. Often the same discounts were available through the AdvancePCS plan, which did not charge an annual fee. The Peoples Prescription Plan justified its annual fee by offering discounts on additional non-pharmaceutical items, such as contact lenses. In addition, Advance PCS might charge a transaction fee on each purchase. There is a similar arrangement between Pinnacle Choice, which charges $50 annually, and FFI Health Services, which has no annual fee for its MatureRx program. These factors make comparisons difficult.

The free programs are not always free. Some charge a transaction fee on each purchase, and that fee is not separately stated in the pharmacy bill. The member sees the bottom-line savings after the fee is included in the price.

Any estimate of savings must be generalized, because prescription drug prices vary by where the customer lives and at which pharmacy medicine is purchased. Not all pharmacies accept all discount plans, and drug manufacturers participate in some plans but not in others.

Lower-income people without prescription drug coverage who are eligible for the manufacturers' plans can get dramatic savings on commonly-used drugs. Eli Lilly, for example, offers a 30-day supply of any of its drugs for $12 to eligible seniors. Pfizer has a similar deal for $15. That means Lipitor, which usually costs $100 or so per month, costs a member only $15 per month. The plans offered by the pharmaceutical companies, however, might not cover all the medicines each produces and are available only to people of certain income levels.

The General Accounting Office surveyed the potential savings from the longstanding discount plans and came away unimpressed. On average, cardholders saved 10 percent or less. That is only the average. The discounts on some drugs under some plans were dramatic. That's why anyone who is serious about cutting prescription costs needs to shop around and do some legwork or telephone work.

How can savings from these plans be maximized?   It is possible to join each plan and go into the pharmacy with a box of discount cards. Then let the pharmacist find the best savings, if he or she is willing. The best approach for those who already are taking a particular medicine regularly is to contact several plans and ask the final price after all charges and discounts for those drugs. If more than one drug is used, inquire about each of them. Some plans give a higher discount based on the member's total spending. Always keep in mind that the highest discounts are available on generic drugs.

Are these plans only for the retired?   Many of the discount plans are open to everyone. Because many health insurance plans exclude or limit prescription drug coverage, even those who are covered by health insurance might benefit from a plan. Even contraception, which is not covered under most health insurance plans, is covered under some of the discount plans.

Are there other ways to save?   There are many other ways to cut prescription drug costs that should be considered before joining a discount plan. Generic drugs, when available, cost significantly less than their brand name counterparts. Many brand name drugs lost their patent protection in recent years and more are scheduled to lose the protection in coming years. Once patent protection expires, generics can be sold. The generics often have prices that are 50 percent or more below those of the brand name drugs.

There are retail discount pharmacies, such as Costco Warehouse stores, that offer substantial discounts over most pharmacies. Active or retired military might be eligible to purchase medicine through the Veterans Administration or the local base pharmacy. For medicine taken regularly, consider a mail order or Internet pharmacy. On my web site (www.RetirementWatch.com) you'll find more details about the prescription discount card plans in addition to information about some mail order pharmacies, Internet-based pharmacies, and Canadian pharmacies that fill orders from U.S. customers.

The Medicare Drug Card

Prescription drug coverage under Medicare will expand in stages. The first stage was the availability of Medicare-endorsed prescription drug discount cards starting in June 2004. The programs, offered by private firms, are Medicare-endorsed and the Medicare logo is on the cards when the programs meet federal government guidelines. Seniors will pay $30 or less annually for a card. Seniors with annual incomes of less than $12,123 receive $600 annually toward medicine with their cards and the fee will be waived.

Discounts vary from card to card and drug to drug. The card providers negotiate with drug suppliers for the discounts. The government has estimated that the average discount will be 10 percent to 15 percent, but some discounts will be significantly more or less than the average. In addition, card issuers generally give higher discounts for generic drugs and to some brand-name drugs over competing brand names.

Because each card-issuer negotiates its own discounts, all drugs and even all categories of drugs are not covered by each card. That means the best card for one Medicare participant might not be the best card for another participant. Each senior should shop among both the new cards and preexisting discount programs to determine the best deal. The discount cards also need to be compared with any existing prescription drug coverage.

Each beneficiary can have only one Medicare-endorsed discount card. But each beneficiary can use other discount cards (mentioned earlier in this chapter) in addition to or instead of a Medicare-endorsed card.

Actions to Take

Each Medicare participant should make a list of all medications taken and the out-of-pocket cost. Consider adding other medications that might be taken in the future based on family history or current symptoms. Study the available discount plans, both Medicaid-endorsed and other types. When examining a new card, be sure to get the specifics of which drugs are covered under a plan and what the cost out-of-pocket cost would be.

The New Prescription Drug Coverage

In 2006, Medicare beneficiaries will be able to sign up for a Medicare drug plan or join a private health plan that offers drug coverage. There also is the option to make no change, because the new Medicare prescription drug coverage will be optional. The cost and benefits of the private plans will be decided by the firms offering the plans. The Medicare medicine program will have several levels of benefits:

- The monthly premium will be $35 monthly, $420 annually. There will be a $250 annual deductible.
- After the deductible is paid, Medicare will pay 75 percent of the next $2,000 of medicine costs, until the total expenses for the year are $2,250. That means the beneficiary will pay $750 of the first $2,250 of medicine expenses, plus the monthly premium. The monthly premium and deductible are waived for individuals earning less than $12,123 ($16,362 for couples).
- Then, the beneficiary pays all medicine costs between $2,250 and $3,600. The coverage gap is waived for individuals earning less than $12,123 ($16,362 for couples).
- Finally, catastrophic coverage kicks in. The beneficiary will pay only 5 percent of the costs that exceed $3,600 each year.
- A little-known provision doesn't allow beneficiaries to buy insurance to cover the gaps in the Medicare prescription drug coverage after January 1, 2006. A beneficiary cannot even buy a policy to cover individual drugs that are not covered at all by Medicare or by the beneficiary's main policy.

Actions to Take in 2006

The new Medicare prescription drug coverage is optional. Those covered by Medicare will need to decide if they want the Medicare prescription drug benefit or any private options that become available in their areas. Keeping any existing medicine coverage also is an option.

Compare more than costs.   A prescription drug plan, including Medicaid's, does not have to cover all prescription drugs. Compare plans to be sure your plan covers all the prescription drugs you use or might use in the future.

About 75 percent of Medicare beneficiaries had some kind of drug benefit besides Medicare in 2003. One concern about the new law was that many corporations and unions would drop their retiree prescription drug benefits and shift the cost to Medicare. To prevent that, the Medicare prescription drug law will make tax-free payments to corporations to encourage them to maintain their retiree prescription medicine benefits. This is estimated to be the biggest expense in the new Medicare law.

Health Savings Accounts

Another feature of the 2003 Medicare prescription drug law adds a useful tool for those under age 65. This tool is the Health Savings Acccount (HSA).

An HSA is a tax-free savings account. The account owner or the owner's employer can make tax-free contributions to the HSA. If the employer makes contributions, the contributions are not included in the employee's taxable compensation. If the employee makes the contributions, they are tax deductible. Investment income in the account is not taxable. Withdrawals from the HSA are tax free if used to pay medical expenses.

In other words, an HSA is much like an individual retirement account, except the HSA is used to pay medical expenses instead of retirement expenses. The HSA must be sponsored by a qualified financial institution, such as a bank or insurance company.

An HSA provides two major advantages. First, it allows the individual to use pretax dollars to pay for medical expenses that are not covered by insurance. Second, it allows a younger person with few medical expenses to begin saving money for medical expenses later in life. A pre-retiree can begin putting the maximum amount into an HSA, invest the account balance, and use the money to pay for retirement medical expenses.

To be eligible to open an HSA, an individual must be covered by a health insurance policy with a deductible of at least $1,000 for a single person or $2,000 for a family policy. Preventive care cannot be subject to the deductible, and out-of-pocket expenses under the policy must be limited to $5,000 annually for an individual and $10,000 for a family.

The annual contributions to the HSA can be no more than twice the deductible, up to a limit of $2,600 for individuals and $5,150 for families. These amounts are indexed for inflation. Account owners aged 55 through 65, inclusive, are allowed an extra "catch up" contribution that is $500 in 2004.

Retired Americans have many decisions to make regarding health care coverage. They need to decide on their basic medical expense coverage.

Then they need to consider supplemental insurance policies. Finally, retirees need to determine how they will pay for prescription drugs.

There is one more important action a retiree must take. After making these decisions and putting a plan in place, the health care insurance market must be monitored. Things are changing rapidly. A sound arrangement this year could be a bad one next year, or there might be a better option available. Be sure to stay informed about the changes in basic health care coverage, supplemental coverage, and prescription drug payments.

8

Solving the Long-Term Care Puzzle

Americans are seriously misinformed about long-term health care—what it is, the probability of needing it, and how to pay for it.

The oldest Americans—those most likely to need long-term medical care—are the most misinformed. In a 2001 survey, 63 percent of respondents age 65 and older either didn't know or gave the wrong answer to a basic question about the extent of Medicare's coverage of nursing home care. This is similar to the results in many other surveys over the years. Even those Americans who are most likely to need long-term care are not well-informed on the subject.

This is understandable. Long-term care coverage is complicated and expensive. Most people don't want to discuss it and report that the possibility of needing long-term care is among their greatest fears. The topic brings up unpleasant possibilities for the future, especially the lack of independence. Also, long-term care and the ways of paying for it are changing rapidly.

Most people think of long-term health care primarily as nursing home care for the very elderly. While that once was true, it no longer is. The very elderly tend to be healthier than in the past, yet the average age of nursing home residents is declining. About 40 percent of people who need long-term care are aged 18 to 64. Many people don't realize that the need for long-term care can arise from sources other than aging, such as accidents, major illnesses and surgeries, or chronic diseases. Half of strokes, for example, occur in those under 65.

Another change is that today there are alternatives to nursing homes, such as home care, adult day care, and assisted living. Only 1.5 million people are in nursing homes, and many of them are in for short-term rehabilitative care. Some estimate that presently, only about 20 percent of long-term care is given in nursing homes.

The means of paying for long-term care also is a source of misunderstanding. Most Americans believe Medicare will cover the bulk of the cost. Medicare, in fact, covers very few long-term health care bills. Medicare's nursing home coverage is only for short-term and skilled care, such as rehabilitation after an injury or illness. Medicare will not cover more than 100 days of long-term care per benefit period. A benefit period starts the day a participant enters a hospital for at least three days of covered care and ends when the participant has been out of a hospital or skilled nursing facility for 60 consecutive days. A new benefit period does not begin until the participant has entered a hospital again for at least three days of covered care. Medicare does not pay for long-term maintenance or custodial care—that's the extended, expensive care that worries most people—whether it is provided at home, in an assisted living facility, or in a nursing home.

Medicaid, the program for the impoverished, will cover long-term maintenance care. To be eligible for this coverage, a person must spend or give away most assets or sell them and buy an annuity. Congress restricted the ability to give away assets and qualify for Medicaid, but it still is possible for those who start far enough in advance. We'll cover that in more detail later in this chapter.

The fact is that family assets and long-term care insurance are the main sources of paying for long-term health care needs.

Long-Term Care Facts and Costs

Long-term care insurance policies have existed for a number of years, but relatively few people own them. Estimates are that only about 3 percent of Americans over age 50 own a long-term health care policy. There are many reasons for the limited participation.

Most people are not aware that the policies have improved in recent years—they are no longer "nursing home policies." They cover more than nursing home care. Standard long-term care policies now will pay whether the long-term care the insured needs is given at home, in an assisted living facility, or in a nursing home. In fact, the policies to some extent are designed to keep the insured out of a nursing home, partly because nursing home care costs more than other options.

The older long-term care policies paid benefits only after a hospital stay or only when the care was needed for specific reasons. Alzheimer's disease, for example, wasn't always covered. Now, most long-term care policies automatically cover Alzheimer's. Few policies now limit their coverage to long-term care caused by specified diseases or conditions; benefits are paid whenever long-term care is needed. Also, most policies don't require a hospital stay before coverage kicks in. That is important, because many people who enter long-term care—especially those who need long-term custodial or maintenance care—don't enter the hospital immediately before the need for care arises.

Long-term care insurance policies are expensive, and that no doubt deters many potential buyers. A 40-year-old in 2002 would have paid approximately $850 in annual premiums. At 50, the average cost rises to $1,100; at 60 it is $1,800; and at 70 the premium is $3,500. That's *per person*. Those costs have to be doubled if a married couple wants to cover both spouses. Obviously a significant part of a family's or retiree's budget can be devoted to long-term care insurance.

Cost of Premiums versus Cost of Long-Term Care

The long-term care average daily cost nationally is $181. That puts the annual cost of a stay at a nursing home at over $66,000. Those who live in higher-cost metropolitan or suburban areas will pay well over $200 per day, putting the cost well over $70,000 annually.

The daily fee doesn't cover all costs. There are additional charges for items such as prescription drugs, physical therapy, special diets, some personal care, and extra nursing care. Estimates are that these extra costs increase the daily charge by about 20 percent. Some of these costs might be covered by Medicare or other insurance; some won't be. The extra costs bring the national average to about $217 per day or more than $77,000 annually. Assisted living facilities and home care usually are less expensive, but they still won't be cheap. Assisted living also charges for most extras beyond the basic room and meals, so depending on an individual's needs it might not be less expensive than a nursing home.

In addition, the cost of long-term care has been increasing by about four times the rate of inflation or almost 8 percent annually. A $66,000 annual cost would rise to over $142,600 in ten years or $307,600 in 20 years, if costs continue to increase at current rates.

Who Needs Long-Term Care?

The final factor to consider is the probability of needing long-term care. This is where it is important to study the statistics. A commonly quoted statistic from The Health Insurance Association of America says that everyone at age 65 has a 50 percent probability of needing some type of long-term care during his or her lifetime. While that is literally true, it doesn't tell the whole story.

Most long-term care, despite the name, is actually for the short term. Over the years, the length of the average stay in a nursing home has declined. About half of nursing home stays now are for 90 days or less because they are for short-term rehabilitation after an injury or illness. Three quarters of nursing home stays are estimated to be for less than one year. Even those numbers don't tell the whole story. While the average stay in a nursing home is declining, those who stay in a nursing home beyond a short-term stay tend to be there for a while. The average extended nursing home stay is for over two years. That is the average, so bear in mind that many long-term residents are in a nursing home for longer than two years. About 9 percent of nursing home stays are for five years or more. Women dominate this group by a ratio of three to one.

These figures don't cover home health care. Nonrehabilitative home care tends to average four years. The numbers also don't include stays in assisted living facilities. Those stays tend to be longer than at nursing homes.

Retirees and pre-retirees need to put all these factors together when making decisions about long-term health care. Consider the probability of needing an extended stay for long-term care and the cost of the care. Compare that with the cost of insurance premiums. Then decide how long-term care should be financed if the need arises. Unfortunately, to be effective a long-term care insurance policy must be purchased before a need arises. That's why paying for long-term care must be planned in advance. The certainty of paying expensive insurance premiums for life must be balanced against the uncertainty of paying an unknown amount for long-term care in the future. Those who eventually use the insurance policy to pay for extended care will come out ahead. Other policyholders will get some benefit from the policies. The benefit to some long-term care policy owners, perhaps to the majority of them, will be only peace of mind.

Insure or Self-Insure?

There are some general rules that can help solve the dilemma of whether or not to purchase a long-term care policy. These general rules divide Americans into three groups.

Those with relatively low incomes and net worth don't have much choice. They cannot afford long-term care insurance without significantly reducing their standards of living. Their best approach would be to use personal assets to pay for any long-term care expenses that arise, then rely on Medicaid or family members for any additional long-term care needs.

The net asset level for this group varies, based on the area of the country and the cost of long-term care in that area. Most advisors put the top net worth of this group somewhere between $250,000 and $500,000. Even so, some in this group buy long-term care insurance because they want to leave money for their children and grandchildren. They don't want to take the risk of having their entire estates absorbed by long-term care costs. A better solution for them would be to buy life insurance. Usually it is less expensive than long-term care insurance and is guaranteed to pay benefits at some point.

A second group is the wealthy. These people have high enough net worths that they don't need to worry about long-term care expenses bankrupting the family or leaving a spouse with a reduced standard of living. This group can simply self-insure. Long-term care expenses, if they are incurred, can be paid from current income and assets.

There is some argument over the net worth level at which this group begins. Some advisors peg this group as beginning with a net worth of $2 million or more. Others put the beginning net worth much higher, at $10 million or so.

The beginning net worth for automatically self-insuring should be relatively high. That's because long-term care expenses are rising much faster than the net worth of most people. As we saw earlier, $66,000 of annual long-term care expenses today easily could become $142,400 in ten years and $307,600 in 20 years. In the meantime, a person's net worth and income are likely to increase at a slower rate and periodically will decline in a recession or bear market. Someone who has shifted from the saving to the spending years also might spend enough to cause a general decline in net worth each year.

Because of the rapid growth of the cost of long-term care, the threshold at which one self-insures should be high. In fact, an argument can be made that there is no wealth level at which self-insurance automatically is an option. After all, someone with $10 million in assets probably can easily afford a few thousand dollars of insurance premiums each year to avoid spending $100,000 or more per year on long-term care in the future. In addition, that $10 million net worth might not be in liquid assets. After the second or third year of long-term care, the family might have to consider selling or refinancing assets such as a family business or real estate in order to pay for the care.

Most Americans, however, are in the middle group for which long-term care insurance cannot be rejected automatically as being either too expensive to afford or not necessary. Those in this group must seriously consider purchasing a long-term care insurance policy. Then, the decisions become how much coverage to purchase and which policy provisions to choose. As we'll see, a long-term care policy can be designed to reduce the premiums to an affordable level. Before we cover that, however, I'll review some alternatives to an insurance policy.

Alternatives to Long-Term Care Insurance

Before rushing to buy a long-term care policy to cover possible future expenses, consider a couple of other strategies.

- Buy life insurance instead. Life insurance generally is less expensive than a similar amount of long-term care insurance. (And remember, life insurance is certain to pay a benefit.) After buying life insurance, if the need for long-term care arises the insured can spend current income and assets to pay for the care. When those are exhausted, Medicaid takes over. Then, the life insurance policy pays benefits to survivors. The insurance benefits replace the assets that were spent on the care. Even better, because life insurance costs less than long-term care insurance, more life insurance can be purchased than health care insurance. The heirs could end up with more assets this way, and they end up with substantially more assets if long-term care expenses are never incurred because they'll get both the assets and the insurance benefits.

There are potential drawbacks to this approach, though. Suppose the insured is married, and the spouse needs the couple's income or assets to meet living expenses. Then it would not be feasible to spend the bulk of family resources to pay for the long-term care of one spouse, because the healthy spouse might suffer financially until the life insurance policy pays benefits. The strategy might be viable only for single people or those who have enough resources to cover both long-term care and a spouse's needs for a number of years.

Also, relying on Medicaid as a backup might not be an attractive idea. We'll see why later in this chapter.

A problem also is created if the long-term care is not a permanent or final need. Suppose the individual spends income and assets for long-term care for a year or two, then no longer needs long-term care. Will there be enough assets left to maintain the previous lifestyle?

- Make long-term care a family affair. The reason most people give for purchasing a long-term care policy is that they want to be sure they have some assets to leave their children. They don't want long-term care expenses to absorb their estates and leave little or nothing for their heirs. If long-term care insurance is meant to protect assets for the children, perhaps the children should contribute to the insurance premiums. The cost of insurance might be much more affordable if each family member contributes a share.

- Combine insurance and self-insurance. Long-term care insurance doesn't have to cover all the potential costs of care. For example, many people have catastrophic medical care insurance. They pay the routine medical expenses themselves and count on the insurance to cover major surgeries or other expenses. Long-term care insurance can be designed the same way, as I'll demonstrate in the following section.

- Insure only the wife. Women far outnumber men among long-term nursing home residents. When paying for the longest-term stays is the concern and money for premiums is limited, statistically, it makes sense to buy insurance covering only the wife. A less risky option is to insure both spouses but to purchase more extensive coverage for the wife than for the husband.

- Plan to use a reverse mortgage. When a home is owned debt free, the owners can borrow against the equity, receiving a lump sum, monthly payment, or line of credit. No payments are due during the owners' lifetimes as long as they own the home. That means when one spouse enters a nursing home, the other can continue to live in the home and keep other income and assets. They use the reverse mortgage proceeds to pay for the long-term care. After both spouses pass away, the loan payments are due. The children or other heirs can convert the reverse mortgage into a regular mortgage. Or the house can be sold and the proceeds used to pay the loan.

Reverse mortgages used to have a bad reputation. But now there are reverse mortgages backed by Fannie Mae and the Department of Housing and Urban Development. Greater disclosure of costs is required. HUD also requires prospective borrowers to meet with counselors to review the full cost and consequences.

Reverse mortgages are expensive and are not recommended until the owners are in their late 70s and after they have exhausted other financial options. A reverse mortgage is not for a younger person or couple. And it is not for someone who wants to leave the home equity to the children. The average reverse mortgage borrower is a single woman in her late seventies. In addition, there might not be enough equity in the home to cover the needed long-term care.

Buying and Designing a Policy

Many of the long-term care insurance policies issued over the years have not paid benefits. There are some estimates that less than 5 percent of policies issued have paid benefits to date. Part of the reason is that the bulk of the people who purchased the policies still are healthy. Another reason is that apparently a large percentage of long-term care policies are allowed to lapse after a few years. The policy owners decide that they cannot afford the premiums or that the premiums are not worth the potential benefits, so they stop paying premiums. Some probably switch to policies they find more attractive. Other policies haven't paid benefits because the policy terms were restrictive. The owners might have needed help with care-related expenses, but their care didn't qualify for reimbursement under their policy terms.

Once a decision is made to buy a long-term care insurance policy, careful consideration must be given to the design of that policy. Always remember that some of the provisions in the policies can be dropped, added, or changed. The terms selected determine the premiums charged and the coverage received. There are five key policy terms that can be adjusted to make the premiums more affordable, while still ensuring that expenses the family cannot afford are likely to be covered.

Customizing a Policy

Following are some key terms and how they can be adjusted to design a custom-made long-term care insurance policy.

Daily benefit.   Long-term care policies promise to pay a maximum daily benefit for each day of covered care. There usually is one daily benefit level for home health care and one for nursing home and assisted living facility care. The insured picks the daily benefit and counts on personal or family income and assets to make up any difference between that amount and the actual cost.

The national average daily cost of a nursing home is $181 for a semiprivate room, plus the additional 20 percent most residents are charged for expenses beyond the basic room and board, such as prescription drugs. Costs are higher in urban areas and lower in rural areas. The home health care benefit is set at a percentage of the nursing home benefit, usually 75 percent to 100 percent of the nursing home benefit.

Survey nursing home costs before picking a daily benefit, but give careful thought to the area surveyed. The choice of a nursing home or other care facility often is made by a woman in her 40s or 50s. In other words, a daughter or daughter-in-law usually decides where a parent or an in-law resides. When an insured's children live in a different area from the insured, the relevant costs might be those in the area where the children live. The children are likely to move the parent to a nursing home in their area instead of in the parent's area.

Once the cost for an area is determined, decide whether or not the policy should cover the full cost. An individual might not be able to afford $130 or more per day for an indefinite period, but insuring for the full amount might make the policy premium too high. On the other hand, the insured might be able to pay $20 or more per day indefinitely if the need should arise, and reducing the daily benefit by that amount might make the policy affordable. For example, suppose Social Security pays the insured $10,000 annually. If there is not a spouse who would need that income, it is available to pay for long-term care. That means the daily benefit can be reduced by about $27 per day ($10,000 annually).

Keep inflation in mind. Long-term care costs are rising about 8 percent annually, which is faster than the rate of general consumer price inflation. The insured would have to pay the future inflated value of the $27 per day.

Waiting period.   This also is known as the deductible or elimination period. It is the length of time that the insured receives covered care before the policy starts paying benefits. Insurers usually offer waiting periods from 0 to 365 days. Most people choose 90 days. The insured pays for all long-term health care during the waiting period. Then, if care still is needed, the insurance company begins paying its obligations under the policy.

The insured selects the waiting period, and it is a form of self-insurance. Selecting a longer waiting period is similar to selecting a higher deductible on a home or car insurance policy. The longer waiting period reduces the premiums on the policy.

The insured might decide that the policy is only for the worst-case scenario when long-term custodial care is needed for years. In that case, the owner would select a waiting period of 365 days. That turns the policy into a catastrophic long-term care policy and should substantially reduce premiums. The reduction might make the policy affordable or might allow the daily benefit to be raised high enough so that none of the insured's assets are used after the waiting period.

Benefit period.   This is the length of time the policy pays benefits. Many policies call this the maximum lifetime benefit. For example, a three-year benefit period is a maximum lifetime benefit of 365 days times three years times the maximum daily benefit. A $150 daily rate would make the lifetime benefit about $165,000.

The maximum lifetime benefit has a great influence on a policy's premium. A maximum of three years of coverage costs about half that of unlimited lifetime coverage. A five-year limit reduces the premium by about 25 percent below the unlimited amount.

While most long-term care these days is for a relatively short time, those whose needs extend beyond the short term tend to need care for a considerable length of time. One study reported that long-term home care in general lasted on average 4.5 years, while long-term nursing home care lasted for 2.4 years. About 9 percent of nursing home stays are for five or more years, though some studies put that number higher.

The issue for the insured is how much to reduce premiums by taking on the longer-term risk. Those who are using the insurance to protect against the worst case will keep the unlimited lifetime benefit and use other provisions to reduce premiums. Other policy buyers might be comfortable reducing premiums by assuming they won't exceed the average long-term stay of two and a half to three years. Still others might pay a little more and take the chance that they won't be among those whose long-term stay exceeds five years.

Inflation protection.   The younger the insured, the more important it is to protect against inflation. Even relatively older insureds, however, should seek inflation protection. At 8 percent inflation, the cost of care doubles in nine years, which is why most people should not skimp on inflation protection in a long-term care policy.

The standard inflation protection is a maximum of 5 percent annually. Some policies offer a simple interest option, but be sure to get the 5 percent compound protection. After ten years, the difference is substantial. Compound interest protection is worth the cost if it does not make the premiums unaffordable. If simple inflation protection is the only option, a better choice might be to drop inflation protection and opt for a substantially higher daily benefit. Usually this offers more protection for the premium dollar.

Someone age 70 or older might consider a higher daily benefit as an alternative to inflation protection. Because of the way insurers determine their premiums, the premiums are likely to be lower when taking this approach. Someone who is age 70 is likely to need long-term care within ten to 15 years or not at all. It can make sense to pick a daily benefit that exceeds the current average cost and is close to what the cost is likely to be in ten or 15 years after inflation. That way the insured is well covered without having to pay for expensive inflation protection.

Covered care.   This used to be a big hole in long-term care policies but now is less of a problem. The policy should cover both skilled and custodial care. The care should be covered whether it is given in a nursing home, assisted living facility, or at home. The daily benefit might be lower for home care, but home care still should be covered. Avoid home-care provisions that say only professional home-care services will be covered. Someone who needs home care needs help with chores such as cooking and cleaning.

These five provisions can be used to structure a policy that meets an individual's needs and is affordable. The insured must estimate the amount of income and assets that can be devoted to long-term care in the future. Some people will decide they can pay expenses for only a limited time, say 90 days or a year. After that, insurance will have to take over. Others will decide that they can pay a small portion of the expenses indefinitely but that insurance will have to cover most of the cost. Policy provisions can be adjusted to accommodate those two scenarios as well as many others.

There are two more factors to consider before buying a policy:

Financial condition.   Be sure to check on the financial safety of the insurer. This should be available from any insurance agent or broker, as well as from your local library or the Internet. Lower premiums probably are available through the less-sound insurers. However, these policies are designed for long-term protection, so the insured should make relatively certain that the insurer will not be around for many years.

Premium increases.   Premiums will increase. Long-term care policies are fairly new, and insurers are learning. They made mistakes in the past by grossly underestimating claims. In the last few years, premiums on many policies increased annually by 20 percent or more, and subsequently many people dropped their policies. An indication of probable future increases is how closely the company checks out a prospect before issuing a policy. An insurer that checks out a prospect's health carefully before issuing a policy probably will have a good premium history. An insurer that does little more than require a short questionnaire is likely to be surprised by higher claims than anticipated and to resort to sharp increases in premiums.

Premiums will increase even if it is a level premium policy. That term simply means the premium cannot increase as an individual ages. Premiums still can be raised for all policyholders in the same class in the same state. If the insurer incurs higher costs or earns less from investments than anticipated, it can raise the premiums.

The insurance company or broker should provide a history of rate increases for the type of policy being considered. The state insurance department also can provide a premium increase history.

If someone can barely afford a policy now, odds are that after premium increases it won't be affordable in five or ten years and will be dropped—probably just when it is needed most.

These are the key decisions that determine the cost of long-term care insurance and its benefits. What they boil down to is determining the risks the insured is willing to retain and which should be shifted to an insurance company. The specific terms of the policy can mean the difference between making a policy affordable and not being able to purchase one.

When to Buy

The ideal time to buy a policy probably is between ages 60 and 70. Premiums will be much lower for a younger person, but long-term care insurance is changing rapidly and probably will change quite a bit more before today's younger person needs long-term care. The major reason to buy early is that health developments might make a person uninsurable by age 60. Also, someone who can barely afford a policy might want to wait to buy and save the money in the interim. That might enable the person to pay the premiums in a few years when the need for the policy is likely to be greater.

Compare Group and Individual Coverage

Many employers are offering group long-term care policies to employees. Employers rarely pay any of the premiums, but use their purchasing power to negotiate favorable terms and premiums for the employees. If a group policy is available, certainly compare it to the individual offerings.

A big advantage of group policies is that an applicant is less likely to be denied coverage for current health problems. Another advantage is that the premiums are likely to be lower than for comparable nongroup policies. Also, the employer has done most of the hard work of the buying process.

Group policies are not without disadvantages. A group policy usually limits the available options. That's one way employers streamline the process and cut costs. There's no disadvantage unless the applicant wants a feature that is not offered. For example, the federal government's offerings to its employees automatically reimburse home health care for 75 percent of the nursing home daily rate. That might or might not be a good provision for everyone. Home health care might be just as expensive as nursing home care.

Also, group policies are not always less expensive. Group policies tend to attract people with medical problems who would not qualify for policies or for low premiums on individual policies. A healthy individual might be able to get cheaper rates through a separate policy.

Another consideration: A married couple buying two individual policies often gets a premium discount of up to 20 percent. That discount is not available under most group plans.

Be sure to review the underwriting. A healthy person wants an insurer who thoroughly checks an applicant's health before issuing a policy. Inexperienced insurers and those seeking to boost market share will issue a policy with little investigation. They come to regret it when claims far exceed estimates. The result is sharply rising premiums on policies issued by the insurer in the future. Tough underwriting provides protection against dramatic premium increases. An applicant should want a medical review and exam before a policy is issued.

Tax Qualified or Nonqualifed Policy?

One more factor to consider before choosing a long-term care policy is whether or not it should be tax qualified. Tax qualified policies were created in the 1996 tax law. Their premium payments can be deductible, and any benefits received from these policies are tax free. That looks tempting, but let's dig a little deeper.

- The tax deductions are limited. The first limit is by age. In 2003 the maximum premium deductions were: age 40 and under, $250; ages 41 to 51, $470; 51 to 60, $940; 61 to 70, $2,510; over 70, $3,130. The amounts are indexed for inflation, and the latest amounts can be found in IRS Publication 502 each year. Another limit is that the deduction is available only to those who itemize expenses on Schedule A.

  A further limit is that the premiums are included with other medical expenses and are deductible only to the extent that when added to other medical expenses, the total exceeds 7.5 percent of adjusted gross income. Few people deduct any of their medical expenses because of these limits.

- Qualified policies have certain required terms and provisions. One requirement for a qualified policy is that it pays benefits only if the insured cannot perform at least two of the activities of daily living (eating, dressing, bathing, walking, etc.) or is suffering from Alzheimer's disease. In addition, a doctor must certify that care will be needed for more than 90 days. A nonqualified policy, on the other hand, often pays benefits if the insured has a medical necessity, and a minimum need period of 90 days is not required. Thus, nonqualified policies can provide more coverage.

  Because the coverage is a bit broader, a nonqualified policy generally costs 5 percent to 20 percent more than a comparable qualified one. Insurers supposedly expect to pay 20 percent to 40 percent fewer claims under the tax-qualified policies, so they charge lower premiums.

■ While the benefit payments from a tax-qualified policy clearly are tax free, it is not clear whether benefits from a nonqualified long-term care policy are taxable. The IRS, courts, and Congress have not ruled on the issue. Recipients of benefits under nonqualified long-term care policies usually treat the benefits as tax free, and the IRS has not challenged this treatment to date.

For all these reasons, it is possible that tax breaks under qualified long-term care policies cost more than they are worth.

Medicaid Trust Strategies

Many older Americans have seen promotions for seminars and publications on how to shift assets to qualify for Medicaid's nursing home coverage. Here is a guide to those strategies and the angles to consider before pursuing them.

Medicaid, the program for the poor, covers long-term nursing home stays. Seniors have to be impoverished in order to qualify for Medicaid's nursing home coverage. Medicaid uses both income levels and asset ownership to determine who qualifies for coverage.

The income limits vary a bit from state to state, but can be met by giving as many income-producing assets as possible to a spouse and children. Likewise, the net worth or resource limit can be met by giving away assets that are not on Medicaid's list of exempt property. Exempt property includes a residence of any value plus household goods, a car, and a few other items up to certain amounts. For example, the car for an unmarried person can be worth no more than $4,500 unless it is needed to commute to work or to receive medical care. The specific limits of the types of assets and their values vary from state to state.

For married couples, the resources of both spouses are added, and each spouse is considered to own one-half of the total assets. But married couples also get special asset limits. There is no limit on the value of the house, car, household furnishings, and personal effects that they can retain.

The first of the Medicaid strategies is to put wealth into an expensive house. Other assets are sold to buy a house that is bigger than needed and would otherwise be unaffordable. That way, the wealth is kept but is not counted against Medicaid qualification. Married couples also can load up on an expensive car, personal effects, and household furnishings.

Another strategy is to transfer to individuals or to trusts any other assets that exceed the Medicaid resource limits. These have to be irrevocable transfers under which the original owner is not legally entitled to get the assets back or receive income from them. To discourage these strategies, any assets transferred to a trust within the 60 months of applying for Medicaid or to an individual within 36 months generally are considered owned by the applicant when determining Medicaid eligibility.

That means to qualify for Medicaid, either the trust must be funded more than 60 months before entering a nursing home or enough assets must be retained to fund up to the first 60 months of nursing home care. Medicaid then is applied for after 60 months of long-term care.

Remember that the specific income and asset limits and other details vary from state to state. A local attorney will have to verify the details of the strategy.

But before implementing these strategies, consider the potential drawbacks. The biggest drawback is that Medicaid's reimbursement to nursing homes is less than it costs to adequately care for someone. Nursing homes that take primarily Medicaid residents generally provide care that is inferior to care in other nursing homes. Those contemplating these strategies should compare a Medicaid nursing home with one that takes primarily private pay residents. Then those who have resources to pay for non-Medicaid care should decide if they really want to be cared for in a Medicaid facility.

Also, even if the strategies are followed precisely, a state has the option of arguing that transfers made under a Medicaid impoverishment strategy were fraudulent. That has not been seriously tested in the courts, but no one can rule out a state's winning that argument.

The strategies also might generate extra taxes. Transfers to individuals or trusts are gifts which, after exceeding the annual exemption amount, either are applied against the lifetime estate and gift tax credit or incur gift taxes. The person transferring the property must pay the gift taxes. In addition, the person receiving the gift takes the same tax basis in the property as the prior owner had. That means when the donee eventually sells the property, he or she will pay capital gains taxes on all appreciation that occurred during the donor's ownership. If the property were held until death instead and received by inheritance, the basis would be increased to its current market value and capital gains taxes on the past appreciation would be avoided.

Finally, consider the ethics. Medicaid was set up for poor people, not for people who have the resources to pay for nursing home care but don't want to spend their money that way. Some people think it is unethical to arrange assets so that taxpayers pick up the tab.

Multibenefit Policies: Worth the Cost?

Insurers have had trouble selling long-term health care insurance policies. To boost sales, they created multiple benefit policies. Let's take a look at them.

Insurers face a dilemma. During most of the average person's life, he is more likely to become disabled or need long-term care than to die prematurely. Yet, fewer people purchase disability and long-term care insurance than buy life insurance. Insurance industry sources estimate that only 3 percent to 5 percent of the target market purchases long-term care insurance.

Long-term care insurance is expensive. But what seems to bother many people is that, unlike life insurance, there is a probability they will pay premiums for years and never receive a cash benefit from the policy. A homeowner's policy also has a low probability of paying cash benefits, but people are much more likely to buy homeowner's insurance than disability or long-term care insurance. By combining life insurance with long-term care and disability insurance, insurers hope the policies might be more appealing to consumers.

Here's how a multiple benefit, or multiple risk, insurance policy might work. The insured buys a permanent life insurance policy with a death benefit. Let's say the benefit is $200,000. The policy also carries a long-term care benefit with a monthly payout of up to $8,000. If the insured needs long-term care, the insurer advances the death benefit at a rate of $8,000 monthly up to a total of $200,000. The payments are structured to be tax-free. If long-term care still is needed after the death benefit is exhausted, the policy will pay up to an additional $200,000 of long-term care expenses at $8,000 per month. The expenses covered are the same as those covered by traditional long-term care policies: nursing homes, assisted living facilities, and home care.

With a traditional permanent life insurance policy, the insured also can tap the benefits early. A loan might be available. Or the insured could cancel the policy and get the cash value. Or the life policy might be sold in a transaction known as a viatical settlement. But in each of these cases, the insured would not get access to the full death benefit. In all but the loan, the insured has to give up ownership of the policy. So the multibenefit policy provides more coverage without giving up ownership of the policy.

A multiple benefit policy also might cover disability or be an all-risk policy. Under these policies, when a covered chronic or critical illness or injury is diagnosed, the policy begins paying a monthly benefit. The amount of the benefit depends on the diagnosis. There usually is a maximum disability payment, up to a percentage of the death benefit. The death benefit and cash value are reduced by the amount of the benefits paid. The payments can be used for any purpose. The insured does not have to be terminally ill, confined to a nursing home, or even hospitalized.

There are obvious advantages to multiple benefit policies. If you do not use the lifetime benefits, the death benefits will be paid. The insured is less likely to think premiums are wasted. Yet, there are some potential disadvantages to be considered:

■ Any benefits paid during life reduce the death benefit. If the amount of death benefit definitely will be needed to pay estate taxes or for some other purpose, you don't want that benefit reduced by lifetime benefits.

- In at least some of the policies, the death benefits are reduced first. Suppose a policy has a $200,000 death benefit and a $200,000 maximum long-term care benefit. If the insured needs long-term care, the payments for that will first reduce the death benefit. If the insured passes away after having received $150,000 for long-term care, the beneficiaries will receive $50,000 of life insurance benefits and the long-term care benefit technically won't have been used. An insured should know how any lifetime benefits will affect the death benefits and the cash value of the policy.
- Multiple benefit policies are relatively expensive. Premiums are higher when several benefits are covered in one policy instead of in separate policies. The insurer is taking more risk in multiple benefit policies, plus there probably is some markup for the convenience and additional administrative costs of the policies. An insured definitely will overpay for some of the benefits and might be paying for unnecessary benefits.
- The benefits might not be high enough. The non-life insurance benefits available are based on the amount of the life insurance selected. For example, to insure for unlimited lifetime long-term care benefits, a lot of life insurance might have to be purchased.

On the one hand, a multiple benefit policy provides more flexibility, has only one premium, and the insured has a greater probability of getting a cash benefit at some point. On the other hand, the insured also might pay more than for separate policies, might buy coverage that isn't needed, and their eventual life insurance benefits could be reduced.

The Grandkids Need Your Help More Than Ever

One of the prime financial goals of many older Americans is to help their grandchildren. They believe that the grandchildren's generation will have a more difficult time financially than either their parents or grandparents did. The adult children, meanwhile, either have established themselves or have shown that they won't make good use of money that is given or left to them.

The grandchildren are expected to inherit less from their Baby Boomer parents than the Boomers are likely to inherit from their parents. The cost of college education and the price of the average home continue to climb to levels unimaginable a few decades ago. Many young people enter their twenties with tens of thousands of dollars of higher education debt. The grandchildren also face the prospect of bailing out the failing Social Security and Medicare systems while dealing with the likelihood that those programs won't be nearly as generous to them as they were to previous generations.

Financial services firms are aware of this interest in helping the grandchildren and offer programs to assist. Unfortunately, not all the programs carry strong benefits. A strategy that benefits one family could be inappropriate for another. There are heavily promoted strategies aimed at grandparents that are more like gimmicks than smart financial planning. In addition, some strategies that were tried and true only a few years ago are no longer the best choices. It takes more knowledge and deliberation to choose the appropriate method for helping the grandchildren.

Consider the following developments in the quest to help grandparents provide for their grandchildren.

- Mutual fund companies offer special funds marketed to parents and grandparents. The funds lock in shareholders for at least ten years. Unfortunately, the returns of many of these funds became dreadful after the bull market ended in March 2000, creating negative returns over the five years ending in 2003. Most investors in these funds now realize they would have been better off buying regular mutual funds for their grandchildren.
- Special trusts are marketed as a way to help grandparents provide for grandchildren. Upon close examination, these really are clever ways to sell high-commission, high-fee products, such as annuities.
- Uniform Gifts to Minors Act or Uniform Transfer to Minors Act (UGMA and UTMA) accounts are longstanding favorite vehicles for helping children and grandchildren. The accounts are easy to set up and are available through virtually every financial institution. Unfortunately, they can create several problems. They give full control of the wealth to a youngster at age 18 or 21, depending on the state, whether or not the individual is able to handle it. They also can make financial aid for college more difficult to receive. After the 2003 tax law, the tax benefits of these accounts might not be significant enough to warrant their use.
- A standard way to invest a youngster's account is to buy a few good stocks or mutual funds and hold them for years. Times have changed. Stocks and mutual funds are more volatile than they used to be. Today's safe investment can be tomorrow's dog. Ask those who bought Xerox, Kodak, Polaroid, and a number of other safe, solid stocks only a few years ago. Those stocks now are well below their historic highs and not likely to reach anywhere near those prices again. The markets and economy change too rapidly to leave a portfolio unmanaged for years.
- Minimum investments for mutual funds and brokerage accounts are rising. It is harder to begin helping a grandchild by setting aside a small amount of money.
- Many of the strategies designed to help pay for a grandchild's education actually hurt, because they reduce the amount of financial aid available. Potential financial aid is one factor that must be considered when establishing a strategy.

A Small Sum Builds a Large Legacy—the Installment Plan to Building a Legacy

It is remarkably inexpensive and easy to establish a meaningful legacy for a grandchild. Two of the most powerful tools in investing can leverage a small amount into a large sum. Those tools are time and compound returns. You can open a relatively small account today for a grandchild, and when the grandchild really needs the money, the compounded returns over time probably will have greatly increased in value.

Suppose an account is opened with $2,000, and $75 is added to it each month. If the account earns an average of 8 percent annually, at the end of 20 years it will be worth almost $55,000—though the total contributions were only $20,000. Time and the compounded returns of the investment markets can more than double total wealth. A higher return would, of course, result in more money for the grandchild. That $55,000 should be enough for the down payment on a new home, to start a business, pay off college loans, or pay for other early-adulthood expenses. See Chart 9.1.

What if the $55,000 is left untouched until the grandchild retires? The grandchild might be disciplined enough not to spend the money, or the account could be created within a trust that limits access to it. If the money compounds at 8 percent for another 30 years, the grandchild will have over $500,000—all on the grandparent's $20,000 investment. That's quite a legacy to leave and quite a financial load to take off the grandchild.

Almost any grandparent can use time and compound returns to build a substantial legacy on the installment plan. There is little or no risk that the standard of living of the grandparent will be lowered. This plan also avoids gift taxes, because the annual contributions should qualify for the annual gift tax exemption ($11,000 per recipient in 2004). Estate taxes also can be avoided if the gifts are put in an account that is not in the grandparent's name or legal control. Annual income taxes also should be low. The money can be invested so that there are few taxable capital gains and dividends in most years. Income that is taxable can be taxed at the grandchild's rate.

Table 9.1 shows how the installment plan can work with monthly contributions of $50 and $75. It assumes that the initial investment is $10,000,

CHART 9.1   How a Small Sum Builds a Legacy

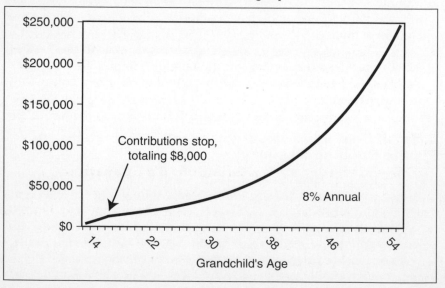

TABLE 9.1   Monthly Deposit

Years	$50	$75
5	$18,522	$20,334
10	$31,294	$35,842
15	$50,321	$58,947
20	$78,669	$93,370

and the account earns 8 percent annually after taxes. Subsequent monthly investments of $50 and $75 are shown.

The main impediment to this plan in recent years is that many brokers and mutual funds raised their minimum investment requirements. Not long ago $100 could open an account in a quality no-load mutual fund. Now, the minimum investment at most financial service firms is $2,500 or more. The few firms that allow low initial investments generally impose higher fees and other expenses. Once the hurdle of the initial deposit is cleared, however, small additional investments can be added on a regular schedule or when money is available.

Brokers and mutual fund companies make it easy to set up these plans using their automatic investment programs (AIP). Under an AIP, once an account is set up, the broker or fund company automatically drafts a set amount from a checking account each month and invests it according to preset instructions (which can be changed). The minimum monthly investment usually is between $50 and $100, though some allow monthly investments as small as $25 and some require as much as $250. The regular investments can be stopped, usually with 30 days notice.

Those are the basics of how to make a small investment become a significant legacy. There are, however, details to consider. Different vehicles can be used to establish this legacy, and the final financial results can vary considerably depending on which vehicle is used. Factors that must be considered are income taxes, estate and gift taxes, control over the account, flexibility, and the effect on financial aid for higher education.

We'll look at how all these factors come together. First, we'll examine the best ways to help fund higher education expenses for a grandchild. Then, we'll look at establishing a legacy that will cover more than just college expenses.

Guide to Helping with a Grandchild's Education

Most grandparents want to help pay for all or some of a grandchild's higher education. So let's look at and compare the different ways available to help fund higher education. Many of these tools also are available to provide wealth in general to a grandchild, so this is a good review even for those who don't want to limit their legacy to higher education. All these strategies, by the way, can be used by parents to help their own children.

The strategies available to help fund college costs—or to provide a legacy in general—have different advantages and disadvantages, which not everyone realizes when choosing a method. Every grandparent needs to carefully consider all the possible effects and choose carefully.

Direct Gifts of Investments

The easiest way to help a grandchild is to make a gift of cash or of an investment. The gift later can be used to pay for higher education expenses. Until the expenses are incurred, the gift should be invested to appreciate.

The benefits of the direct gift are that the property is out of the donor's estate, and any income and capital gains earned by the gift are not attributable to the donor's income tax return and are likely to be taxed at the grandchild's much lower rate. There are no restrictions on the money or how it can be invested or withdrawn.

The disadvantages are that the grandchild has direct control of and unfettered access to the money. It can be invested in whatever strikes the grandchild's fancy. The grandchild may even decide to convert the account to cash and withdraw it.

If the grandchild still is a minor, an account cannot be established solely in the grandchild's name. The assistance of a parent or other adult is required. The easiest approach is for the parent and child to set up a joint account. That arrangement gives either the parent or child the ability to withdraw the money or change how the account is invested. An alternative is to set up a custodial account, such as a UGMA, which is discussed below.

Because of the lack of controls with the direct gift and joint account, they rarely are used to help a grandchild pay for higher education expenses.

The Classic UGMAs

For decades the only vehicle to help fund a minor grandchild's (or child's) education was the Uniform Gift to Minors Act (or Uniform Transfer to Minors Act) accounts, known as UGMAs or UTMAs. (The name depends on the state in which it is set up.)

These accounts have many advantages. An adult serves as custodian of the account until the child reaches the age of majority. The account is in the minor's name, but the adult controls the investments and withdrawals. Also, a deposit into the account automatically qualifies as present interest under the gift tax law. That means the transfer qualifies for the annual gift tax exclusion, so the transfer is free of gift taxes until all the donor's gifts for the year to that minor exceed the annual limit ($11,000 in 2004). Normally, a gift is not a present interest that qualifies for the annual gift tax exclusion unless the recipient has full legal title and control of the property. The tax law carves out a special exception for UGMAs.

Income and capital gains from the account are taxed to the grandchild. That can result in significant income tax savings to the family, because the grandchild is likely to be in a 0 percent or 10 percent income tax bracket, allowing the family to accumulate more after-tax wealth for education.

The disadvantages of UGMAs are less well-known. One disadvantage occurs when the grandchild is ready to attend college and applies for financial aid. Under the formula used to determine financial need at most colleges, a student is expected to spend on college expenses up to 35 percent of assets held in his or her name. The parents are expected to contribute only up to 5.64 percent of their assets each year. Grandparents aren't expected to contribute anything. Not all higher education institutions use this formula, but most do.

A UGMA is considered an asset of the grandchild for whom it was established. That means if $20,000 is in the student's name, up to $7,000 must be spent on college during the first year before the student can qualify for financial aid. If the money is in the parents' names, only about $1,000 counts against aid. If the property is in the grandparents' names, none of it is considered during the financial aid qualification process.

If financial aid is a possibility, grandparents and parents should carefully consider whether they want to put assets in the future student's name. Doing so could reduce the amount of financial aid available and require the family to spend more on college expenses than they otherwise would have.

Another disadvantage is that once money or property is placed in a UGMA, the donor cannot get it back. It is important that the donor not contribute money that might at some point be needed to meet emergencies or living expenses. In addition, the UGMA cannot be used to pay expenses that are the legal support obligation of the parents. If the family runs into hard times, the money cannot be used for these legal support items, such as food, clothing, shelter, and medical care.

Another potential disadvantage of the UGMAs is that the youngster gets full legal title to the account immediately upon reaching the age of majority. This is 18 in some states, and 21 in others. There is nothing the parents or grandparents legally can do to keep the youngster from spending the money however he or she wants. Instead of paying for college, the money could be used to purchase a new car, take expensive trips, or on even more alluring items. Because of this feature, many grandparents look for strategies that provide more restrictions on the grandchild's access to and use of the money.

Creating a Trust

Combining the advantages of a UGMA without incurring most of the disadvantages can be achieved by creating an irrevocable trust. A trustee will control and invest the money. Cash will be distributed or used to pay expenses as directed in the trust agreement. Either the trust or the grandchild will be taxed on the income and capital gains, not the parents or grandparents.

Gifts to the trust are present interests and qualify for the annual gift tax exclusion if the trust has a Crummey clause. This clause allows the grandchild to take from the trust any new contribution within a certain time after the contribution was received by the trust. Usually 30 days is the time set. If the money is not taken out within that time, it stays in the trust under the terms of the trust agreement. If the child does demand distribution of the money, the grandparent isn't likely to make future contributions.

The trust agreement, which is written by the grandparent, determines when the money is distributed. There are many options available.

Here's one example. The trust agreement might say that money may be spent only for certain purposes—such as education or emergencies—until the child reaches age 21. After 21, the annual income or a percentage of the trust's value is distributed. At age 25, one-third of the principal is distributed. Additional principal is distributed at ages 30 and 35, after which the trust terminates. Those terms are classics for trusts set up to aid youngsters.

Some trusts provide that money is distributed to pay only for education. Other trusts make distributions as the grandchild achieves certain milestones, such as earning a college degree, holding a job, or reaching a certain age. Trust law is very broad. The standards for distributing and withholding money generally are limited only by your imagination.

Another option is to give the trustee complete discretion over how income and principal will be distributed. The creator of the trust can give the trustee a letter stating the principles to be used, but the trustee is charged with the ultimate decision. That allows the trust to adapt to changing, unplanned circumstances.

An irrevocable trust should contain a clause providing that no distributions will be made when the trustee determines that withholding the money would be in the best interests of the grandchild. This clause protects the money in case the grandchild drifts into substance abuse, gambling, high-risk business ventures, or similar activities. The trustee can resume distributions after determining that doing so again would be in the grandchild's best interest. The trust also should have a clause that allows the trustee to distribute money under special circumstances, such as becoming disabled, needing special medical attention, or wanting extended education.

There are some disadvantages to an irrevocable trust. It costs money to create and maintain the trust. A lawyer must prepare the trust agreement. The trust also has to file separate tax returns and keep separate records. The tax returns can get complicated. In addition, a trustee is needed to manage the trust. To get the maximum tax benefits, an independent trustee is needed. A professional trustee, such as a bank, will do the administrative work, tax returns, and money management for a fee. The administrative and tax work can be split from the investment and distribution management. Whatever the arrangement, creating the trust and having a trustee manage and maintain it will cost money. That's why an irrevocable trust is not a viable option unless a lot of money is involved. Attorney and trustee fees vary around the country, so the advisable minimum size for a trust varies by region.

Another potential disadvantage of a trust is that it reaches the top tax bracket much faster than individuals do. The tax brackets are indexed each year, but a trust paid the top tax rate in 2003 when its taxable income exceeded $9,350. The trustee might be able to manage the investments to avoid the top tax bracket. Otherwise, the family might not get any income tax benefits from setting money aside in a trust for the grandchild.

The trust also might affect the amount of financial aid available. The exact effect will depend on the terms of the trust and whether or not a school chooses to treat the trust as an asset of the grandchild.

Section 529 Savings Plans

The newest tool available to help fund education expenses is the Section 529 college savings plan. These plans were created by a 1997 amendment to Section 529 of the tax code and have become extremely popular.

The 529 savings plan carries a number of benefits to both the adult who funds it and the future student who is the beneficiary of the account. The plans double as both an education funding tool and an estate planning strategy.

In a 529 plan, a state sets up a college savings trust. An adult opens an account and contributes to it, naming a child or grandchild (or anyone for that matter) as beneficiary. The state invests the money, and the gains earned by the account compound tax-deferred. There are no taxes until money is withdrawn from the account. If distributions are made for qualified education expenses, all compounded income and gains are tax free. If distributions are used for nonqualified purposes, the income and gains are taxed at the beneficary's tax rate. There are additional benefits.

- Contributions to the trust are considered gifts of present interests, qualifying them for the annual gift tax exclusion. In addition, tax-free gifts can be front-loaded. Up to five years worth of gift-tax-free contributions can be put into the account in one year and still qualify for the gift tax annual exclusion. When the annual exclusion is $11,000, up to $55,000 per beneficiary can be put into a 529 plan in one year free of gift taxes. A married couple can each put that amount into each account gift tax free in one year.

  Front-loading gifts means that the tax-free exclusion for gifts to that beneficiary are exhausted for the five years. In addition, if the donor dies before the five years have ended, a pro rata portion of the gifts will be included in the donor's estate. Otherwise, the money and all its future appreciation are not considered part of the donor's estate.

- The donor is considered the account owner and can get the money back when needed under most states' plans. Some states impose an early withdrawal penalty of up to 10 percent of the account's value, some don't.
- The donor can change the beneficiary. If a grandchild decides not to go to college, a new beneficiary can be named.
- The account in one state can be used to pay for education expenses in any state if the state sets up the plan that way.
- Some states give a deduction against state income taxes to their residents who contribute to the 529 plans sponsored by the state.
- There is no preset limit on the earnings under most plans. The money is invested, and most state plans give the donor some ability to choose the investments. If the markets do well, so will the account. On the other hand, there are no guaranteed earnings. An account could lose money, and many did from 2000 to 2002.
- Some states require that the account be spent by a particular time, usually when the original beneficiary reaches a certain age, such as 30. Others let the account compound indefinitely, changing the beneficiary several times. This type of strategy can substitute as a trust for part of an estate plan.
- The U.S. Department of Education stated that for financial aid purposes, the assets will be considered those of the owner. That means the student will not be considered the owner for financial aid calculations. If the grandparents set up the 529 account, the account will not count in financial aid considerations. Individual schools, however, can set their own policy on this issue.

These provisions make the 529 plans more attractive in many ways than other investment-oriented plans such as UGMAs, trusts, and direct gifts of money or investment accounts. The donor gets gift and estate tax benefits, yet can get the money back if needed. The donor still has some control over the account and can change the beneficiary. The grandchild does not get legal title to the account after reaching the age of majority.

However, there are three potential disadvantages to 529 plans. One is that the state usually decides how the account will be invested. In most plans, well-known money management companies such as Fidelity, Vanguard, and TIAA-CREFF invest the money. The donor might have some ability to select the initial investment options, but usually the choice cannot be changed after it is made. In a few states the state treasurer invests the accounts, and some states have only one investment plan.

To counter this disadvantage, many states offer additional versions of their 529 plans in conjunction with financial services firms. The account is opened through a firm, usually a broker or mutual fund that has established a relationship with the 529 plan. These accounts generally offer more investment options than the state-managed version of the plan, and investments usually can be changed more frequently. These versions of the plans, however, charge higher fees than the state-managed version.

The second potential disadvantage is that Congress might change the rules. This provision was created only in 1997, and withdrawals for education expenses weren't made tax-free until the 2001 tax law. We are not yet in the period when significant tax-free withdrawals are being made and the government is losing the potential revenue. It is hard to evaluate what Congress might do when that happens.

The third potential disadvantage is cost. Each state imposes fees and expenses on the accounts in its plan. The level of these costs varies. Some states set the fees at low levels that cover only their costs. Other states try to make a profit from the 529 plans. In addition, a state can have several plans with different levels of fees for each plan. Many states now have plans that can be sold through brokers and financial planners. These professionals get fees from the plans, and the fees under these versions are higher than for the plans purchased directly from the states.

Most states now offer at least one 529 plan. The terms, costs, and fees of the plans vary, though most have modest fees. Most states also now accept contributions from residents of any state and allow the accounts to finance higher education in any state. That enables everyone to shop around for the state plan that best suits their needs, investment preferences, and fee levels. The main disadvantage to using an out-of-state plan is the potential loss of a state income tax deduction. States that allow residents deductions for their 529 plan contributions generally allow the deductions only for contributions to their own plans. Also, a few states consider distributions to be tax free only if used to pay for education at a college in their state.

Because most states will open accounts for residents of any state, diversification of plans is possible. Rather than settling on one state plan, a grandparent can split contributions among plans from different states with attractive features. A grandparent might, for example, contribute enough to his own state's plan to get the maximum income tax deduction, then contribute additional amounts to another state's plan with more attractive features.

The details of the available plans are collected on the Internet for comparison at www.collegesavings.org. It is important to review all the terms before settling on a plan. For example, not all plans allow the owner to get the contributions back. Some plans allow the return of contributions but only after a penalty is subtracted. Some plans will transfer an account to another state's plan if desired; others won't.

Prepaying College

Before the Section 529 college savings plan was created, section 529 of the tax code provided only for prepaid college savings plans. These plans still are available. They are not as well-known because financial services firms do not have an incentive to promote them. Yet, they do provide significant benefits to grandchildren. In some ways they are more attractive than the savings plans, especially after the bull market in stocks ended in March 2000. In fact, as the bear market dragged on, states that offer both types of plans began reporting that new accounts for prepaid plans far exceeded new savings plans.

Under a prepaid college savings plan, the person opening the account names a beneficiary and tells the state the beneficiary's age. The plan determines how much has to be paid in. The plans generally offer payment options ranging from a lump sum to fixed annual payments. When an account is fully funded, the state guarantees it will pay four years of tuition and mandatory fees at public colleges within the state.

In 2003, a group of private colleges formed their own prepaid plan, called the Independent 529 plan. A list of participating institutions and other details are at www.independent529plan.org. Cash put into the plan earns tuition certificates that can be used to buy tuition at the participating schools. How much education each dollar buys depends on the school the child chooses to attend, because tuition and fees vary among the schools. A disadvantage of the plan arises if the child chooses to attend a public university or a private school that does not participate in the plan. In that case, the plan pays back the original investment plus a 2 percent annual return.

The major advantage of prepaid tuition plans is certainty. If the cost of college grows faster than the plan anticipated, the state makes up the difference. Likewise, if investment returns lag behind expectations, the state suffers the loss. On the other hand, if the actual results are better than the projections, the state benefits.

Certainty can be a major advantage. The 2001 recession and 2000–2002 bear market crimped state government budgets. Many governments reduced subsidies for higher education, causing institutions to raise tuition and other fees at a higher rate than in the past. Buying into a prepaid plan early locks in the current inflation rate and lets the plan take the risk of higher inflation.

A potential disadvantage is that the guarantee covers only the cost at public colleges within the state sponsoring the plan. Private colleges and those in other states aren't guaranteed. If the grandchild does decide to go to an institution that isn't covered, the state will determine a value for the account and transfer that amount to another institution to be applied to costs there.

A prepaid plan won't cover all the costs of college. Additional costs that aren't covered include room and board, textbooks, a computer, and expenses other than tuition and fees.

For financial aid purposes, the prepaid plan is considered the student's asset, and generally will reduce the aid available to the student dollar for dollar.

A prepaid tuition plan has less flexibility than a savings plan. Money generally cannot be withdrawn as it can with a savings plan, other than to transfer it to a college to pay expenses. There also might be limits on the ability to change the beneficiary.

Prepaid savings plans ran into problems during the bear market of 2000–2002. When determining how much a parent needs to pay into the prepaid plan, each state estimates the investment return it will earn on that money. The state also estimates the rate at which tuition and fees will increase. Both sets of estimates turned out to be far too optimistic. Of course, the bear market returns were far less than the estimates. The recession also caused states to reduce tuition subsidies, so colleges and universities compensated by substantially increasing their fees.

A number of state plans now are projecting deficits for a few years because of the poor returns. Many significantly raised the amounts that must be paid by new enrollees in the plan. A few states stopped accepting new enrollees until they could resolve the financial issues. It is possible that in some cases the plan might not have enough money to pay all the promised expenses at some point, and the state government will have to decide if it is obligated to fund the deficits.

Coverdell Savings Accounts

Coverdell savings accounts initially were called Education IRAs. The name was changed in the 2001 tax law to honor the late U.S. Senator from Georgia, Paul Coverdell. The 2001 tax law also dramatically increased the benefits of these accounts.

Up to $2,000 per child can be put into a Coverdell account each year. There is no deduction for contributions to the account, income and capital gains are tax deferred, and they are tax free when withdrawn, if used for qualified education expenses. The account must be spent by the time the beneficiary is 30.

Qualified education expenses include tuition, fees, books, supplies, and equipment that are required for enrollment or attendance. Room and board are included if the individual is at least a half-time student. The expenses can be incurred for undergraduate or graduate level courses and also can be used to purchase tuition tax credits under a qualified state tuition program. Beginning in 2002, the accounts also can pay for elementary and secondary school expenses.

An account balance can be transferred or rolled over tax free from the account of one beneficiary to another beneficiary in the same family.

The $2,000 annual contribution limit is phased out when the contributor's adjusted gross income is between $190,000 and $220,000 on a joint return.

The nice thing about Coverdell accounts is that virtually any relative can open an account for the benefit of another relative. If a grandparent's income exceeds the limit, he can give money to a parent to contribute to an account for the grandchild.

A problem with the Coverdell accounts is opening one. Many financial services firms do not offer the accounts. They do not foresee there being enough interest to make the accounts profitable. It was hoped that increasing the contribution limit from $500 to $2,000 would help the situation, but that has not been the case so far. Coverdell accounts also have trouble competing with 529 savings plans and even with taxable accounts when all the features and benefits are compared.

U.S. Savings Bonds

Those saving for college education get a special benefit from U.S. Savings Bonds. Normally interest on the bonds is tax deferred until the bonds are redeemed. Then the interest is taxable. If the interest is used to pay for college expenses, however, the interest is tax free. The tax-free status of the interest is phased out for bond owners whose adjusted gross income for the year exceeds $86,400.

Savings bonds generally offer safe, solid interest rates. The returns won't be spectacular, and higher interest often can be earned on other types of bonds. The safety of the savings bonds, however, cannot be matched, and the tax-free interest feature can make them a good alternative for a conservative investor.

Let the Grandkids Pay

The tax law and some other factors can make it advantageous to have the grandkids pay for college. The grandchildren would pay taxes at their own rates and also might qualify for tax breaks for which the parents' and grandparents' incomes are too high. There are several ways to make this strategy work.

The grandparents can invest in their own names. This carries with it the disadvantages of keeping the property in their estates and having income and gains reported on their tax returns. It does, however, avoid the problem of searching for a vehicle that helps the grandkids but doesn't give them too much control, reduce financial aid, or create other problems.

One advantage of the taxable account is that the grandparent retains control of the account. The account also can be set up at any mutual fund or broker the grandparent wants. In addition, after the 2003 tax law, the account can be invested in a tax-wise fashion so that the after-tax returns will rival those of the tax-favored vehicles such as 529 savings plans. The maximum 15 percent tax rate on capital gains and dividends is a big help.

In fact, the grandparent does not have to incur taxes on gains. When the college expenses need to be paid, the grandparent can transfer appreciated assets to the grandchild. The grandchild can sell the assets and pay the capital gains taxes. The capital gains taxes to the grandchild are likely to be 5 percent. By paying the expenses themselves, the grandchildren also might qualify for tax breaks such as the Hope or Lifetime Learning tax credits for education expenses. Applying those credits to the grandchild's income could make the gains tax free.

An option that builds on this strategy is to have the children pay at least half their living expenses for the year. That makes them independent. They claim their own personal exemptions, the credits for college expenses, and deductions for any loan interest. They aren't likely to hit the income limits at which those tax breaks are phased out. Be sure to keep track of their annual living expenses and be able to show that the children paid at least half their expenses.

The grandchildren's living and college expenses could be paid with gifts received from the grandparents, and the grandchildren still would qualify for the tax breaks. The key is that the gifts must be unrestricted. The grandparents must take the risk that the money will be spent on something else.

Bringing it All Together

You can see that there are many ways grandparents can help pay for a grandchild's education. There is no one right vehicle. A number of factors must be balanced before making a decision. Here are some general rules to consider.

- When money will be invested in the markets to be used years from now, a section 529 savings plan can be the best choice. For a relatively low cost it provides tax advantages and estate planning benefits. The 529 plan also makes it unlikely that the grandchild will spend the money on something more alluring than college. It has minimal impact on eligibility for financial aid and has a great deal of flexibility.
- When the child can be trusted or the grandparent is willing to assume the risk, a good choice is to invest in a taxable account in the grandchild's name. Once the child turns 14, all income and gains are taxed at the grandchild's tax rate, which might be as low as 5 percent. The tax savings can be substantial when the capital gains rate can be reduced that low. The grandparent can invest in his or her own name until sometime after the child turns 14, then give the account to the grandchild. As discussed, if the grandchild still is a minor, an adult will have to be responsible for the account in some way. There would have to be a joint

account or a custodial account. This approach could severely reduce available financial aid, because the assets are in the student's name.

- If financial aid is a possibility, the grandparents might want to consider investing in their own names. Saving in either the grandchild's name or even in the parents' names could reduce financial aid. Investments could be given directly to the grandchild when college expenses are due. The grandchild could sell the investments, incurring taxes at his or her own rate. A disadvantage is that the grandparents would pay taxes on the investment income at their rates in other years. Under the 2003 tax law, however, a taxable account can be managed to keep annual taxes on the investment returns extremely low. Another disadvantage is that the property would be included in their estates if they pass away before the money is spent. Normally the amount saved for college, however, is not enough to incur sizeable estate taxes.

- Investing in the grandparent's name keeps many options open. The education expenses can be paid for as they are incurred by making gifts of appreciated investments to the grandchild. The taxes on gains are paid at the grandchild's tax rate. In addition, the grandchild might qualify for the Hope and Lifetime Learning tax credits. Saving in the grandparent's name also keeps the grandchild eligible for the maximum financial aid. The saving can be done either directly in the grandparent's name or through a Section 529 plan.

- A prepaid tuition plan provides the most certainty. The payment of tuition and fees is guaranteed in return for fixed payments from the parent or grandparent. Additional expenses, such as room and board, can be funded through the other strategies.

How to Use the 2003 Tax Law

After the 2003 tax law bigger family tax savings are possible by using new and different strategies than those that produced the best savings under prior law.

The 2003 law reduced the top tax rate on ordinary income from 39.6 percent to 35 percent. In addition, the maximum rate on long-term capital gains was cut from 20 percent to 15 percent. The maximum rate on dividend income fell from a top rate of 39.6 percent to 15 percent.

Income taxes might be cut even more if investment income can be shifted to children and grandchildren. The lowest tax rates on ordinary income now are 10 percent and 15 percent. Even better, in these lower brackets the tax rate on long-term capital gains and on dividends is a mere 5 percent.

Clearly, with this great difference between the highest and lowest brackets there are significant benefits to shifting income to the youngsters. More importantly, the low rates might make taxable accounts for children and grandchildren more valuable than some popular tax-advantaged vehicles such as Section 529 plans.

In 2004 for single taxpayers, the 10 percent bracket applied to taxable income (after deductions and exemptions) up to $7,150; for married couples the bracket ended at $14,300.

The Kiddie Tax provides special rules for taxing youngsters through age 13. For any dependent under age 14, the first $750 (indexed for inflation each year) of income and gains is tax free. The next $750 is taxed at the child's tax rate, either 5 percent on long-term capital gains and dividends or 10 percent on other income. Any income above $1,500 is taxed at the parents' top rate. Once the child hits age 14, however, all income and gains are taxed at the child's own rates.

Minimize Tax Implications

These rules and the new tax rates open up some profitable planning opportunities. Here are the new strategies for splitting income among family members to minimize taxes.

Limit income until age 14.   Under the Kiddie Tax rules it can be profitable to transfer a relatively small amount of investment income to a young child or grandchild, but there is no benefit to transferring too much income. Any investments in the name of a child under 14 should be structured to limit dividends, interest, and capital gains so they are not taxed at the parent's rate. Invest for growth until the child is at least 14. That means buy stocks that pay low or no dividends. Or invest in mutual funds that traditionally have low or no annual distributions. Buy only stocks or mutual funds that are unlikely to be sold until the youngster is age 14 or older.

Shift bonds to youngsters.   No one gets a tax benefit on bond interest income. The interest is taxed at ordinary income rates. There can be very significant tax savings, however, by shifting interest income from a top-bracket adult (35 percent rate) to a youngster (0 percent to 15 percent rate). If a family is holding a diversified long-term portfolio for a grandchild's benefit, it might make sense to have the bonds held in the grandchild's name while other investments are in the parents' or grandparents' names.

Give appreciated property.   Parents or grandparents can invest for growth in their own names until a child or grandchild needs money. Then, the family can reap substantial tax benefits by transferring the appreciated property to a youngster who is age 14 or older. The youngster sells the property. If the adult sold the property, a long-term capital gains tax of 15 percent would be due. The youngster, however, likely would pay taxes at only a 5 percent rate. On a $10,000 gain that drops the family tax bill from $1,500 to $500.

Before giving, adults want to be sure that the gains plus any other income of the youngster won't push his or her income above the limit for the 15 percent bracket. If it does, there is no tax advantage transferring the capital gains to the youngster.

Of course, once property is given to the youngster, it is his or hers. If the child is at least the age of majority (18 or 21, depending on the state), he or she can do anything with the wealth. Before that, the money can be put into a custodial account and managed by an adult for the child's benefit. But with the custodial account, once again the youngster gets full control of the property at the age of majority. In addition, money in a custodial account cannot be spent on a legal support obligation of the parents.

Reconsider Section 529 plans. The lower tax rates dim some of the luster of 529 plans. A taxable account in the parents' or grandparents' names won't get the 0 percent rate of a 529 plan. But if dividends and long-term capital gains are the only investment income in the account, the maximum tax rate is only 15 percent. In addition, taxes can be deferred by letting gains in stocks and mutual funds compound tax deferred until the money is needed. Further, the taxable account will have unlimited investment options instead of the limited choices imposed by a 529 plan. A taxable investment account also might have lower fees than a 529 plan. The fees could be much lower if the taxable account is invested in no load mutual funds. The 2003 tax law reduces the tax advantages of the 529 plan. The total control over the taxable account plus its flexibility and lower costs might make up for the lower taxes of a 529 plan.

Don't forget financial aid. College financial aid will be more significant than tax savings for many families. Determine if the future student might be eligible for financial aid. If he or she might be, it makes sense to keep money out of the child's name despite any tax benefits of family income splitting.

When financial aid is computed, the formula assumes that most of the wealth in the student's name will be spent on education expenses. A much smaller portion of wealth that is in the parents' names will be used to reduce an aid award. No wealth in a grandparent's name will be used to reduce financial aid. An adult who wants to maximize financial aid for a youngster and who wants control over the wealth should avoid transferring money to a child's or grandchild's name.

Plan for the truly long term. Most reports about the 2003 law have not noted that in 2008 for one year only the lowest tax bracket drops to zero for all types of income. That's right. Those in the lowest tax bracket will pay 0 percent tax on ordinary income, dividends, and capital gains realized in 2008. If the law doesn't change, that would be a good year to shift some appreciated property to a grandchild or child and have it sold. Be sure that the child doesn't earn enough income to exceed the lowest tax bracket that year.

Don't forget gift taxes.   Any transfer from one person to another is a gift. Each person can give any other person up to $11,000 annually (indexed for inflation) free of gift taxes. A married couple can give jointly up to $22,000 annually per individual donee. Gifts above that amount each year reduce the giver's lifetime estate and gift tax exemption. If the lifetime exemption is exhausted, gifts above the annual exemption are taxed.

Most parents and grandparents should take a multiyear approach to helping a youngster. In the first years, investments should be kept in the adult's name. The adult can invest to minimize taxes, avoid interest income and short-term capital gains, and earn primarily long-term capital gains and dividends. Later, after the child is 14 or older, the adult can decide if it makes sense to shift all or some of the investments to the youngster.

There isn't even a need for the property to be in the child's name for long. As money is needed, give appreciated property to the youngster, either directly or through a custodial account. The youngster can sell the property and pay the lowest long-term capital gains tax rate. This way, the property can be controlled by the parent or grandparent until the child needs it, say, when a tuition bill is due. Then a gift of enough property to pay the child's expenses plus the taxes can be given.

Helping Beyond College

Most grandkids can use help beyond college. Assistance could be used to buy the first home, start a business, or even prepare for retirement decades away. Some of the strategies that help save for college also could be used to establish a general legacy for grandchildren. Prepaid college savings plans aren't useful for saving beyond college, and neither are Coverdell Savings Accounts. UGMAs can provide wealth beyond college, though whether or not that happens is completely at the discretion of the grandchild. He or she gets full legal control at the age of majority. Good use can be made of direct gifts, trusts, and even 529 savings plans. Most of the 529 savings plans don't require the money to be spent until the original beneficiary is age 30; some allow accumulations even longer.

Let's look at how some other vehicles can help establish a legacy for a grandchild.

Best Way to Help a Grandchild

Perhaps the best tool for providing financial help to a grandchild is a Roth IRA. They were created as retirement accounts, but it is tough to beat the Roth IRA for estate planning and transferring wealth.

The advantages of the Roth IRA are that income and capital gains earned by the account are not taxed. Also, neither the owner nor the subsequent beneficiary pays income taxes on distributions in most cases. These advantages mean investment earnings compound tax free, then the accumulated amount can be withdrawn without incurring income taxes.

A Roth IRA's advantages are back-end loaded. There is no benefit for creating a Roth IRA, such as a deduction for contributions. There is no age limit on contributions to a Roth and no required minimum distributions (RMDs) for the original owner. With a regular IRA, contributions cannot be made after age 70 1/2, and required distributions must begin after that age. A beneficiary inheriting a Roth must begin RMDs, but they can be made over the beneficiary's life expectancy. That means for a grandchild, the required annual distributions would be small, usually much smaller than the earnings and the appreciation of the Roth IRA. So the account's value can appreciate for many years until the beneficiary really needs the money.

Those are powerful advantages that cannot be found in any other vehicle. There are several ways the Roth IRA can be used to help loved ones.

Start a new Roth IRA for yourself. A new Roth IRA can be started with annual contributions of up to the annual limit. The limit is scheduled to rise. (See Chapter 11 for details.) For married couples filing jointly, the full contribution can be made if their adjusted gross income is below $150,000. Partial contributions can be made when AGI is between $150,000 and $160,000. Single taxpayers can make full contributions up to $2,000 when AGI is below $95,000, and make reduced contributions when AGI is between $95,000 and $110,000. No contribution is allowed for a single taxpayer when AGI is above $110,000.

The owner also must have earned income for the year at least equal to the amount contributed to the Roth IRA. Earned income is salary and wages, not investment income. A contribution also can be made to a Roth IRA for a nonworking spouse as long as the working spouse has earned income at least equal to the contributions. The earned income requirement keeps a completely retired person from pursuing this strategy.

A grandparent can begin a Roth IRA, name the grandchild as beneficiary, and make regular contributions. After the grandparent passes away, the grandchild becomes the owner. The grandchild must begin taking minimum annual distributions from the Roth and can take additional amounts when desired. Instead of taking additional distributions, the grandchild can let the account continue to compound tax free. If the investment returns exceed the required annual distributions, by the time the grandchild is ready to retire the Roth IRA should provide a meaningful source of tax-free income.

Also, a grandparent who already has a traditional IRA can convert all or part of it into a Roth IRA, naming a grandchild as the beneficiary. This would generate all the Roth IRA benefits for both the grandparent and grandchild. There is a cost to converting a regular IRA to a Roth IRA: The amount converted must be treated as though it were distributed. That means the converted amount must be included in the grandparent's income and taxes paid on it.

To be able to convert a regular IRA to a Roth IRA, adjusted gross income for the year must be no more than $100,000 (excluding the conversion amount). This limit applies whether the grandparent is single or married filing jointly. (AGI actually is modified AGI. The modifications are in IRS Publication 553, available by calling 800-TAX-FORM or at www.irs.gov.)

When does it make sense to convert a regular IRA to a Roth IRA? First, the grandparent should be able to pay the taxes from sources other than the IRA. As much money as possible should be left in the new Roth IRA to earn compounded tax-free returns. Second, the grandparent should be able to leave the converted amount untouched for at least seven years, preferably longer. That's how long it takes for the benefits of tax-free compounding and distributions to make up for paying the taxes early. The longer the converted amount is left alone, and the higher the return that can be earned on the Roth IRA, the greater the benefit of converting.

If a grandparent expects to be in a lower tax bracket in the future, it might not make sense to pay the taxes now and convert to a Roth IRA. By not converting, lower taxes could be paid later. Before converting, a grandparent should be sure to check the state's tax rules. Many states follow the federal rules on Roth IRAs and conversions, but not all of them do.

The entire IRA does not have to be converted. It might make sense to convert only part of the IRA. Considering all the trade-offs can get complicated. A financial planner or accountant can help with the calculations. There also are conversion calculators on the Internet, such as at www.rothira.com. T. Rowe Price and several other mutual fund and brokerage firms offer free Roth IRA calculators. More details on converting IRAs can be found in Chapter 11.

Grandparents can help set up a grandchild's IRA. There is no minimum age for setting up a Roth IRA. All the taxpayer needs is earned income. It doesn't even have to be enough income to incur taxes. Suppose a grandchild earns a bit of money from babysitting, mowing lawns, or a part-time job. The grandchild naturally wants to spend most of that money. The grandparent can match the earnings with a cash gift that is used to set up a Roth IRA. The youngster then lets the income and capital gains compound tax free in the Roth IRA and is still able to spend the money he or she earned.

This can be the best deal for the grandchild. Because the grandchild is setting up the IRA and not inheriting it, there are no required minimum distributions at any time during the grandchild's life. The income and gains can compound for as long as the grandchild lets them. In addition, the money does not have to be left in the IRA until retirement. Distributions from a Roth IRA are tax-free if the money has been in the Roth IRA for at least five years and it is withdrawn for one of the following reasons: death, disability, after reaching age 59 1/2, or to pay first-time homebuying expenses of up to $10,000. A grandchild can take a tax-free withdrawal to help buy his or her first home. Or the money can compound until after the grandchild reaches age 59 1/2. After that, all distributions are tax free. Money can be withdrawn for other reasons as needed. The gains and income would be taxable, but it would have benefited from tax-deferred compounding over the years.

Don't overlook Roth IRAs just because they don't fit into your retirement plan. Roth IRAs are extremely powerful estate planning tools and can be used by individuals of almost any income level to enhance the future of their loved ones.

No-Tax, Low-Cost Way to Help a Grandchild

A grandparent doesn't need to give away money or property to help a grandchild. Money can be lent to let a grandchild build something with the principal.

Here's one plan. Lend $50,000 to a grandchild for five years. The grandchild invests the money and earns 10 percent annually. At the end of five years, the grandchild has accumulated over $80,000 before taxes. The grandchild can repay the $50,000 and still have about $30,000, minus taxes, left as a nest egg. Taxes should be quite low, because the grandchild should be in the lowest tax bracket and the gains should be long-term capital gains. The grandparent's only cost is the earnings from the $50,000 for five years, and the grandchild has accumulated a nice starter fund after only five years.

This is such an attractive deal for taxpayers at any income level that the tax code has imposed a number of hurdles.

A lender is required to charge a minimum interest rate on most loans. If the minimum isn't charged, then it is a below market loan on which a minimum interest rate based on current market rates is imputed. We'll discuss the effects of imputed interest shortly.

There are several key exceptions to the requirement of a minimum interest rate. The first is that a gift loan between individuals, which is what is described here, does not have interest imputed when loans between the individuals do not exceed $10,000, and the loan is not used to purchase or carry income-producing investments.

Another important exception provides no imputed interest on gift loans between individuals when the loans do not exceed $100,000 and the borrower's investment income for the year does not exceed $1,000. If the borrower's net investment income does exceed $1,000, interest will be imputed but only in the amount of the borrower's net investment income for the year.

This obviously is an important exception for loans to grandchildren. A grandparent can lend up to $100,000 to a grandchild interest free, if it is invested primarily for long-term capital gains so that there is little or no taxable annual income. If there is annual investment income, the grandchild should be sure to keep track of investment expenses such as broker's commissions. Those expenses are subtracted from investment income to arrive at net investment income. After five years, the grandchild sells enough of the investments to pay back the loan. There are no tax consequences to anyone, except taxes when the grandchild sells the investment.

Suppose a loan doesn't meet one of the exceptions and has interest imputed. Even then, the results are not bad.

When interest is imputed, the grandparent will be treated as having made a gift to the grandchild equal to the interest that should have been charged but wasn't. Then the grandparent will be treated as having received a payment of that amount of interest income from the grandchild. Because the grandparent can give the grandchild up to $11,000 annually free of gift taxes, gift taxes aren't a problem until the imputed interest is over $11,000. If the imputed rate is 8 percent, for example, there won't be a gift tax unless the loan exceeds $125,000.

The grandparent will have interest income equal to the amount of the imputed interest, though it won't be paid in cash. Suppose the imputed interest is $2,000 and the grandparent is in the 40 percent tax bracket. The cost of making the loan will be $800 in taxes on phantom interest income each year.

If a gift loan is made to a grandchild (or any other relative), there must be appropriate paperwork. The IRS doesn't like loans between related parties and tries to treat them as gifts. There must be a real expectation of repayment and the intent to enforce collection. The note should spell out an interest rate and repayment schedule and contain an unconditional promise to repay. The repayment schedule, which can be a balloon payment at the end, must be followed as much as finances permit. There also must be a reasonable expectation that the loan could be repaid. For example, a loan made to a relative with a failing business that is unlikely to recover might be treated as a gift rather than a loan.

One word of caution is that the assets the grandchild purchases might decline in value. I know one wealthy individual who lent money to an adult child and suggested the purchase of a stock he knew well. Unfortunately, the market did not agree with his assessment of the stock. The child soon owned a stock worth half its previous value and still owed the father the full amount of the loan.

New Ways to Invest for Grandchildren

The markets have sent a message to grandparents in the last few years. To ensure the success of a plan for leaving the grandchildren wealth, grandparents should heed the message.

A time-honored practice when setting up an account or trust for grandchildren was to buy shares in a few favored companies or mutual funds, then leave them alone. The grandchildren and their parents were told to hold the stocks or mutual funds until the money was needed. This was fine advice in the days when many companies became dominant after World War II, expanded that dominance around the globe, and enriched their shareholders for decades. Even the bear market of the 1970s merely slowed the effectiveness of this strategy.

But the changing economy of recent years should force grandparents to reconsider their strategy. These days, it is very difficult for a company to maintain its dominance for decades. Even companies that do maintain prime positions in their industries might see the growth of their industries or their pricing power or the dominance of their brand name decline. Starting in the late 1990s, the world's greatest brand name, Coca-Cola, saw its sales growth slow rapidly. Its ability to raise prices also disappeared in the deflation of 1998–2000. Coke's stock price fell by half. Likewise, in a short time Procter & Gamble's stock price was cut in half in the late 1990s. McDonald's has been limping along for years as the company struggles for ways to increase earnings growth. It recovered some of its luster in 2003 and 2004, but the stock price still has been stagnant for years. The list of former solid blue chips whose stock prices have declined substantially or stagnated is a long one. It is difficult to find a stock that one would feel comfortable locking into a portfolio for 20 years or more.

Likewise, mutual funds have seen many changes. Managers who build a fund's record move to other firms or retire. Or a manager's success disappears as the fund's size grows. The fund company might merge with another. These and other factors often cause a winning mutual fund to become a mediocre one or a loser.

In addition, even if a stock or fund is a good long-term holding, the market or economy might drag the value down at the time the investment needs to be cashed in to pay expenses.

Because a buy-and-hold strategy is no longer a sure bet, grandparents should consider a different approach for increasing the wealth they can leave to their grandchildren. It still is possible to increase a legacy by putting quality stocks or mutual funds in an account. Just don't count on leaving the portfolio untouched—someone should be watching it regularly. The stocks don't need to be traded frequently, but they should be reviewed regularly for shrinking markets, reduced pricing power, and other signs that growth might slow dramatically or even stop. These days, four to five years is a long time to hold a stock. Mutual funds also should be reviewed for signs that a long-term change in performance is occurring or is likely to occur. Such signs include a change in investment philosophy, new fund managers, a change in the fund company, and rapid growth of a fund's size.

Simple, Low-Cost Ways to Help

A grandparent doesn't need to be a multimillionaire to help the grandchildren. The grandparent doesn't even need to be wealthy. There are many simple, low-cost ways to help, and they are tax free. With many of these strategies, the grandparent can see the benefits now instead of imagining how the wealth will be used in the future.

The use of property is a great way to help future generations. For example, a grandparent might have a vacation property or recreational vehicle. The adult children (the grandchildren's parents) might save significant expenses if these assets can be used for family vacations. That savings can be used to help pay for the grandchildren's education or other future needs. Letting others use property costs the grandparents very little, and it usually has no tax consequences.

An increasingly popular strategy is to pay for family vacations. Travel can be fairly expensive, and many families with children have to stretch for or cannot afford a nice trip. A family trip paid by the grandparents can give the family an experience they never would have had or save them thousands of dollars. Grandparents who cannot afford to pay for an entire trip might be able to pay for a portion. Sometimes grandparents will pay for a cruise or a stay at a resort. All the children and grandchildren have to do is get to and from the location.

Technically, paying a share of someone's vacation costs is a gift to them and counts against the annual tax-free gift amount. But the IRS in the past has looked only at gifts of money and property. It has not tried to add up holiday gifts, meals, and travel.

Another way grandparents can help loved ones is to have their financial advisor's help. Suppose a grandparent gets professional advice on an estate plan, financial plan, or investments. The advice can be tailored to ensure that the needs of the children and grandchildren are considered in the plan. The grandparents also can pass on any advice received.

A further step is for the grandparent to offer to pay the advisors to work with the children or grandchildren. The loved ones would meet with the advisor, and all the information would be confidential between them. But the grandparent will have rendered a valuable benefit, and the advisor can ensure that what the children are doing is consistent with what the grandparent is doing and that the plans are coordinated.

The grandparent also should be able to get a break on fees. Even if the grandparent doesn't pay for everything, the family should get a break by using the same advisor. A family buying as a group probably can negotiate a lower fee than could each individual family member.

Another benefit is that together the family learns more and sees how finances work. That's a big improvement over leaving your loved ones your assets and expecting them to know how to manage them. Often, being unprepared to handle the family's assets can do more damage than taxes or probate costs.

A grandparent who is in business or is an investor can help family members by letting them benefit from opportunities that come the grandparent's way. When family members are in the same or related businesses, the grandparent can send some potential business or clients to other family members instead of keeping the opportunities for themselves.

Teaching Grandkids Wealth Management

It is nice to give wealth to grandchildren. But an even better gift can be to teach them how to multiply and manage wealth for the rest of their lives.

Youngsters today are more financially savvy than any prior generation. They own investments, have such high discretionary income that retailers make pitches to them, and even financial services firms are catering to the younger generation. Despite this attention, money, and information, most grandchildren know just enough about money management to be dangerous. That's where grandparents come in. Grandparents can help subsequent generations become better, shrewder financial managers. An additional benefit is that by managing their own funds, the grandchildren will learn to be more responsible people in general.

To help grandchildren on their way, consider these steps:

- Open basic accounts for the youngsters. Start with a savings account. It could be an account at a local bank or a money market fund that is easy to access. The grandparent can put in the start-up capital to meet the minimum investment amount, but can tell the grandchild that the start-up money is either the grandparent's or is available only for college. Review the account statements with the grandchild from time to time, so that he or she can see how the money grows just by being left alone in the account.
- Use the account to teach the youngster to save for the long term. For example, the grandparent could say that only up to 20 percent of the balance can be spent, and the rest is being saved for college. Also, instead of depositing gifts to the account that the grandchild doesn't know about, give money directly and encourage him or her to save all or most of it.

  Some people prefer separate accounts—one for spending money, one for long-term expenses such as college, and maybe another for other expenses. Each time the child receives money, a portion is put into each account.
- Give simple lessons to the grandchild. Explain how compound interest and regular savings work, using examples and explanations that the child can understand. Some brokers and mutual funds have education materials to help explain a point. A good book is *The Richest Man In Babylon* by George Clayson, a classic that explains savings and compounding of wealth.
- Encourage the grandchild to save by offering to match new savings with additional gifts to the account.
- Help the grandchild pick stocks for a hypothetical portfolio. It can be a

game, but the child will learn and might become interested. Over time, review the selections and how they performed.

- Buy mutual funds in the investment account. Teach the grandchild how to check prices in the newspaper or on the Internet. When the reports from the mutual fund arrive, use these to show the grandchild which companies the fund owns and how they have affected the price.
- Buy a few stocks with the grandchild. This is how a child learns to think like a business owner. When the company reports arrive, the grandchild won't be able to understand most of them. But the grandparent can point out some highlights, such as descriptions of the company's activities and how a few key numbers changed over time.

A grandchild needs to save and invest for a lifetime. Grandparents can get them off to a good start with a few easy steps and some early lessons on how wealth works. With any luck, the grandchild will be able to benefit from a grandparent's wisdom long after the grandparent is gone.

CHAPTER 10

Beware the Retirement Tax Ambush

T axes will be lower in retirement. That used to be true. Now it is one of the most dangerous myths in retirement planning. It is likely to become an even bigger myth in the coming years.

These days, it is rare for a person's tax rate to decline after retiring. In many cases, the income tax rate actually increases in retirement. For years, Congress and the IRS have looked to older Americans to increase government revenues. After all, today's older Americans are the richest generation in history and also a very large generation. That's where the money is. As the Baby Boomers age and inherit wealth from their parents, those over age 50 will become an even bigger target. Taxes are likely to be one of the larger expenses in a retiree's budget—if not the largest.

Retirees face the same tax burdens and rules as other Americans. Retirees also face a number of special tax rules directed specifically at them. Some of these rules are complicated and require decisions. At times, once choices are made, they cannot be changed.

As a result, retirees today face some of the highest marginal tax rates in U.S. history. For example, not too long ago, Social Security benefits were tax free. Since 1993, when a couple's income is greater than $44,000 ($34,000 for single taxpayers), up to 85 percent of Social Security benefits are taxed for each additional dollar earned. Earn an extra dollar of investment income, and not only is that dollar taxed but 85 cents of Social Security benefits also are taxed. (See Chapter 4 for more details about taxes on Social Security benefits.)

These are the types of rules that can create a marginal tax bracket (the tax rate on the last dollar earned) higher than 70 percent for many seniors. A retiree can face a marginal tax rate of 90 percent or higher if he or she lives in a state with high income tax rates.

More Social Security beneficiaries pay taxes on their benefits each year because the income levels at which the tax takes effect are not indexed for inflation. The IRS reported that over 20 percent of recipients paid income taxes on their benefits in 1999, a record 9.6 million people. Those numbers are estimated to increase steadily every year.

That is just one example of how the income tax burden increases and the tax code becomes more complicated after retirement. The 2003 tax law improved things a bit by enacting a number of tax reductions. Income tax rates were cut across the board. The maximum tax rates on dividends and on long-term capital gains were reduced to 15 percent. Yet, for the most part the law did not change the extra taxes that are imposed on most older Americans.

In addition to the taxes on Social Security benefits, there are several areas of the tax code that affect older Americans more than other taxpayers or that are specifically directed at post-retirement taxpayers. We'll cover those parts of the tax code in this chapter. The taxes on IRAs and other tax-qualified retirement plans are so important that they are covered separately in Chapter 11.

The Stealth Taxes

The tax law is replete with stealth taxes. These are hidden taxes that take money out of people's pockets without increasing tax rates or changing the law. The taxes are hidden because they can be incurred by actions many taxpayers don't even realize can trigger higher taxes. It used to be that only the wealthy worried about stealth taxes. In recent years, however, these taxes snared more and more taxpayers, and older taxpayers are among those most likely to pay stealth taxes.

There are four main stealth taxes: the alternative minimum tax (AMT), the Pease tax (the itemized deduction reduction), the PEP (personal exemption phaseout), and the tax on Social Security benefits.

- In 1999 a record 999,790 taxpayers paid $5.9 billion under the AMT. That's 21 percent more taxpayers than in 1998, and the dollar amount was 34 percent higher. The AMT is projected to affect 17 million returns by 2010. In 1997, taxpayers with incomes of less than $200,000 were 68 percent of those paying the AMT. That percentage should rise to 83 percent by 2007.
- The Pease tax affected 5.4 million individual returns in 1999, a 13 percent increase, and denied $31 billion in itemized deductions—a 20 percent increase over the prior year.
- The PEP tax reduces personal exemptions for high-income taxpayers.

Though rarely directed specifically at older Americans, stealth taxes are especially important to retired taxpayers. For example, IRA distributions and capital gains are discretionary income that can trigger higher taxes under the Pease and PEP provisions. Also, because of the way it is computed, the AMT is more likely to trap older taxpayers than younger ones.

The 2001 tax law advertised an end to the stealth taxes, but its efforts have proven meager. There was a small change made in the AMT that wasn't scheduled to take effect until 2005 and would reduce but not eliminate the tax. The 2003 tax law accelerated that change by immediately raising the AMT exemption amount to $40,250 (from $35,750) for single taxpayers and $58,000 (from $49,000) for married couples filing jointly. Yet, the new exemptions take effect only for tax years 2003 and 2004 unless Congress acts to extend them. Elimination of the Pease and PEP are phased over several years starting in 2005. The tax on Social Security benefits will not change.

Fortunately, taxpayers can avoid or minimize stealth taxes if they know about them ahead of time and take action.

The Alternative Minimum Tax

The AMT basically is a separate tax system and is almost a flat tax. A taxpayer computes both the regular tax and the AMT, then pays the higher of the two. The IRS also computes the AMT for all returns it processes. That's how many taxpayers end up paying it, even though they have never heard of the AMT and didn't compute the tax.

The AMT is computed on Form 6251. The tax starts with regular taxable income. Then a number of adjustments and preferences listed on the form are added back to taxable income. After adding the adjustments and preferences, the exempt amount is subtracted. The reason more and more people are subject to the AMT is that the exemption hasn't kept pace with inflation or income growth. Even the relief in the 2001 and 2003 tax laws is only a partial adjustment. The AMT is computed on the income remaining after subtracting the exemption. The AMT is close to being a flat tax because the tax is a 26 percent rate on the first $175,000 of AMT income and 28 percent on any additional income.

Originally the AMT was designed to ensure that the wealthiest taxpayers did not make generous use of tax breaks to eliminate all income taxes. It was created after IRS data revealed that about 500 taxpayers earned more than $1 million but paid little or no taxes.

Unfortunately, the AMT now traps taxpayers in most income brackets when they have enough deductions—even if they have a sizeable tax liability under the regular tax. Unexceptional deductions that are added back to taxable income under the AMT include personal and dependent exemptions, state and local taxes, most miscellaneous itemized expenses, and incentive stock option gains.

Upper-income and middle-income residents of states that have high income or real estate taxes (or both) are very likely to pay the AMT. So are people with a lot of dependent exemptions. In New York, a family with five children and less than $100,000 in income could pay the AMT. Their high number of exemptions and the large deduction for state taxes trigger the AMT, though the family is hardly wealthy. One study concluded that almost 75 percent of the difference between the regular income tax and the AMT is due to personal exemptions, the standard deduction, and itemized expenses. That means taxpayers who have significant exemptions or itemized expenses could pay a higher tax under the AMT than under the regular income tax. Those write-offs aren't restricted to the wealthy.

When hit by the AMT, a taxpayer can lose the benefit of personal and dependent exemptions and state income tax deductions. The benefit of the 15 percent top tax rate on long-term capital gains is reduced. Also chopped will be part of the tax benefit for charitable contributions, some medical expense deductions, and deductions for miscellaneous itemized expenses such as tax preparation fees and investment management fees. Almost all tax credits are disallowed under the AMT. For most taxpayers, mortgage interest and charitable contributions are the only deductions permitted under the AMT. Medical expenses must exceed 10 percent of adjusted gross income to be deductible under the AMT.

Ironically, the 2003 tax cut means even more people are likely to pay the AMT. That's because taxpayers pay the higher of the regular tax or the AMT. If the regular income tax goes down and no other changes are made, more people will owe the AMT. People who narrowly avoided the AMT under the old law will pay the AMT after the 2003 tax cuts.

The number of people snared by the AMT is forecast to rise each year. By 2004, 19 percent of those with adjusted gross incomes between $100,000 and $200,000 will pay the AMT, as will 7 percent of those with incomes between $75,000 and $100,000. By 2010, 18 percent of taxpayers with incomes between $50,000 and $75,000 will pay the AMT.

Retirees are especially susceptible to a sneak attack from the AMT. A retiree usually receives less taxable income in retirement. Yet, most deductions will remain the same for at least the first few years. Real estate taxes and mortgage interest won't change just because a property owner has retired. Investment advisor fees and other miscellaneous itemized expenses probably will be stable and might even rise. State income taxes will decline a bit with income, but charitable contributions generally stay the same. Even worse, a retiree might have purchased a second home. That increases real estate tax deductions and perhaps mortgage interest expense, and with that comes the risk of paying the AMT.

Most retirees believe that tax-exempt bonds are exempt from all income taxes. They are only partly right. General obligation bonds do not affect the AMT. A number of exempt bonds, however, fund private activities. Interest from these is tax free under the regular tax but is taxed under the AMT. A number of tax-exempt bond mutual funds have about 80 percent of their portfolios in these private activity bonds. A private activity bond is one that is backed not by the general obligation of a government but by an activity that is not considered an essential government function. These activities include airports, stadiums, many commercial properties, and the like.

A retiree also is likely to have more capital gains from the sale of investments than during the working years, and increased capital gains puts the retiree at risk for triggering the AMT. The result for too many retirees is that income declines while tax deductions remain stable and might perhaps increase, which also can trigger the AMT.

Planning to Avoid the AMT

Here's what to do to avoid the AMT:

Several tax years should be planned at one time. The AMT depends on the ratio between income and tax breaks. If there are too many tax breaks for the amount of income, the AMT will be triggered. The simple rule is to try to match income and expenses to minimize the AMT. Ideally, expenses should be moved into a year with higher than usual income or income moved into a year that will have extra tax breaks.

Often, taxpayers conclude that they cannot beat the AMT every year. They will have too many tax breaks for their level of income. Instead, they decide to pay the AMT once every two or three years. They look to maximize income in an AMT year, knowing it will face a maximum tax of 28 percent. They try to defer some deductions to a year when they aren't likely to be paying the AMT. This ensures that more of the deductions are deducted against the ordinary income tax and are not lost under the AMT.

Here are more specific steps:

- During the year, estimate both the regular tax and the AMT to see if the AMT might be triggered this year. Those with incomes above $75,000, especially those who live in high tax states, are most likely to pay the AMT.
- If the AMT might be triggered, consider deferring some deductions to the next year. Doing so might avoid the AMT this year. Even if it does not avoid the AMT, deferring the deductions might ensure that they are used fully next year instead of being fully or partially lost under the AMT this year.

  Many deductions that might trigger the AMT can be deferred. Some state and local income tax payments often can be paid in January instead of December. Real estate taxes also might be delayed. Some taxpayers find that it is cheaper to pay a penalty for making these payments late if it avoids the AMT. Charitable contributions can be made at any time; delaying a contribution from December to January might save considerable taxes. Large charitable contributions might need to be spread over several years. Examine the other expenses that might trigger the AMT and see which of those payments can be deferred.

- When the AMT clearly will be paid this year without changes, accelerate income into this year. Bringing extra income into one year could increase the regular income tax and might avoid the AMT. If that happens, tax breaks won't be lost under the AMT. The other possible effect is that, if the AMT cannot be avoided, a maximum marginal tax rate of 28 percent on the additional income is assured, instead of the usual maximum 35 percent rate.

  There is a potential trap to this strategy. The AMT exemption amount is phased out at higher incomes. The phaseout occurs between $150,000 and $346,000 on joint returns ($112,400 and $255,500 on single returns). Within the phaseout range, 25 cents of the exemption is lost for each additional dollar of income. That converts the 28 percent AMT rate into a marginal tax rate of 35 percent on each additional dollar of income. A taxpayer should not accelerate income if it will put income into this phaseout range.

- Plan state and local tax payments. Most taxpayers can control when at least some of their state and local taxes are paid. For example, the final payment of a year's estimated income taxes might not be due until the following January. The check, however, can be written in December of the tax year if the taxpayer chooses. Similar payment flexibility often is available with real estate and personal property taxes. This flexibility can be used to move state tax payments into the year that provides the most tax benefits.

- Time capital gains. The 15 percent long term capital gains tax rate can trigger the AMT in a year when the taxpayer has a lot of capital gains. The large gains could cause the loss of deductions and increase the effective tax rate on the capital gains. Be careful about taking a lot of capital gains in one year and avoid large investments in mutual funds that have histories of making significant capital gains distributions. Reevaluate tax planning for the year if a mutual fund declares a large capital gain distribution. As year end draws near, try to get estimates of capital gain distributions from mutual funds and be prepared to readjust your tax plan.

- Examine exempt bonds and bond funds. Yields from private activity municipal bonds are higher than from regular exempt bonds, partly because the higher yield is taxable under the AMT. Most tax-exempt bond funds invest at least part of their portfolios in private activity bonds and let shareholders worry about the tax consequences. A fund that labels itself tax exempt must earn at least 80 percent of its interest from genuinely exempt bonds. A fund that calls itself municipal, however, can be completely invested in private activity bonds.

- Watch stock options. Exercising incentive stock options could trigger the AMT. Even worse, holding the stock after exercising the options could trigger taxes based on the value on the exercise date, even if the stock price subsequently declines.

- When the AMT won't apply this year but might next year, accelerate some deductions into this year. Deductions can be accelerated, for example, by prepaying some miscellaneous itemized deductions or state and local taxes.

Itemized Deduction Reduction

The Pease provision (named after the congressman whose idea it was) affects far more taxpayers than the alternative minimum tax. Pease disallows part of a taxpayer's itemized expense deductions when the taxpayer's adjusted gross income (AGI) is too high. The level at which the itemized deduction reduction kicks in (known as the threshold amount) is indexed for inflation, so it changes each year. In 2004, the provision kicked in when adjusted gross income exceeded $142,700 on most returns, and $71,350 for a married individual filing separately.

Computing the Pease deduction can get complicated. Itemized deductions are reduced by 3 percent of the difference between the threshold amount and AGI. Up to 80 percent of itemized deductions can be eliminated under the Pease provision. For example, a married couple in 2003 with AGI of $209,450 could lose almost $3,000 of itemized deductions.

The Pease provision is particularly hard on taxpayers with volatile incomes or who have one-time income boosts. A large capital gain or retirement plan distribution could make a lot of itemized deductions disappear. Someone who has a high income each year knows he or she will be subject to the itemized deduction reduction and can reliably estimate ahead of time the amount of a deduction that would be lost before writing a check for an itemized expense. But someone with a volatile income or one-time change in income is likely to get trapped by the Pease provision and lose the benefit of a lot of tax deductions. Some of those deductions, such as charitable contributions, could have been delayed until the next year.

The strategy for avoiding the itemized deduction reduction is to keep track of income and expenses. When AGI is near the threshold, carefully consider all financial transactions before taking action. For example:

- Don't make large charitable gifts or other discretionary itemized expenses until income for the year can be estimated reliably and the status of the tax deduction is clear.
- Before taking extra retirement plan distributions or realizing capital gains, be sure to consider the effect this would have on itemized expense deductions.
- When income is going to be high enough to trigger the Pease provision, try to defer some itemized expense deductions to a year with lower income. For example, if a large capital gain is going to be realized, consider deferring large charitable contributions to the following year.

Saving Personal Exemptions

Personal and dependent exemptions also are phased out as income increases under the Personal Exemption Phaseout (PEP) rules. Each taxpayer gets a personal exemption deduction, one for a spouse, and one for each dependent. The exemption amount is indexed for inflation and was $3,100 in 2004. These deductions are allowed whether expenses are itemized or the standard deduction is taken.

The personal and dependent exemptions are reduced when AGI exceeds a threshold amount. That amount in 2004 was $214,050 on a joint return and $142,700 for a single taxpayer. The formula for reducing the exemptions is complicated. It works out to losing 2.25 cents of each exemption for each dollar income rises above the threshold amount. The formula is that exemptions are reduced 2 percent for each $2,500 or part of $2,500 that AGI is above the threshold. For those who don't use computer software or a tax preparer to do their returns, the IRS offers a worksheet along with the instructions to compute the exemption reduction.

The PEP is scheduled to be phased out over five years beginning in 2005. In the meantime, there is little a taxpayer can do. A taxpayer who has flexibility in recognizing income can keep track during the year and defer some income when there is a risk of exceeding the threshold amount. Income could be deferred by not taking distributions from retirement plans or realizing capital gains.

Another way to avoid the PEP is to increase deductions that are subtracted before adjusted gross income. There are only a few deductions in this category. The commonly-known itemized expenses (charitable contributions, mortgage interest, state and local taxes) won't help. They are deducted after AGI. The best deductions for this purpose are capital losses and business losses. For example, the PEP might be avoided by selling investments that show paper losses and deducting the losses against capital gains. Losses that exceed capital gains can offset up to $3,000 of other income.

Retirees' Special Tax Problem

A special tax problem for many retirees, especially new retirees, is the required quarterly payment of estimated income taxes. After decades of having taxes automatically deducted from their paychecks, many have trouble adapting to a system of writing a check for estimated taxes each quarter. Too often, retirees' payments are late or aren't high enough, resulting in unnecessary penalties. Some retirees prepay too much, providing an interest-free loan to the government.

Those who expect to owe more than $1,000 in federal income taxes that are not prepaid through withholding must make quarterly estimated tax payments. The payment for the first quarter of the year is due by April 15.

The other three payments are due June 15, September 15, and January 15. If the fifteenth of the month falls on a weekend or holiday, the deadline is delayed until the next business day.

The penalty for a late or low payment is interest compounded daily at a rate announced by the IRS each month. The interest rate changes with market treasury rates. Interest is charged from the day the payment was due until the earlier of the date the tax return for the year is due and the date the payment actually is made.

Estimated tax payments must cover all types of taxes due: income, self-employment, and any others that will be reported on Form 1040. Estimated tax payments are determined by projecting the taxes that will be due for the year, dividing the total by four, and paying that amount each quarter. Payments can be made through the mail by filing Form 1040-ES or can be made by credit card over the phone by calling 800-2PAYTAX.

The first goal is to make payments that are high enough to avoid any penalties. Taxpayers can avoid the penalties by qualifying for at least one of three safe harbors. High income taxpayers must qualify for the third safe harbor to avoid the penalties. The safe harbors are:

- Pay at least 90 percent of the current year's tax liability through timely estimated tax payments;
- Pay an amount equal to at least 100 percent of last year's tax bill through timely estimated tax payments;
- A high-income taxpayer must pay an amount at least equal to either (1) 90 percent of the current year's tax liability or (2) 110 percent of last year's tax liability. A high income taxpayer is one whose adjusted gross income on the previous year's tax return was over $150,000 ($75,000 for married individuals filing separately).

Another way to avoid an underpayment penalty is through the annualization method. For example, suppose estimated tax payments for the first three quarters of the year were accurate based on the income to date, but income increased during the last quarter of the year. Then, the taxpayer can make a higher estimated tax payment for the fourth quarter and avoid a penalty. This method is for anyone whose income varied during the year and who made payments based on the income as it actually was received. To use this method, Form 2210 with Schedule AI must be filed as part of the tax return for the year. This form requires a showing of when income was received during the year and that quarterly estimated payments were sufficient for the income received each quarter.

Penalties for failure to pay estimated taxes cannot be avoided by paying the year's taxes with a big check in the last quarterly payment. The IRS expects estimated taxes to be paid equally throughout the year. When payments are not equal, the only way to avoid penalties is to use the annualization method.

Retirees should choose the payment schedule that allows them to retain money as long as possible and keep it working for them, not the government. If income is likely to stay the same or decline this year, prepay 90 percent of this year's tax liability. That way, 10 percent to 20 percent of the final tax liability can be invested until the tax return for the year is filed. The trick with this approach is to make an accurate estimate of the tax bill for the year. If prepayments are too low, the taxpayer will be hit with a penalty. A taxpayer might want to figure the 90 percent amount, then pay a little extra each quarter to ensure there won't be penalties.

If income is likely to increase this year, make payments based on last year's liability. That way, penalties will be avoided and cash will be conserved for as long as possible.

If income will fluctuate and the taxpayer doesn't mind keeping careful track of the cash flows and related tax liabilities, then the annualized method is best. Taxpayers whose income is primarily from capital gains or retirement plan distributions that are discretionary instead of on a schedule might choose this method. It is too much work for most people, but it can save money when income varies throughout the year. The goal should be to estimate income well enough to hold on to the cash as long as possible without incurring any penalties.

Beat Taxes on Social Security Benefits

Social Security benefits originally were tax free. In the 1980s, taxpayers with adjusted gross incomes above $32,000 began to have up to 50 percent of their benefits taxed. In the 1993 tax law, those with incomes exceeding $44,000 began to have up to 85 percent of their benefits taxed. The threshold levels are not indexed for inflation, so a greater percentage of Social Security beneficiaries pay taxes on their benefits each year. The details of computing the tax are complicated, and can be found in IRS Publication 915 (call 800-TAX-FORM). More information about this tax and how to avoid it can be found in Chapter 4.

Deducting Investing as a Business

The only job many retirees have is managing their portfolios. It is one of the most important jobs many have held. The portfolio has to help meet expenses for the rest of their lives, and it will be part of any legacy they leave.

Many retirees and pre-retirees have a separate space in the home to store investment records and resources. They generally do research and make decisions there. A computer might help manage the portfolio. A typical retiree probably spends some time on the portfolio every week, and many give the portfolio some attention each day.

These retirees are treating portfolio management as a part-time business and it is their means of supporting themselves—therefore, shouldn't they be able to report it as a business on their tax returns? Let's take a close look at this tax strategy.

There can be substantial tax advantages to treating portfolio management as a business. The taxpayer could file a Schedule C and deduct directly from investment income the home office expenses and the cost of publications and other resources used to make investment decisions. The taxpayer also might be able to set up another pension plan to shelter investment income and gains that exceeded spending needs. A spouse or child could be hired to help out, and the salary would be deductible from the investment income.

When investing is not a separate business, no home office deduction is allowed, and other investment expenses are reported as miscellaneous itemized expenses. They are deductible only if the taxpayer itemizes deductions and only to the extent that all the miscellaneous expenses exceed 2 percent of adjusted gross income. For example, if adjusted gross income is $45,000, the taxpayer deducts only the miscellaneous itemized expenses that exceed $900. Not many people are able to deduct miscellaneous itemized expenses.

Unfortunately, retirees who want to treat investing as a business face a stacked deck. The IRS and the courts distinguish between traders and investors. Traders can treat portfolio activities as a business; investors cannot. The IRS and the courts don't care how large a portfolio is, how much of the investor's income or net worth it comprises, or even how much time is devoted to portfolio management. Instead, the following three factors are what matter.

- Investment goals. To treat investing as a business, the intent must be to invest for the short term and capture profits based on daily or, at most, weekly changes in values.
- Type of income. If the investor is earning long-term capital gains, he or she is an investor, not a trader. Investing for income, such as interest and dividends, also means the investor cannot treat the portfolio as a business. The courts want to see the taxpayer earning primarily short-term capital gains before they will allow deductions of investment expenses as business expenses.
- Frequency, extent, and regularity of transactions. The taxpayer needs to make a lot of transactions and make transactions frequently to qualify as a trader. To the tax authorities, a week is a long time to let an investment ride if someone is in the business of investing. Trades have to be made at least several times a week before investing is considered a business.

These standards are tough. In one case the taxpayer made 326 sales during the year involving $9 million worth of stocks and options, and the Tax Court still ruled he was an investor and not a trader in the business of investing. To meet the tax law's standards, an individual must be a short-term speculator, not an investor. Not many people profit that way, and those that do don't have time or energy for much else.

Health Care Tax Strategies

Health care or long-term care can eat up a big part of a retiree's budget—or the budget of a retiree's children. Fortunately, the tax law can help pay for a big part of that burden.

Deductions for medical expenses seemed to disappear when the rules were changed in 1986. Medical expenses can be deducted only by those who itemize deductions. Even then, only the medical expenses that exceed 7.5 percent of adjusted gross income can be deducted. For example, if adjusted gross income is $50,000, only those medical expenses that exceed $3,750 can be deducted.

But those who know the tax rules and how to structure their affairs can get big tax deductions for medical expenses. Following are some examples of how to get the most medical expense deductions.

Suppose Rosie Profits is in a nursing home at a cost of $60,000 annually. Rosie has income from Social Security and her investments that cover most of the cost, and the rest is paid from selling some investments. Deducting the cost as a medical expense wipes out her tax bill.

What if Rosie's adult son, Hi, is in a higher tax bracket? The medical expense deduction is much more valuable in the higher tax bracket. In addition, adding the nursing home expense to the other medical expenses of Hi's family could make those family expenses deductible. In these circumstances, the best solution is for Hi to pay Rosie's nursing home expenses.

Here's how the numbers could work. Suppose Hi's adjusted gross income is $250,000. He needs medical expenses to exceed $18,750 to deduct any of them. If Hi pays all Rosie's nursing home expenses, he'll deduct $41,250. In addition, Hi's other medical expenses now might be deductible. The medical expense deduction reduces Hi's taxes by more than $16,000. Rosie could give Hi $44,000 annually to pay the nursing home expenses. Rosie might now have an income tax bill of over $8,000 annually, leaving the family net savings of around $8,000 by restructuring this way. Rosie would need to file a gift tax return when she gives Hi $44,000 annually. The first $11,000 of the gift annually would be tax free. The remainder would reduce her lifetime estate and gift tax exemption.

A taxpayer can deduct another relative's medical expenses if the taxpayer provided over half that person's support during the year. IRS Publication 502 Medical and Dental Expenses lists the relatives that qualify and the expenses that count as support. (Call 800-TAX-FORM or check www.irs.gov.) If that relative also has non-Social Security income less than the personal exemption amount, the taxpayer might also get a dependent exemption. Check IRS Publication 17 for details on the dependent exemption.

Suppose all of Rosie's children contribute to her nursing home expenses. To ensure that someone gets the medical expense deduction, they should all make tax-free gifts of up to $11,000 to one sibling who pays the expenses and takes the deduction. The amount they all contribute should take the tax deduction into account.

Knowing the rules also can maximize the nursing home expenses that are deductible, regardless of who deducts them. When a person resides in a nursing home because of his or her physical condition and the availability of medical care is the primary reason for residing there, the entire cost of the nursing home is deductible. But if medical care is not the primary reason for residing in the nursing home, only the costs attributable to medical or nursing care are deductible. Payments for food, lodging, and other personal expenses are not deductible in that case. Most nursing homes give itemized bills for their services. Whoever is paying the bills should request an itemized bill if it is not given.

Deducting the cost of an assisted living facility is trickier. Deductions are most limited for those who can perform at least five of the six activities of daily living (eating, toileting, transferring, bathing, dressing, and continence). These individuals get deductions only for the portion of the costs related to nursing care or other health care. These should be itemized in the bill.

But when the assisted living resident cannot perform two or more of the activities of daily living, the entire cost of the facility can be deducted if the resident also has a plan of care in place. A physician, a nurse, or a physical therapist can draw up a plan of care.

Home health care expenses also might be deductible. Naturally, direct medical expenses can be deducted. These include medical care—even simple tasks such as blood pressure monitoring—performed by a licensed health care worker. But those who require home health care often require help with personal tasks such as meals, bathing, dressing, and bed-changing. The cost of this help might also be deductible if the patient is unable to perform two or more of the six activities of daily living and there is a plan of care that specifies help with these tasks. Check IRS Publication 502 for details.

Sometimes a medical expense can be deducted twice. Suppose Max Profits purchases a medical device such as a wheelchair or crutches. That is deductible as a medical expense. Then Max recovers or his needs change. Max can contribute the medical device to a charity and deduct the fair market value of the item as a charitable contribution.

In recent years, the IRS eased deductions for some expenses that previously weren't deductible. The cost of smoking cessation programs, whether or not prescribed by a doctor, and the cost of prescription drugs to alleviate the symptoms of nicotine withdrawal are now deductible (Rev. Rul. 99-28). A weight loss program also might be deductible when prescribed by a physician to treat a specific illness or ailment, though it is not deductible when undertaken to improve general health.

By restructuring some activities and knowing the rules, a retiree might be able to greatly increase deductions from medical expenses. There can be a lot of money at stake, so be sure to read the IRS Publications and consult with your tax advisor.

Making IRAs Last

Individual Retirement Accounts (IRAs) began as simple investment vehicles to help investors set aside a little bit extra for retirement. They aren't so simple any more. The contribution limit for IRAs began at $500, but it will grow to $5,000 in 2008 ($6,000 for those over 50). Congress also created several different types of IRAs over the years and loaded on new rules. In addition, 401(k) accounts often are rolled over into IRAs at retirement, making many IRAs the largest financial asset most people have ever owned.

IRAs now are essential to the retirement plans of many Americans. IRA owners need to know how to take maximum advantage of these accounts, keep up with the ever-changing rules, and learn how to avoid some of the traps of IRA ownership. They also should consider some strategies that are counterintuitive. Sometimes these unconventional moves can increase the benefits from IRAs and other tax-deferred accounts.

This chapter will examine the critical decisions that must be made by owners of IRAs and other tax-deferred accounts. We'll discuss how to choose from among different tax-deferred vehicles, how to invest a tax-deferred account, and how to take distributions from IRAs. Each decision could change the after-tax wealth of the account owner by tens of thousands of dollars. The decisions also greatly affect the amount that can be left to heirs or charity.

Choosing Among Tax-Advantaged Vehicles

Congress periodically gets concerned about the reported low savings rate of Americans and creates another tax incentive to save and invest. Sometimes a new vehicle is created; sometimes an existing vehicle is enhanced. The result is an array of sometimes confusing choices for investors. It takes some work for each investor to determine the best choice. Here's how to choose.

401(k) First

Most employers of any size offer 401(k) savings accounts to their employees. A provision in the 2001 tax law allows even one-person businesses to offer 401(k)s. These accounts usually are the best first choice for long-term savings.

In a 401(k) plan, an employee elects to have part of his or her salary deposited in an account. The deferred salary is not subject to current income taxes, though Social Security and Medicare taxes are imposed. Investment earnings in the account compound tax deferred until they are withdrawn, then they are taxed as ordinary income. Loans can be taken from the accounts under certain circumstances. Those who qualify for a hardship withdrawal can take money out before age 59½ without paying the 10 percent early distribution penalty (though income taxes still are due).

The 401(k)'s benefits are comparable to those of a deductible IRA. Each allows before-tax dollars to be invested in the account, and income and capital gains to compound tax deferred. Distributions from each type of account are taxed as ordinary income. A 401(k) carries with it the additional benefit of allowing loans and penalty-free hardship distributions. Loans from an IRA are taxed as distributions, and only a few types of IRA withdrawals before age 59½ are subject to the 10 percent penalty. A 401(k) also has higher annual contribution limits.

Perhaps the biggest advantage of many 401(k) plans is that the sponsoring employers match their employees' contributions. The most common match is 50 percent of the amount of salary an employee defers, up to a percentage of salary that usually is 3 percent to 6 percent. So if an employee earns $50,000 and the employer has a 50 percent match up to 3 percent, each year the employer will contribute $0.50 for each dollar the employee defers until the employee has deferred $1,500 of salary. The employee might be able to defer more than $1,500 under the tax law, but the employer will not match the additional amount. The matching contribution is not taxed to the employee until it is distributed, and it is invested tax deferred along with the employee's own contributions. The matching contribution in this case is a guaranteed 50 percent return on the employee's first $1,500 of contributions. The employee can lose money on the investments and still come out ahead.

Some employers have more generous matching provisions. Not all 401(k) plans, however, are such attractive deals. Some employers, especially smaller ones, do not make any matching contributions. Some firms also have employees pay the annual maintenance fees on the accounts, usually $25 to $50. Other fees also might be charged. In those cases, a deductible IRA could be more attractive. Even so, the higher contribution limit for the 401(k) and the ability to borrow from the account still might make the 401(k) an essential part of a retirement saving strategy, especially for those who plan to defer a relatively large amount into the account. See Table 11.1.

Which IRA to Choose?

When a good 401(k) is not available or its limits are exhausted, the next vehicle to consider is an IRA. As the national savings rate declined during the 1990s, Congress increased the types of IRAs available. Now, there are about six types of IRAs open to at least some taxpayers. Following is a discussion of each type.

The traditional deductible IRA still is open to many taxpayers. The deduction is allowed without restriction, however, only to taxpayers who are not covered by an employer retirement plan, including a 401(k). If either spouse is covered by an employer plan, both spouses are considered covered. When a taxpayer is covered by an employer plan, IRA contributions still are deductible but only if the taxpayer's adjusted gross income does not exceed a certain level. The AGI limits are adjusted for inflation each year. For 2003, the limit for a married couple filing jointly was $60,000. The limit for a single taxpayer was $40,000. Above these levels, the deduction is phased out, until no deduction is allowed when AGI is $10,000 above these levels. Contributions to a traditional IRA cannot be made in the year one reaches age 70½ or in later years. After the owner passes age 70½, required minimum distributions must be taken at last annually.

Taxpayers whose incomes are too high to deduct their IRA contributions still can make nondeductible contributions. The income and gains on the nondeductible contributions are tax deferred. When nondeductible contributions are withdrawn, they are not taxed. That makes it important to keep track of the amount of nondeductible contributions made to an IRA over the years. Other than the treatment of contributions and their distribution, the nondeductible IRA has the same advantages and disadvantages as the traditional deductible IRA. Distributions of the accumulated income and gains are taxed as ordinary income. Again, anyone over age 70½ cannot make IRA contributions, and required minimum distributions must be taken at least annually after age 70½.

The Roth IRA is the newest option. There is no tax benefit for making a contribution to the Roth IRA. The contribution is made with after-tax dollars. The eventual benefits of the Roth IRA, however, are substantial. The income and capital gains compound tax free as with a regular IRA. When distributions are made, they are free of income taxes if the distributions are made more than five years after the first contributions to the IRA and after

TABLE 11.1   Maximum Contribution

Account Type	2004 Over 50/Under 50	2006 Over 50/Under 50	Comments
401(k) or 403(b)	$16,000/$13,000	$20,000/$15,000	Employer can lower maximum. Employer can match employee contribution.
Deductible Keogh	$40,000	$40,000	For self-employed. Maximum 20% of self-employment earnings.
Deductible IRA	$3,500/$3,000	$5,000/$4,000	No deduction if have an employer retirement plan and earn too much. Limits increase to $6,000/$5,000 in 2008.
Deductible Spousal IRA	$3,500/$3,000	$5,000/$4,000	Working spouse can contribute for unemployed spouse if family income not too high.
Roth IRA	$3,500/$3,000	$5,000/$4,000	Tax-free withdrawals. Not eligible if income too high. Limits increase to $6,000/$5,000 in 2008.
Nondeductible IRA	$3,500/$3,000	$5,000/$4,000	For those with incomes too high for deductible IRAs. Limits increase to $6,000/$5,000 in 2008.

Note: When the taxpayer contributes to more than one IRA, the contributions to all IRAs are aggregated to determine the limit for the year. In other words, in 2006, total contributions to all IRAs cannot exceed $4,000 for someone under age 50.

the owner is age 59½. In addition, unlike other IRAs, the owner of a Roth IRA is not required to begin taking required minimum distributions after reaching age 70½. The owner can let the income and gains compound as long as desired. A beneficiary who inherits a Roth IRA must begin required minimum distributions, but the distributions can be scheduled based on the beneficiary's age. Also unlike a traditional IRA, an owner can make contributions to a Roth IRA after age 70½.

A Roth IRA has the same annual contribution limit as the other IRAs. The different types of IRAs potentially compound to the same amount over the years. With distributions from the Roth IRA being free of income taxes, the after-tax value of the Roth IRA far exceeds the value of a traditional IRA, whether deductible or nondeductible. Even if the tax savings from a deductible IRA are invested separately, the Roth IRA usually will generate more after-tax wealth.

Not everyone is eligible to open a Roth IRA. There are income limits, as with deductible IRAs. Anyone whose adjusted gross income exceeds the limits cannot open a Roth IRA. In 2003, single taxpayers had their ability to make Roth IRA contributions phased out at adjusted incomes between $95,000 and $110,000. For married taxpayers filing jointly, the phase out occurred between $150,000 and $160,000.

Another benefit of the Roth IRA is that the owner has better access to funds. Loans still are not allowed. The Roth IRA owner, however, can withdraw contributions made to the account tax free and penalty free at any time. Owners of other IRAs and 401(k)s do not have that level of access to their money.

Rollover IRAs for the most part are traditional IRAs. When someone leaves an employer, there are several options regarding the 401(k) or other retirement account. Many employers allow the account to be maintained with the employer. Another option might be to transfer the account to a retirement plan at the new employer, if the new employer will accept the transfer. A third option is to transfer the account to an IRA, known as an IRA rollover. This option is used most frequently, and most people roll over their 401(k)s to IRAs at retirement.

There are a couple of ways to do an IRA rollover. The employer can give the departing employee a check for the account balance. The former employee then has up to 60 days to get the entire amount deposited in an IRA. If the deadline is not met, the entire balance is included in income for the year. In addition, the employer is required to withhold taxes equal to 20 percent of the account balance. If the entire account balance is rolled over to an IRA, the employee gets a refund of the withheld taxes. To qualify, however, the employee must roll over to the IRA not only the check received from the employer but also the 20 percent that was withheld. If the employee cannot come up with that much money, the withheld amount will be included in income for the year.

The easier approach is to have the former employer transfer the balance directly to an IRA custodian designated by the employee. That way, there is no withholding and the employee doesn't have to worry about the 60-day deadline.

Generally, when leaving an employer it is a good idea to roll over the 401(k) balance to an IRA. The IRA is likely to have more investment options. In addition, at retirement an employer is allowed to limit the distribution options from a 401(k) plan. As we'll learn later in this chapter, an IRA can be managed to last for a long time, even after the required minimum distributions begin after age 70½. The law only requires the employer to allow a 401(k) to last up to five years. After that, the employer can require full distribution of the account.

When a 401(k) or other retirement plan is rolled over into an IRA, it is a good idea to roll over the account into a brand new IRA instead of an existing IRA. If the owner decides to work for another employer, that employer might accept transfers from other 401(k)s to its 401(k). Such a transfer also can be made from an IRA rollover account only if the rollover account contains only the proceeds from a previous employer's plan. If the IRA also contains other contributions, then none of the IRA can be transferred to a new employer's 401(k).

Other types of IRAs also might be available to self-employed individuals, such as SIMPLE plans and SEP IRAs. These options must be considered along with Keogh plans and corporate retirement plans. Comparing these options is best left for a book on business planning instead of a book on retirement planning.

The tax-advantaged accounts must be compared with taxable accounts. There can be advantages to taxable investment accounts. The money invested in a taxable account can be withdrawn at any time and used for any purpose. Access to money in the tax-advantaged plans tends to be limited, as described above. Also, with the exception of the Roth IRA, distributions from the IRAs and other tax-advantaged accounts are taxed as ordinary income at the owner's individual income tax rate. A taxable account, on the other hand, often can be managed so that income taxes are not incurred until the owner wants to incur them. In addition, the income can be taxed as long-term capital gains or dividends facing a maximum tax rate of 15 percent. The access to the money and the possible top tax rate of 15 percent need to be considered when considering contributions to investment accounts. Calculations I've done indicate that, as a general rule, income and gains need to compound at an average annual return of 8 percent or higher for 10 or more years in order for using a deductible traditional IRA to be a better choice than a taxable account. That is because the tax-deferred compounding of returns needs time to overcome the disadvantage of converting some capital gains and dividends into ordinary income.

Converting a Regular IRA to a Roth IRA

The Roth IRA is one of the most attractive tax-advantaged investments Congress ever created. Congress went a step further and gave many people a chance to convert their regular IRAs to Roth IRAs. It doesn't matter if the regular IRA contributions were made because the owner was unaware of the Roth's advantages or was not eligible to make Roth contributions. It also doesn't matter if the regular IRA was opened before the Roth IRA was created in 1997 or as a result of rolling over a 401(k) or other retirement plan into the IRA. The IRA can be deductible or nondeductible. In any of these cases, the IRA owner might be able to convert the regular IRA into a Roth IRA. In addition, the IRA owner can choose to convert the entire IRA or any portion of it into a Roth IRA. Once a traditional IRA is converted into a Roth IRA, it is treated the same as an original Roth IRA.

There are two requirements for converting a regular IRA into a Roth IRA. First, taxes on the IRA must be paid as though the amount converted were distributed to the taxpayer. For example, suppose there is a deductible traditional IRA with a balance of $100,000. If the owner decides to convert the entire amount, then $100,000 must be included in gross income in the year of the conversion. If $50,000 is converted, then $50,000 is included in gross income. If the IRA has nondeductible contributions, then the conversion of the nondeductible contributions is not taxed. (If the IRA owner is younger than age 59½, the 10 percent early distribution penalty does not apply to amounts that are included in income because of the conversion.)

Second, the adjusted gross income on the tax return for the year cannot exceed $100,000, excluding any IRA conversion amount that is included in gross income. The IRA owner's filing status doesn't matter. The $100,000 limit is the same whether the taxpayer is married filing jointly, single, or head of household. This means that each spouse's income is counted as the other spouse's income when determining the income limit. If one spouse earns over $100,000, neither spouse will be able to convert an IRA as long as they are married, regardless of the other spouse's income level. If the taxpayer is married filing separately, the income limit is $0. In other words, a conversion is not possible unless the taxpayer has no other income at all.

The rules are simple. The trick is determining when it makes sense to incur the cost of converting an ordinary IRA into a Roth IRA. The answer depends on several factors. The IRA owner has to make assumptions about these factors and compare the results of continuing to own the traditional IRA with converting to a Roth IRA. Here are the factors to consider and how they affect the decision.

- Is money outside the IRA used to pay the conversion taxes? The more money that is left inside the IRA to benefit from tax-free compounding, the more advantageous it is to convert to a Roth IRA. A conversion is less beneficial if money is taken out of the IRA to pay the taxes—though it still can make sense to convert if the remaining balance is left in the IRA to compound for 10 years or more after the conversion. In addition, if the owner is under age 59½ and uses an IRA distribution to pay conversion taxes, the 10 percent early distribution penalty will be owed on the amount that actually was distributed in addition to income taxes. In that case, it will take longer for the conversion to make sense.

- How long will the money be left in the Roth IRA to compound before distributions begin? The longer the money is left in the Roth IRA before beginning withdrawals, the more sense a conversion makes. For a conversion to pay, the owner should be prepared to leave the Roth IRA alone for at least seven to ten years after the conversion, if the average annual total return is at least 8 percent. A lower return will take longer to make the conversion pay off. The payoff period also is affected by whether the money eventually is withdrawn in installments or in a lump sum. The longer the distributions can be delayed or stretched out, the more sense it makes to pay taxes to convert to a Roth IRA.

- Is there a difference between the tax bracket at conversion and the tax bracket when distributions are made? The more the tax rate is expected to decline at distribution time, the less sense it makes to pay taxes at today's rate. Keep in mind that the conventional wisdom about tax rates decreasing during retirement frequently is not true, as discussed in Chapter 10.

- How much of the IRA will be converted? Conversion is not an all-or-nothing question. Any percentage of the IRA can be converted to a Roth IRA (depending on the IRA custodian's minimum account requirements). Suppose the owner is using the IRA to pay living expenses now and cannot wait seven years or more after the conversion to begin taking distributions from a Roth IRA. Then the owner might decide to leave enough in the regular IRA to cover expected expenses for seven years or more, and convert the rest into a Roth IRA. Or if the owner doesn't have enough cash to pay taxes for converting the entire IRA, a smaller amount can be converted. The entire IRA can be converted in stages over the years.

- Will Social Security benefits be taxed? Converting to a Roth IRA also can reduce taxes on Social Security benefits. Distributions from a regular IRA are included in gross income, boosting the amount of Social Security benefits that are taxable (see Chapter 4). Nontaxable distributions from a Roth IRA are not included in gross income, so they won't make Social Security benefits taxable.

- How does the state tax the Roth IRA? About 29 states automatically conform to federal law, but other states have yet to pass specific legislation to make Roth IRA distributions tax free and not all states are willing to do that. Check your local tax law.

- Will required minimum distributions from a traditional IRA exceed spending needs? Minimum annual distributions (discussed later in this chapter) are required from a traditional IRA but not from a Roth IRA. The required distributions can dramatically increase income taxes as one ages. If the owner anticipates that required minimum distributions will significantly exceed spending needs, then a Roth IRA should be considered.

How to Decide

Deciding whether or not to convert a traditional IRA into a Roth IRA obviously involves some projections and number-crunching. There are some general rules that can be used as guidelines. The longer the Roth IRA will be allowed to compound before distributions begin, the more sense a conversion makes. The higher the expected investment rate of return on the Roth IRA, the more sense a conversion makes. A conversion also makes more sense if the taxes are paid with funds that are outside the IRA. A conversion makes less sense if the tax rate will decline after distributions begin.

Fortunately, there are many convenient ways to do the number-crunching so that general rules don't have to be relied on. A number of web sites offer free calculators for examining the results of a Roth IRA conversion. These calculators allow the user to quickly change the assumptions on the key factors. Most mutual fund firms and brokers have calculators on their web sites. The best probably are at vanguard.com, fidelity.com, and troweprice.com. T. Rowe Price also has a separate program called IRA Analyzer that is more sophisticated. It can be downloaded from the web site for $4.95 (www.troweprice.com) or is available through the mail for $9.95 (availability and prices subject to change). Many financial publication web sites also have calculators, such as www.forbes.com.

The mutual fund and brokerage firm calculators often are not full-featured or what the programmers call robust. A more sophisticated Roth IRA calculator can be found at www.rothira.com. A couple of other calculators with no ties to financial products or services are at www.datachimp .com, www.volition.com, www.dinkytown.com, and www.customcalculators.com. I recommend using at least two different online calculators. They almost certainly will get different results, and using different calculators allows you to see which calculator items are variable and which are assumed to be true for all users. Most financial planners also have software calculators that have many features and allow comparisons of many different scenarios. Having a financial planner or CPA do the calculations makes sense when the IRA balance is large. For those who don't use computers, many mutual funds and brokers also have worksheets or workbooks that enable the user to make similar calculations on paper.

There is one trick to conversions for those already over age 70½. Taxpayers who already are subject to the required minimum distributions must take the required distribution for the year of the conversion. A required distribution cannot be avoided by converting a traditional IRA to a Roth IRA.

The best candidate for converting a traditional IRA to a Roth IRA is a wealthy individual who really doesn't need the IRA income, plans to pass the account to the next generation or two, and wants to reduce income and estate taxes. But that is not the only situation when a conversion is appropriate. For example, someone who won't take distributions from the IRA for at least seven to ten years and who has enough cash outside the IRA to pay the conversion taxes also could benefit from a conversion. The only way to decide with considerable confidence is to make forecasts using estimates for the factors outlined above.

Changing Your Mind

Once a decision is made on whether or not to convert a regular IRA to a Roth IRA, the IRA owner should continue to monitor the results. Changes in the value of the IRA should trigger a reevaluation of that decision.

- Suppose a conversion was made. The law allows this decision to be reversed as late as the date the tax return for the year is due. This is known as a recharacterization. The Roth IRA can be converted back to a traditional IRA and no taxes would be due on the transactions for the year. A recharacterization should be considered when the value of the IRA decreases significantly after the conversion. If the conversion is not reversed, then taxes still are due based on the IRA's value on the conversion date. The owner would be paying taxes on wealth that no longer exists. It makes sense to reverse the conversion. Then, the owner can decide to reconvert into a Roth IRA at the new value or leave the account as a traditional IRA for the rest of the year. A reversal and reconversion can be done up to once annually per IRA, provided that at least 30 days passes between the recharacterization and the new conversion.
- Suppose a traditional IRA was converted into a Roth IRA. The owner then becomes unemployed or for other reasons suffers a decline in income. The owner determines that the reversal of fortune is likely to continue into the following year and will be severe enough to drop him or her into a lower tax bracket that year. Then it makes sense to recharacterize the Roth IRA as a traditional IRA before the year closes. The conversion can be made the following year when the owner will be in a lower tax bracket and the cost of conversion will be lower.
- Suppose the owner decided not to make a conversion. Again, if the value of the IRA drops significantly later in the year, the decision should be reconsidered. If the conversion was not made because the owner did not have enough other assets to pay the taxes, then the lower value of

the IRA might make the conversion affordable. In addition, making the conversion when the value is lower means that all appreciation from the new lows will be tax free when eventually distributed from the Roth IRA. Without the conversion, those gains would be taxed as ordinary income.

A recharacterization is simple. A conversion may be reversed any time until the final due date for the tax return for the year, including extensions. That means the decision can be delayed until as late as October 15 of the year following the conversion. The recharacterization is done on Form 8606 filed with the regular tax return, or with Form 1040X (amended tax return) if the regular return already was filed.

When the calculations show that conversion makes sense, the biggest risk is that the government will change the rules. Once many people have accumulated significant wealth in Roth IRAs, Congress might impose some kind of income taxes on future distributions.

Which Investments for Tax-Deferred Accounts?

Most people own their retirement savings in several different types of accounts. Often there are several types of tax-advantaged accounts, such as IRAs and 401(k)s. There also are likely to be one or more taxable accounts. Each of these accounts is treated differently under the tax law, both while the money is accumulated and invested and when it is withdrawn. That raises the question of how to invest the different types of accounts. The overall after-tax wealth an individual can accumulate changes depending on which investments are in the tax-advantaged accounts and which are in the taxable accounts. The results surprise many people.

The longstanding conventional wisdom was very simple. It stated that income-producing investments—those that paid regular, taxable interest and dividends such as bonds and stocks with high dividend yields—should be purchased through tax-deferred accounts such as IRAs and 401(k)s. Investments that can earn tax-advantaged capital gains should be purchased through taxable accounts.

The rationale was that in a taxable account, interest and dividends were taxed as ordinary income at the taxpayer's highest tax rate. That didn't leave much income after taxes to compound over the years. Therefore, income investments should be in tax-advantaged accounts where the full income can compound tax-deferred. Stocks and equity mutual funds, if held for more than one year, were subject to a maximum tax rate of 20 percent on their capital gains when held in taxable accounts. If stocks were held in tax-deferred accounts, such as traditional IRAs, the gains would compound tax deferred but the distributions would be taxed as ordinary income. Putting assets with the potential for long-term capital gains (such as stocks) into tax-deferred accounts had the effect of converting tax-advantaged long-term capital gains into higher-taxed ordinary income. Tax-wise investors generally want to do the opposite.

While the conventional wisdom was logical, it wasn't always the best advice. I demonstrated this in my monthly newsletter, *Retirement Watch*. In addition, the 2003 tax law changed the equation. Dividends and long-term capital gains are taxed at only a maximum 15 percent rate. Meanwhile, tax rates on ordinary income were reduced but not as much as the taxes on long-term capital gains and dividends. The best advice on how to divide investments between IRAs and taxable accounts depends on the individual investor involved.

The conventional advice still works best for investors who buy individual stocks and hold them for a long time. Those investors will be able to take advantage of the lower long-term capital gains rates on investments held for more than one year. The conventional approach also is good for investors who own equity mutual funds and hold them for more than one year, if the mutual funds make no or small taxable distributions each year.

The problem is, many investors do not fall into these two categories. Studies show that whether they own individual stocks or equity mutual funds, individual investors buy and sell too frequently to take advantage of the long-term capital gains rates on most of their equity gains. While that is not the best way to maximize investment returns, it is the way many investors manage their portfolios. Other investors own mutual funds and hold them for more than one year. Many of those funds, however, make taxable distributions each year of a significant portion of their total returns. In these two situations, most of the gains from the stocks and mutual funds would be taxed as ordinary income.

Investors in these situations often can be better off keeping their income-earning investments, such as bonds, in taxable accounts. Their investments with potentially higher returns—such as stocks that are traded after less than one year—that will be taxed as ordinary income should be purchased through tax-advantaged accounts. The tax-deferred accounts protect the annual gains from taxes and allow the gains to compound to a much higher amount than would be possible in a taxable account. Even after paying the taxes when the money is distributed from the tax deferred account, the investor has more after-tax wealth than would have been accumulated by holding the stocks in a taxable account. The more gains that can be compounded before taxes are incurred, the greater the investor's lifetime after-tax wealth will be.

Another factor to consider is the difference between the investor's ordinary income tax rate and the long-term capital gains rate. An investor who faces the top ordinary income tax rate of 35 percent and a top long-term capital gains rate of 15 percent has a lot at stake in this decision. An investor in a lower tax bracket has a smaller difference between the two rates. He or she still would benefit from getting the allocation right, but the benefit would not be as great.

Perhaps even more important is any difference between the ordinary income tax rate during the accumulation years and during the distribution years. While fewer people see their tax rates decline after retirement, it is possible an investor will be in a much lower tax bracket at retirement. Someone who believes he or she would be in a significantly lower bracket in retirement could come out ahead by putting the highest returning investments in tax-deferred accounts. Taxes would be paid at a much lower rate in the future when the gains are withdrawn.

Putting It All Together

Let's look at a specific example to see how all these factors work together. Suppose Max Profits has $200,000 that he plans to split evenly between stocks and bonds. His portfolio already is split evenly between taxable and tax deferred accounts. Max is an average mutual fund investor, so he assumes that because of trading and distributions 20 percent of his equity mutual fund returns in the taxable account are taxed annually at the 15 percent long-term capital gains and dividend tax rate. The rest of the gains are taxed in the future when Max needs the money. Max expects to earn 9 percent annually from stocks for the long term and 4 percent from bonds. After 20 years Max will take annual distributions equal to $25,000 in today's dollars, and he assumes 3 percent inflation. Initially, withdrawals will be from the taxable account. Max will be in the 25 percent ordinary income tax bracket (the second highest bracket).

Under the assumptions and the 2003 law, Max's money lasts a couple of years longer if the higher returning investments are put in the IRA instead of the taxable account. This is true, though some long-term capital gains are converted into ordinary income.

The amount at stake in this decision becomes even more dramatic if Max changes his investment policy. If Max puts the higher returning stock mutual funds in the taxable account and invests that account so that only 25 percent of the annual return is taxed at the 15 percent rate each year, Max's money will last much longer.

These examples show how the right decision depends on the interaction between the tax law and Max's investment strategy. Given these two examples, Max should invest in equity mutual funds in the taxable account. He also should use tax-wise investment strategies in the taxable account. He should invest in mutual funds that make low annual distributions and hold those funds for at least one year. He should limit his trading of funds so that no more than 15 percent of his annual gains are subject to taxes each year.

Since the end of the great bull market in 2000, many people are expecting lower than average stock returns for the next ten years or more. With that in mind, I took a look at the results if the long-term return from stocks were 6 percent, and the bond return were 4 percent. The percentage of stock returns in the taxable account that were taxable each year remained at 25 percent. Under these circumstances, putting the higher returning stocks into the IRA was a terrible choice. Max's retirement accounts would be depleted much faster than under any of the other scenarios. When the returns on the stocks decline to a lower level, it is important that those gains be kept in a taxable account and managed so that returns are taxed at the lowest tax rates possible. See Charts 11.1 and 11.2.

The results in these examples would not be the same for an investor with a different profile. An investor who trades stocks or funds after owning them for less than one year would pay ordinary income tax rates on the capital gains if they were held in a taxable account. The tax rate effectively is the same whether the stocks are owned in an IRA or taxable account. That investor should put the higher returning investments in the IRA to get the tax-deferred compounding.

Likewise, an investor who holds stock funds for a long time, but whose funds distribute a lot of short-term capital gains each year, would pay ordinary income tax rates on much of the investment returns, even if the distributions are reinvested in the funds. This investor also would be better off putting the higher-returning stock investments in tax-deferred accounts and letting the gains compound tax-deferred for as long as possible.

The higher an individual's ordinary income tax rate, the more important it is to shelter higher return investments such as stocks. The best way to shelter those returns is to hold the investments for more than one year in a taxable account to take advantage of the long-term capital gains rate. If that

CHART 11.1   Lower Returns in IRA

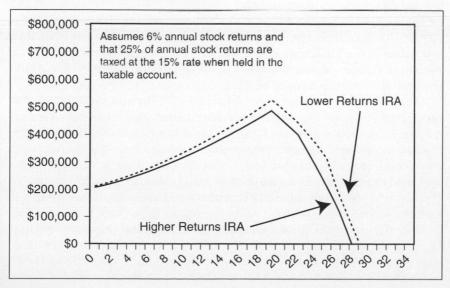

CHART 11.2   Lower Returns in IRA

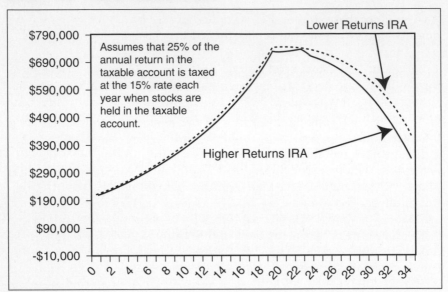

won't be done, the investor is better off putting higher returning investments in tax-deferred accounts.

The answer to the question of how to split investments between taxable and tax-deferred accounts depends as much on the owner's investment policy as on the tax law. An investor who buys individual stocks, holds them for the long-term, and takes losses to offset any realized gains is a tax-efficient equity investor. Equity investments for this investor would be better off in a taxable account. Another tax-efficient investor is one who buys mutual funds that make small taxable annual distributions and holds those funds for longer than one year. A tax-inefficient investor is one who sells mutual funds or stocks after less than a year, or who invests in mutual funds that distribute a large portion of their gains each year. These equity investments probably should be in tax-advantaged accounts.

Estate planning is another factor to consider. Suppose the investments under consideration are ones the investor doesn't anticipate needing during his or her lifetime. Instead, the investor is accumulating an estate for the next generation. If the investments are held in a taxable account, when the investor passes on the heirs will get to increase their tax basis in the investments to their current fair market value. The heirs could sell the investments immediately and have no taxable gain or loss. If the investments are held in a tax-deferred account, however, the basis is not increased. The account is included in the original owner's estate where it might be subject to estate taxes, depending on the size of the estate. In addition, when heirs take distributions from the account, those distributions are taxed as ordinary income.

New Rules for Investing IRAs

As a result of these studies, I've compiled the new rules for investing tax deferred and taxable accounts after the 2003 tax law:

Taxes count.   Investors need to consider taxes when setting their investment policies and deciding how to invest tax-advantaged and taxable accounts. Taking advantage of the tax breaks available in taxable accounts makes wealth last longer than shielding higher returns in a tax-deferred account.

The tax cuts help.   Under any of the scenarios, the 2003 tax cut makes a retiree's nest egg last at least a year or two longer than under the old law.

The IRA advantage is reduced.   There are few circumstances under which higher-returning investments such as stocks and equity mutual funds are better in an IRA instead of in a taxable account. The stock returns need to exceed the returns from bonds by more than a couple of percentage points annually for it to make sense to put stocks in the IRA. Also, stocks are better in an IRA only if the investment policy would result in more than 25 percent of the annual return from equities being taxed at ordinary income tax rates if they were invested in a taxable account.

Tax-wise investing can significantly preserve wealth.   An investor generates the most after-tax wealth by maximizing use of the 15 percent tax rates for long-term capital gains and dividends. There are several ways to do this. Individual stocks can be purchased and held for more than one year before selling. Or equity mutual funds that use tax-wise investment policies can be purchased and held. Tax-wise investment policies include low turnover and holding their stocks for longer than one year. High-yielding stocks and equity mutual funds also should be held in taxable accounts so that the dividends will be taxed at the 15 percent rate instead of the ordinary income tax rate.

Real estate investment trusts probably should be owned in tax-deferred accounts. While REITs will have significant capital gains over time, they also pay high dividends that are not eligible for the 15 percent rate. The taxable portion of the dividends will be taxed as ordinary income in a taxable account.

Even after taking all these factors into consideration, it is important not to let the tax law dictate your investments. First, determine an investment policy. An investor's risk tolerance and required return should first determine how the total portfolio should be split between stocks, bonds, and other investments (see Chapter 5 for details). After that, the rules discussed here should be used to determine the best way to manage that split among the investor's different accounts. Don't fall for theories or rules of thumb.

Instead, decide which investment approach will be followed and divide investments between taxable and tax-exempt accounts accordingly.

Creating a Stretch IRA

Congress decided that IRAs and other retirement accounts should be primarily for saving for the owner's retirement and only the owner's retirement. Congress wanted to encourage retirement saving but did not want to encourage saving to accumulate wealth for the next generation. This policy was not applied as stringently to the Roth IRA, but it still applies to other tax-advantaged retirement savings accounts. To implement the policy, Congress created required minimum distributions (RMDs). The original concept of the RMD was that an IRA should be depleted when the owner reached his or her life expectancy.

The RMD rules require tax-qualified retirement account owners to begin taking annual RMDs by April 1 of the year after they turn age 70½. Another RMD is required by December 31 of that year and by December 31 of each year after that. The penalty for failing to take an RMD is 50 percent of the amount not distributed. The RMD and its penalty now apply to inherited Roth IRAs as well as to all traditional IRAs, 401(k)s and employer retirement plans.

The amount of the RMD is calculated using tables issued by the IRS, and we'll get to the details of the calculation shortly.

Until a few years ago, several key and complicated decisions had to be made before beginning RMDs. The decisions determined the amount of the RMDs, who eventually inherited the account, and how the beneficiary computed his or her own RMDs after inheriting the account. To get the best results, retirement account owners effectively were required by the rules to predict the order in which family members would pass away. Fortunately, the IRS revised these rules in January 2001 and again in June 2002. The result is a much simplified set of rules that greatly ease the choices for account owners, reduce RMDs, give heirs many options, and make it possible for retirement accounts to continue compounding tax deferred for many years, if that is what the owner and beneficiaries want.

Now, the RMD calculations and decisions are relatively simple. To determine the RMD, the value of the account at the end of the previous year is divided by the life expectancy of the owner or the joint life expectancy of the owner and the beneficiary. The life expectancy is listed in tables issued by the IRS. This calculation is repeated each year.

When a retirement account owner passes away, the beneficiary can either have the entire account distributed, continue tax deferral for as long as possible, or do something in between. If the account is distributed, the entire amount other than nondeductible contributions of the owner is taxed as ordinary income (except for a Roth IRA). For whatever part of the account the beneficiary chooses not to distribute right away, RMDs are required (including a Roth IRA).

The IRS regulations greatly simplified RMDs. The choice of beneficiary no longer affects the RMD in most cases, and the calculation method is selected by the IRS instead of by the IRA owner. The only real decision left is the life expectancy table to use.

Most IRA owners now use a life expectancy table that assumes the beneficiary is ten years younger than the owner. This is known as the Uniform Lifetime Table. It is available in IRS Publication 590 and also is available on my web site for subscribers to my newsletter. The only exception to the use of this table is when the beneficiary is the owner's spouse and is more than ten years younger than the owner. In that case, a life expectancy table using the actual ages of each spouse is used. This is known as the Joint Life Table and carries over from the IRS's 1987 regulations. A third life expectancy table, the Single Life Table, is used by sole owners of inherited IRAs.

When a beneficiary inherits an IRA, RMDs must be computed if the beneficiary does not take an immediate distribution of the entire IRA. If there is more than one beneficiary, the oldest beneficiary is used to compute the RMD for the entire IRA. The beneficiaries, however, have the option of splitting the inherited IRA into multiple separate IRAs.

An inherited IRA often is known as a Stretch IRA. That is because if the new owner is younger than the original owner, the longer life expectancy reduces the required payments and allows the tax-deferred compounding to last much longer, assuming the new owner does not take distributions exceeding the requirement minimum. If the beneficiary is a grandchild of the owner, the IRA could last for many decades, because the annual returns of the account are likely to be more than the required annual distributions. The RMDs of an inherited IRA must begin by December 31 of the year following the original owner's death.

To calculate the RMD for a year, an owner simply determines the IRA balance at the end of the prior year. Then the owner locates his or her age on the life expectancy table. The life expectancy for that age is divided into the IRA balance. For example, if an IRA was $100,000 last December 31 and the owner is age 71, 26.5 is divided into $100,000, resulting in an RMD of $3,773.58. The following year, 25.6 is divided into the IRA balance.

Special Rules for Spouses

The revised regulations retain one of the better old rules. A spouse who inherits an IRA can roll it over into a new IRA and get a fresh start on beneficiaries and RMDs. If the spouse is not yet 70½, RMDs do not have to begin until he or she reaches that age. In all other cases, a beneficiary who inherits an IRA must take RMDs. The spouse can name all new beneficiaries and contingent beneficiaries. Obviously, this provides a great deal of flexibility.

A major benefit of the revised regulations is that the beneficiary can be changed at any time without affecting the RMD. In fact, the final beneficiary of the account really doesn't have to be determined until September 30 of the year after the owner's death. The Designated Beneficiary, as the person is known, can be named by the account owner or estate administrator. Also, multiple beneficiaries can inherit the IRA.

A person's will doesn't affect any decisions regarding IRA beneficiaries. Only beneficiaries named on the form kept by the IRA sponsor count in determining who actually inherits the IRA and who counts as a beneficiary with the IRS. As will be discussed shortly, an owner of a large IRA should name many possible beneficiaries and contingent beneficiaries on this form so that the heirs and executor have maximum flexibility in determining the final Designated Beneficiary.

It is important that the owner's estate not be named as beneficiary and that the owner does not fail to name a beneficiary, which would automatically make the estate the beneficiary. When the estate is the beneficiary, the IRA must be distributed immediately. The entire amount of the IRA is subject to income taxes in addition to any estate taxes that were incurred. The result in such cases is that only about 40 percent of the IRA is left after taxes.

An IRA's value is included in the owner's taxable estate. Owners should clarify who pays any estate taxes attributable to the IRA. In most states, if the will does not say anything, the rest of the estate will pay taxes attributable to the IRA. That might mean that other beneficiaries have less money available than the owner anticipated.

The RMD rules apply to more than IRAs. They also apply to 401(k) plans and to other tax-qualified retirement plans, though there are some differences between the plans. Keogh plans cannot stretch payments to a non-spouse beneficiary, and 401(k) plans are not required to allow payments to last beyond five years, though the employer can provide more options. To get the maximum flexibility in the RMD, at retirement owners of employer retirement accounts might need to roll over to an IRA the account balance.

The RMD rules also apply to inherited Roth IRAs. The original owner is not required to take RMDs, but the beneficiary who inherits is required to begin RMDs. The distributions might still be tax free, but they must be made on schedule.

Those are the basic rules. Now let's look at how to use those rules to select the right beneficiaries for the IRA. Then we will examine what heirs need to know to make the most of an IRA or other inherited retirement account.

Naming the Right IRA Beneficiaries

Much IRA planning used to involve navigating complicated tax rules to select the beneficiary who minimized RMDs. The revised rules allow IRA owners to shift the focus of their planning. Owners can name the beneficiary who makes the most sense without considering tax consequences. Owners also have the flexibility to name additional beneficiaries and contingent beneficiaries so survivors can make a final choice that keeps the most wealth in the family and meets the family's needs. Most importantly, to get the best results, owners don't have to guess the order in which people will die.

The section above lays out the basic rules for computing RMDs and selecting beneficiaries. Before selecting or changing beneficiaries and contingent beneficiaries, every retirement account owner who wants to maximize the account's benefits for loved ones should review several factors and consider taking certain steps.

Consider the spouse's needs first.   This should take priority over tax benefits and providing for succeeding generations. If there are not sufficient assets outside the IRA to maintain the spouse's standard of living, the spouse should be sole primary beneficiary of the IRA. Other objects of affection can be contingent beneficiaries who will take over after the spouse passes on.

There are a couple of options available when naming a spouse as primary beneficiary. The main difference between these options is what happens to the remaining account balance after the spouse's demise. One option is simply to name the spouse as beneficiary. That gives him or her maximum flexibility. The best option for the surviving spouse often is to roll over the inherited IRA into a new IRA. The rollover allows the naming of new beneficiaries and the start of a new distribution schedule.

Leaving the IRA outright to a spouse, however, means the original owner does not control who eventually gets the account. There is a risk that a second spouse, children of a second marriage, other relatives, or a charity could become beneficiaries instead of the owner's intended contingent or final beneficiaries. If that scenario concerns an owner, the options are to name a trust as beneficiary or split the IRA into multiple IRAs. We'll discuss both options later in this chapter.

Talk to the beneficiaries and potential beneficiaries.   IRA sponsors report a curious phenomenon. Original IRA owners often do a lot of work to determine the right beneficiaries and distribution method for their IRAs. They design Stretch IRAs so the tax deferral of their IRAs can last as long as possible. Yet, a significant number of beneficiaries want to liquidate the IRAs right away and take whatever after-tax cash they can.

Owners determine who is eligible to receive an IRA by naming beneficiaries and contingent beneficiaries. They can set things up so that the IRA can last as long as possible. The owners, however, cannot keep the new owners from liquidating the IRA when they want, unless a trust is named as the beneficiary. Then, the trustee would determine the distributions.

Determine the goals of the beneficiaries.   Find out if they plan to spend the after-tax cash quickly or let the IRA compound tax deferred for some future use, such as their own retirement. If they plan to spend the account, and the owner doesn't want them to, consider naming a trust as the beneficiary. If the owner doesn't care what heirs do with the IRA, at least a lot of time won't be wasted planning for a deferral that isn't wanted.

Consider splitting an IRA into multiple IRAs.   When more than one beneficiary is named for an account, the IRS regulations allow an estate or the beneficiaries who inherit the IRA to do a split. That permits each beneficiary to have his or her own distribution schedule and to choose how the account is invested. The owner, however, can split the IRA while still alive. There are several reasons for the owner to consider splitting the IRA.

Splitting an IRA now allows the owner to name a separate beneficiary or group of beneficiaries for each IRA. The owner knows which investments will go to each beneficiary. Often, when multiple beneficiaries inherit an IRA, they have conflicts over how the account should be invested. Even if they agree to split the IRA into several, they might disagree over who gets which original assets in the IRA. When the owner splits an IRA, he or she is assured that the preferred beneficiary of each account will get the account as long as he or she survives the owner.

The split also lets the owner name different contingent or subsequent beneficiaries for each account. That gives the owner more control over who gets any remaining money after the first beneficiary passes on.

Splitting an IRA also can reduce estate taxes. When a surviving spouse is the primary beneficiary of an IRA, the marital deduction ensures no estate taxes are due. The IRA uses none of the owner's lifetime estate and gift tax credit; that credit can be used to shelter other assets from estate taxes by leaving them to children or other beneficiaries. The surviving spouse's lifetime credit might be available to shelter the remainder of the IRA at his or her passing. If the original account owner doesn't have other assets that can use up the estate and gift tax credit, consider splitting an IRA and having children or grandchildren inherit enough to use up at least a portion of the lifetime credit. Before doing this, an owner should be sure that the amount of the original IRA inherited by the surviving spouse will be sufficient to maintain his or her lifestyle.

Name a trust as beneficiary.   A trust, as mentioned, can ensure that an IRA supports a surviving spouse and eventually goes to the owner's chosen heirs—not to a new family of the surviving spouse. A trust also is a good way to leave the IRA to children or grandchildren who are not prepared to manage the account. Further, the trust can ensure that the wealth is distributed for the purposes the owner prefers, not the spending preferences of the beneficiaries.

A trust is a valid IRA beneficiary if some conditions are met. The trust must be valid under state law or would be valid except that it doesn't yet own any property. The trust also must be irrevocable or will become irrevocable upon the creator's death. That means the owner cannot get back the property from the trust or change the trust's terms. The owner can, however, change the IRA beneficiary (or have the estate change the beneficiary) at any time, shifting it away from the trust. In addition, all possible beneficiaries of the trust must be clearly identifiable from the trust agreement. Finally, proper documentation as defined in the regulations must be provided to the IRA custodian no later then December 31 of the year after the owner's death.

When these requirements are met, then the oldest beneficiary of the trust will be treated as the beneficiary of the IRA when computing the required distribution schedule.

For this strategy to work, the owner first drafts a trust agreement which names the beneficiaries, the trustee, and the terms under which distributions are to be made. Then the trust is named as the beneficiary on the form filed with the IRA custodian. There are some tricks and traps to naming a trust as IRA beneficiary. It is best to work with an estate planner who is familiar and has experience with IRA Trusts or Retirement Plan Trusts.

Charities and Other Strategies

Make charitable gifts through an IRA.   Few people realize an IRA is a better way to make charitable gifts than a will.

An IRA is included in the taxable estate and is potentially subject to estate taxes. In addition, when the beneficiary takes distributions from the IRA, the distributions are taxed as ordinary income. That means the IRA is taxed twice. The after-tax cash that flows to the beneficiary from an inherited IRA could be a fairly low percentage of the beginning value. When someone inherits non-IRA assets, the receipt of those assets is tax free, and the tax basis usually is increased to current fair market value. The assets might have been subject to the estate tax, but they can be sold free of income and capital gains taxes.

When a charity receives a distribution from an IRA, there are no income taxes on the distribution because the charity is tax exempt. The charity gets the benefit of the entire distribution. The IRA still is included in the owner's estate. The estate, however, gets a charitable deduction for the portion of the IRA that goes to the charity, so the IRA faces no taxes when a charity is named the beneficiary. The charity is indifferent to whether it inherits IRA or non-IRA assets. The rest of the estate's beneficiaries, however, probably are better off inheriting non-IRA assets and letting the charity benefit from the IRA.

Revised IRS regulations make this strategy easier to use. A charity and one or more individuals can be named as co-beneficiaries of an IRA. If the charity's share is distributed to it before required distributions must begin to the other beneficiaries, then the required distribution schedule for the other beneficiaries can be computed as though the charity and its share never were involved.

The disadvantage of naming a charity as IRA beneficiary is that the amount the charity will receive fluctuates with the investment performance of the account. In addition, if the charity is co-beneficiary with one or more heirs, the owner doesn't know how much the heirs will receive. At one point it might seem reasonable to give a charity one-third of an IRA and the owner's children the rest. A few months later the IRA's value might decline substantially, leaving the children less wealth than expected. Or the IRA might increase substantially, giving the charity far more than the owner would have liked.

One way around this disadvantage is for the owner to name the charity as a contingent beneficiary and tell the estate executor and the heirs of his or her desires for the charity. Then the beneficiaries can disclaim part of the inheritance after working with the executor to determine a reasonable amount to leave the charity. Another solution is to draft a detailed beneficiary designation form that leaves the charity the lesser of a stated percentage of the account or a certain amount. For example, the statement could say that the charity is beneficiary for the lesser of one-fifth the IRA or $20,000. Not all IRA custodians, however, accept such customized forms.

Name a lot of contingent beneficiaries. The IRS regulations give the estate and beneficiaries a great deal of flexibility in determining the final amounts received by different heirs. The Designated Beneficiary doesn't have to be determined until September 30 of the year after the owner passes.

Naming multiple beneficiaries and contingent beneficiaries, along with a legal tool known as a disclaimer, allows for some creative planning by survivors.

Suppose the owner desires to help with a grandchild's education. The owner doesn't have a lot of other assets and names his spouse as beneficiary to ensure his or her lifestyle is maintained. The grandchild is named as contingent beneficiary. After the owner passes, the spouse feels financially secure enough to help the grandchild and disclaims the inheritance of enough of the IRA to pay for the grandchild's education. That amount then can be split into another IRA for the grandchild, and RMDs on the second IRA would be computed on the grandchild's life expectancy instead of the surviving spouse's.

This flexibility, however, can be used only if enough contingent beneficiaries are named. The Designated Beneficiary eventually named for the IRA must be among the initial or contingent beneficiaries named on the form filed with the IRA custodian. The beneficiaries and contingent beneficiaries also must be aware of the owner's intentions and be willing to take or disclaim rights to the IRA.

Roll over employer plans to an IRA.   An employer who sponsors a 401(k) plan isn't required to provide all the planning options available through an IRA. A 401(k) sponsor is required only to offer distribution options that stretch the distributions up to five years. For that reason, an account owner might want to roll over a 401(k) to an IRA after retiring or leaving the employer, unless the 401(k) offers some excellent features.

The beneficiaries and contingent beneficiaries can be changed at any time. These changes will not affect the RMDs the owner must take. They will affect only those who eventually inherit the account. IRA beneficiary designations should be part of regular estate plan reviews.

As IRAs grow to become the major assets in many estates, beneficiary designations are among the most important estate planning decisions. Beneficiary designations should be carefully considered along with the possibility of splitting an IRA into multiple IRAs. After making the preferred beneficiary choices, contingent beneficiaries should be added, giving heirs and the estate administrator maximum flexibility.

The final step is to educate the heirs about the owner's desires, the possible options, and the steps that need to be taken. Good planning and taking advantage of the options provided in the law don't mean much unless the heirs know what to do. That's what I'll discuss next.

Heirs and IRAs

IRAs now often equal or exceed the value of family homes. Despite this, IRAs often don't get the attention in estate planning that they should. The IRA and other tax-qualified retirement plans first need to be fully integrated in the estate plan, as described in the previous section. Then the heirs must be educated about the proper handling of inherited IRAs. Many people overlook this last step. Too many IRAs get depleted by taxes prematurely because the heirs are not informed about their options.

Despite the simplified and improved IRS regulations, there still are traps for unwary heirs. Also, many financial advisors and financial institutions aren't well versed in all the rules, or they use the old rules instead of the new ones. It is worthwhile to be sure heirs know a reliable source to consult about the IRAs they inherit. Otherwise, they could lose thousands of dollars.

Here are some things heirs need to know about inherited IRAs. Don't take the deceased's name off an inherited IRA. A major benefit of an IRA is its tax deferred compounding of income and gains. Usually an heir can continue that deferral for many years on most of the IRA's income and gains. The tax deferral ends, however, when the deceased's name is taken off the IRA. The newly-named IRA must be completely distributed to its new owners, who must pay the appropriate income taxes.

A few IRA sponsors still automatically take the deceased's name off the IRA and put it in the new owner's name. IRA owners might want to make sure their IRA custodians are not in that group. Also, they should make sure their beneficiaries know not to switch any inherited IRAs into their own names.

Suppose Max Profits passed away, leaving an IRA to his beneficiary, Hi Profits. The correct new name on the IRA should be similar to: "Max Profits, deceased, for the benefit of Hi Profits." If the beneficiary dies and a successor beneficiary inherits the IRA, the account should remain in Max's name, but for the benefit of the new beneficiary.

Spouses should know about the spousal exception. A spouse who inherits an IRA gets special status. He or she can roll over the inherited IRA into a new IRA in the surviving spouse's name and make a fresh start. This allows the inheriting spouse to begin required minimum distributions under a new schedule and to name new beneficiaries and contingent beneficiaries. If the surviving spouse is under age 70½, required minimum distributions do not have to be made yet, even if the deceased spouse already began the distributions. Because of this, rolling over the IRA to a new IRA in the inheriting spouse's name can greatly extend the account's life and increase the number of potential beneficiaries.

Inheriting spouses should be told about this option ahead of time and be advised whether or not it is likely to be a smart move for that spouse. An advisor or other source of information should be lined up. Otherwise, the inheriting spouse might make the wrong move and incur unnecessary taxes.

Beneficiaries can restart the distribution schedule. Before the IRS changed the rules in early 2001, the distribution schedule used by an IRA's inheritor depended on whether or not the deceased owner had begun required minimum distributions. Now, the beneficiary simply starts a new distribution schedule based on the beneficiary's own life expectancy. If there are multiple beneficiaries of the IRA and they do not choose to split it into separate IRAs, the life expectancy of the oldest is used to determine RMDs. The distributions are determined using the IRS Single Life Expectancy table. The first distribution to the inheritor needs to be taken by December 31 of the year after the original owner's death.

Distributions can be as large as needed. We've been discussing the required *minimum* distribution rules with the idea that the owner and beneficiary want to minimize the required distributions and maximize the tax deferral of the IRA. That might not always be the case. The owner and beneficiary should know that the beneficiary may take out more than the minimum amount. The only maximum limit on the withdrawals is the amount in the IRA. (An IRA custodian might impose its own distribution limit.) Owners should be sure their beneficiaries know that they can tap the IRA for whatever money is needed each year. The beneficiary also should realize that the distributions will be taxed.

Beneficiaries don't have to be designated until after the owner dies. In the old days, the choice of beneficiary was locked in when the owner turned age 70½. Now the official beneficiary, known as the Designated Beneficiary, doesn't have to be named until September 30 of the year after the owner dies. The first distribution has to be made by that December 31. The Designated Beneficiary can be named by the estate administrator. To take advantage of this flexibility, the owner should be sure to name a number of contingent beneficiaries. Only those named by the owner as primary or contingent beneficiaries can become Designated Beneficiaries.

This delay allows heirs to adapt the estate plan to changed circumstances, which is why the beneficiaries should know about it. A beneficiary who doesn't need the IRA could disclaim in favor of another beneficiary or a contingent beneficiary. An older person who is a beneficiary might disclaim the IRA in favor of a younger beneficiary. The older beneficiary then might qualify for other assets in the estate. The younger beneficiary, meanwhile, will face lower RMDs from the IRA than the older beneficiary would have and can continue its tax deferral longer.

While the beneficiary does not have to take a first distribution until December 31 of the year after the owner's death, if the owner already had begun required minimum distributions, the required distribution for the owner's last year must be made by December 31 of that year. It will be taxed to the owner's estate.

More on Splitting IRAs

An IRA can be split into different IRAs. An owner can name multiple beneficiaries of an IRA. The beneficiaries can inherit equal shares, or the owner can designate that they inherit different proportions. If the beneficiaries continue the IRA as one account, then the age of the oldest beneficiary will determine the amount that must be distributed from the account each year.

An alternative for the heirs is to split the IRA into a separate IRA for each of them. Each IRA would have its own distribution schedule based on the age of its new owner. This move can be significant if there are meaningful age differences between the beneficiaries. Splitting the IRA also can be helpful if the beneficiaries have different ideas about spending and investing the account.

Be sure the IRA custodian will allow the account to be split into separate IRAs for each beneficiary. While the tax law allows this, not all sponsors want to incur the cost of maintain separate accounts. Others will charge either for the split or for future maintenance of the accounts.

Distributions don't have to be in cash. While assets have to come out of the IRA under the minimum distribution schedule, a beneficiary does not have to sell investments and distribute cash. The law allows distributions to be made in property, and most IRA sponsors will arrange property distributions. If the IRA has stock or mutual fund shares the beneficiary wants to continue holding, the shares can be distributed into a taxable account. This avoids any buying and selling costs.

Most IRA custodians require the beneficiary simply to open a taxable account at the firm and complete a form identifying the property to be distributed from the IRA to the taxable account. Many sponsors will make the transfer without cost.

When a distribution is made in property, the beneficiary should retain good records to avoid paying taxes twice. The distribution will be taxable income, whether it is paid in cash or property, and the taxable amount will be the value on the date of the distribution. The beneficiary's tax basis in the shares is the value that was included in income, not the original cost of the shares. Forgetting this, or not keeping a record of the property value on the distribution date, could result in overpaying taxes when the shares are sold from the taxable account.

The early distribution penalty doesn't apply. There is a 10 percent penalty for most distributions from an IRA that are made before the owner is age 59½. The penalty, however, does not apply to the beneficiary-owner of an inherited IRA. It doesn't matter if the distribution is a required one or an optional one that exceeds the required amount. Many beneficiaries are incorrectly told that in addition to being taxed on the distributions, they must pay the 10 percent early distribution tax.

All the options might not be available for a 401(k) plan. A 401(k) sponsor is not required to accommodate long-term distribution schedules. The law requires the sponsor only to allow distributions to last up to five years. Some sponsors will allow the long-term options, but many won't. If a 401(k) sponsor does not allow the long-term distribution options, then the owner or the heirs should roll over the account to an IRA.

Inherited Roth IRAs must make required distributions. The original owner of a Roth IRA doesn't have to take required minimum distributions at any time. A beneficiary who inherits a Roth IRA, however, must take required distributions under the same rules as the beneficiary of a regular IRA. The distributions usually won't be taxable, but they must be taken out of the IRA.

Which Account to Spend First?

Most retirement-age Americans have both taxable and tax-deferred accounts. Some have tax-exempt accounts. They can find a lot of information explaining why it is better to save through tax-deferred accounts and even better to save through tax-exempt accounts such as Roth IRAs. They won't be able to find much guidance on how to take money out of retirement investment accounts. Yet, the order in which money is withdrawn from different types of accounts will affect how long the wealth lasts.

Fortunately, in most cases, this is an issue for which the traditional thinking is correct. Most people would say intuitively that money in taxable accounts should be spent first and money in tax-advantaged accounts such as IRAs should be spent after that so that the tax-deferred compounding can continue for as long as possible. Money in Roth IRAs should be spent last since no taxes are incurred.

Most people would be well-served by following that advice. A study published in the *AAII Journal* in May 2002 found that wealth lasted longer when money from taxable accounts was spent first and IRA money was spent only after taxable accounts were exhausted. The higher the rate of return on the investments, the longer wealth lasted by spending taxable accounts first. Also, the higher the individual's tax bracket, the more important it is to allow the tax-deferred compounding of IRAs to continue as long as possible. I've confirmed these results with my own calculations and show in Table 11.2 how long an individual's assets last under different scenarios. The figures assume that the individual's assets are evenly split between taxable and tax-deferred accounts and that each account earns the same rate of return. The table is updated for the 2003 tax law, which did not change the original conclusions.

There is an exception to the general conclusion. The exception is when higher-returning investments are held in the taxable account and the after-tax return is four percentage points or more higher than the return earned by the tax-deferred account. In that case, you want to take distributions from the tax-deferred account first and let the higher after-tax returns compound in the taxable account for as long as possible. See Table 11.2.

The individual's wealth can be made to last even longer when the taxable accounts are managed and liquidated tax efficiently. Some basic rules should be followed when managing taxable accounts for maximum longevity.

Investments showing losses should be sold first. A capital loss first offsets any capital gains realized for the year. If the losses exceed the year's gains, then up to $3,000 of net losses can be deducted against other income. If there still are unused capital losses, they are carried forward to future years to be applied in the same way until they are exhausted. Most investors are hesitant to sell losing investments. They don't want to make the loss of capital final. Instead, they want to hold the investments until the values at least recover to their purchase prices. Investors, however, would be better off selling the losing investments, using the tax losses to reduce

TABLE 11.2   Which Account to Spend First?

Rate of Return	Taxable Account First	Tax-Deferred Account First
6%	18+ years	15+ years
8%	25+ years	18+ years
10%	51+ years	24+ years

The second and third columns show how long the owner's accounts will last under the stated distribution order and rate of return.

gains on other income, and spending the sale proceeds or investing them in something else.

After harvesting losses, the next investments to be liquidated from taxable accounts should be those that would incur the lowest taxes as a percentage of their value. Take the taxes that would be incurred from the sale of the asset and divide them by the market value of the asset. The result is the percentage of the asset that would be taxed, in effect the tax rate on that asset. The asset with the lowest tax rate should be sold first.

By following these strategies, a taxable account can in effect become a partially tax-deferred account. The longer taxes are deferred, the more after-tax wealth can be accumulated before taxes are paid, and the greater the after-tax wealth will be.

There also might be tax-deferred accounts for which distributions are partially taxed. An example is an IRA with nondeductible contributions. Part of each distribution from such an account will be taxable and part non-taxable. These accounts should be liquidated before the fully taxable IRAs.

Of course, these results were derived from examples using assumptions. Individuals need to determine which assumptions apply to them before adopting a strategy and to consider factors that have not been discussed. For example, state tax laws need to be considered. Some states, such as New York, exempt from state taxes some retirement income, including distributions from IRAs. Retirees in those states might want to take distributions from IRAs up to the exempt amount before selling assets in taxable accounts.

Another factor to be considered is the investor's asset allocation. Taking distributions from any account will change the investor's asset allocation, because the assets sold no longer will be in the portfolio. Changes to the other accounts might have to be made to ensure that the desired ratio between stocks, bonds, and other assets is maintained for the long term. Taxes and other costs could be incurred when rebalancing the portfolio.

Empty an IRA Early?

The conventional advice is to delay distributions from tax-deferred accounts for as long as possible so that tax-deferred compounding can continue its work. That advice works for most people. Yet it is not the right advice for everyone. It is not always a good idea to keep money in an IRA as long as possible. There are people who would benefit by taking money out of IRAs first and by taking distributions from IRAs that not only exceed the required minimum distributions but also exceed what is needed to meet spending needs.

The revised regulations for RMDs require lower distributions than in the past. Yet as the owner gets older, the RMD increases sharply each year.

After a few years, that can leave the IRA owner with distributions that far exceed spending needs and also with large tax bills.

For example, Max Profits has a $1 million IRA that earns 9 percent annually, and he is in the top tax bracket. He has to begin RMDs this year, and the first distribution will be $38,168. In five years the RMD will be $58,250, and at age 82 the distribution will be $102,813. If Max lives to age 90, the RMD is up to $176,238. Max's expenses aren't likely to rise at that rate.

Between federal and state income taxes, Max will be paying close to half these distributions in taxes. If Max hadn't already been in the top tax bracket, the RMDs would push him into it. The RMDs also could increase taxes on Social Security benefits and cause Max to lose other tax benefits because of the phase out of deductions and exemptions for higher income taxpayers. (See Chapter 10 for details.)

Suppose Max is only age 65, and the rest of the facts are the same. He has to begin RMDs after age 70½, and the first distribution will be $56,154. Five years later the RMD will be $78,011, and at age 82 the distribution will be $145,308. If Max lives to age 90, the RMD is up to $243,077. At that point the IRA still is worth more than $2.5 million.

Max and others in his situation can slash their lifetime tax burden by taking an unconventional step. They can begin taking more from the IRA than the law and their spending needs require.

To make a point, let's take an extreme example and say that Max in the second case lives to 100 and takes only the RMDs. He'll pay just over $2 million in federal income taxes on these distributions at the 35 percent rate. The exact amount of taxes will depend on Max's other income, deductions, and other factors. He still will have over $1.6 million in the IRA at age 100. That amount will be taxed when distributed to him or his heirs.

Suppose instead that, to avoid the higher income taxes down the road, Max decides not to let the IRA grow as much. Max decides to take large enough distributions so that the IRA grows no more than 4 percent from its original balance. Then, the lifetime taxes on the distributions at age 100 are down to just over $1.2 million. (Under prior law, before the 2003 tax cuts, these taxes would be about $1.5 million.)

Suppose Max puts into a taxable account the after-tax distributions that exceed the RMDs. That account grows 7 percent annually before taxes, and taxes are paid at a 15 percent rate each year. By age 100, the taxable investment account exceeds $2 million. The IRA still is worth over $700,000.

In this scenario, Max's heirs have more after-tax wealth available to them if he limits the growth of the IRA. The IRA still has significant value, and they will be able to spend its after-tax value. All or most of the taxable account is available to them without additional taxes.

Running the numbers until Max is 100 exaggerates the effects. Suppose Max passes away at 80. The IRA would be worth over $1.1 million ($736,000 after income taxes), and the taxable account would be worth over $615,000. By comparison, if Max took only the RMDs, at age 80 the IRA would be worth over $2.2 million. That is about $1.5 million after income taxes at the 35 percent rate and not counting estate taxes.

In this example, at age 80 the benefits of early IRA distributions are a closer call than if Max assumes he lives to 100. Keep in mind, though, that I've skewed the results to favor letting the IRA compound by assuming the taxable account will be invested to earn less than the IRA and will be taxed at 15 percent each year. The rate of return could be the same as the IRA, and the taxable account could be taxed at less than 15 percent each year with tax-wise investment management.

Let's go a step further and have Max decide to take high enough distributions to allow no growth in the IRA's value after age 65. Let's also assume Max lives to 80.

In this case, the lifetime taxes on the IRA distributions are over $472,000. The IRA is worth $1,090,000 ($708,500 after taxes), and the taxable account

TABLE 11.3   Life Expectancy Table for Required Minimum Distributions

Age	Distribution Period	Age	Distribution Period
70	26.2	93	8.8
71	25.3	94	8.3
72	24.4	95	7.8
73	23.5	96	7.3
74	22.7	97	6.9
75	21.8	98	6.5
76	20.9	99	6.1
77	20.1	100	5.7
78	19.2	101	5.3
79	18.4	102	5
80	17.6	103	4.7
81	16.8	104	4.4
82	16	105	4.1
83	15.3	106	3.8
84	14.5	107	3.6
85	13.8	108	3.3
86	13.1	109	3.1
87	12.4	110	2.8
88	11.8	111	2.6
89	11.1	112	2.4
90	10.5	113	2.2
91	9.9	114	2
92	9.4	115+	1.8

is worth almost $700,000. Again, those amounts are close to the $1.5 million after-tax value of the IRA if only RMDs are taken.

Is It Right for You?

The benefits of taking more out of an IRA than the law and spending needs requires depend on the individual situation.

The strategy should be considered by those whose IRAs, after considering other sources of income, greatly exceed lifetime spending needs. In effect, the IRA is operating as an emergency savings account or a supplement to other sources of income. In those cases, benefits can be generated by getting money out of the IRA early instead of letting it compound indefinitely.

The earlier one begins the strategy, the better the results will be. (Don't begin before age 59½, to avoid the 10 percent premature distribution penalty.) You will pay income taxes on the early distributions and be able to invest in the taxable account only the after-tax amount of the distributions. The taxable account will need time for the investment returns to make up for the taxes.

Also important are the assumptions about rates of investment return, tax rates on and turnover in the taxable account, and longevity. Other factors are whether the RMDs would push the owner into a higher tax bracket, cause the loss of itemized deductions and personal exemptions, or increase taxes on Social Security benefits.

The prime beneficiaries are people like Max: A relatively young retiree whose IRA exceeds by a significant amount likely lifetime spending needs. Without extra distributions, future RMDs would force large taxable distributions as the owner ages. Lifetime taxes by the owner and his heirs would be much higher than if the IRA were emptied early, the taxes paid, and investment income compounded in a taxable account.

A good analogy is the conversion of a traditional IRA into a Roth IRA, discussed earlier in this chapter. We found that paying taxes to convert the IRA to a Roth IRA makes sense if the account will compound long enough to make up for paying the taxes early. The same principle works here, especially if the taxable account is managed to minimize taxes. See Table 11.3.

12

Estate Planning Is More Than Taxes

O nly the very wealthy have to worry about estate planning. That myth will devastate many heirs and estates. Sure, under the 2001 tax law fewer people will pay the estate tax—eventually. The estate tax, however, isn't scheduled to be repealed until 2010, and before then will be phased out slowly. More importantly, even those whose estates are exempt from taxes still need an estate plan. Traditionally, estate planning focused on tax reduction. Yet, estate planning is much more than reducing taxes, and the non-tax aspects of estate planning are more important than in the past.

Estate planning ensures that wealth is transferred to those the owner wanted to have it, in the way the owner wanted, and with minimal cost and delay. Estate planning also can ensure that the wealth is protected from waste, mismanagement, the owner's health problems, and other concerns.

Lack of a solid estate plan has destroyed the wealth of many families—even those of modest means. The devastation is more traumatic to families who didn't begin with substantial wealth.

Estate planning after the 2001 tax law focuses more on how much to give, to whom, when, and in what form. Owners can focus less on taxes and more on issues such as: reducing costs and delays; controls that can be put on gifts and inheritances so heirs won't waste them; how to benefit more than one generation of heirs; ways to protect assets from creditors and in-laws; and simplifying the estate. Avoiding probate, with its costs and delays, also might become more important. IRAs also are a more significant part of many estates than in the past. Special strategies for IRAs are covered in Chapter 11.

The point is that changes in estate taxes don't eliminate estate planning.

They free up the process so owners can focus on more important things than cutting taxes. We'll look at those factors, and also ways to reduce estate taxes in this chapter.

The New Estate Tax

Under the 2001 tax law, the estate tax will not apply to the estate of anyone who dies after December 31, 2009, and the generation skipping tax will not apply to transfers after that date. The gift tax, with some modifications, will remain in place. In addition, in many cases those who inherit assets after the estate tax repeal in 2010 no longer will get to increase the tax basis of those assets to the current fair market value. Just as when assets are received as a gift, the recipient will take the same tax basis that the prior owner had. (Under current law, an inherited asset's basis is increased to its fair market value. That means there are no capital gains taxes on all the appreciation during the deceased owner's lifetime.)

But those changes are well in the future. A few changes will take place in the interim. For years after 2001, the two highest estate tax brackets of 53 percent and 55 percent were removed. The top estate and gift tax rate became 50 percent for 2002 and 2003. Also, the 5 percent surtax on large estates was repealed after 2001. The maximum estate and gift tax rate drops by one percentage point each year from 2003 through 2007 until it reaches 45 percent, where it stays until the estate tax is repealed. The same rates apply to the generation skipping tax, which is a tax imposed on gifts directly from grandparents to grandchildren. After 2009, the top gift tax rate will be 35 percent on gifts over $500,000.

The estate and gift tax credit, which often is called the lifetime estate and gift tax exemption, also is increased. Before the 2001 law, the exemption of $675,000 was scheduled to reach $1 million per person in 2006. Under the 2001 law, the exemption for estate and gift taxes jumped to $1 million in 2002 and 2003. The exemption for the gift tax will remain at $1 million. But the exemptions for the estate tax and generation skipping tax will gradually rise to $3.5 million in 2009.

Remember that assets inherited before 2010 get their tax basis increased to current fair market value, while most assets inherited after that date retain the tax basis of the prior owner.

The gift tax is retained with its lower lifetime exemption amount, apparently so that people won't be encouraged to give away a lot of property during their lifetimes—especially before the estate tax might be reinstated.

The 2001 tax law is written so that all of its changes expire after 2010, and the law reverts to the one in place before the 2001 law was enacted. If Congress does not take additional action, then the estate tax will be repealed only for the year 2010. Beginning in 2011, the old estate and gift tax that applied before the 2001 law was enacted will be restored. Obviously, the way to maximize the benefits of the law is to die in 2010 and only in

2010. Those who die before 2010 should leave everything to a spouse who will expire in 2010.

The 20-Minute Estate Plan

That plan isn't a very practical one. For most of us, estate planning still is a key part of our financial planning. We must continue to plan our estates unless we are confident of passing on in 2010, and the planning must take into account the changes and uncertainties of the law.

Estate planning is easier than most people believe. That's because most estate planning experts shroud the topic in complex tax, legal, and insurance jargon. Most people can't get interested in discussions of probate, reversionary interests, split interest trusts, and related topics. Maybe the experts want to add some mystery to the process, or perhaps they don't know how to communicate in plain English. The reason doesn't really matter. What matters is that most presentations on estate planning cause people either to avoid planning their estates or to put together hurried, inadequate estate plans.

That's why I've put together this simple guide I call the 20-Minute Estate Plan. It provides straightforward, practical explanations that will help an individual put together an estate plan. This isn't a complete self-help guide. Meetings with an estate planner still are essential. The guide makes it easier to work intelligently and economically with an estate planner and to make informed decisions about the various options. That will save time, money, and frustration, and also result in a superior estate plan.

Estate Planning Basics

What is estate planning? It's not simply avoiding taxes or probate. Estate planning is deciding how wealth should be transferred to the next generation (or other recipients of the owner's choice), then determining which legal tools to use to transfer that wealth. Only after establishing how the assets should be distributed does the focus move to considering ways to reduce taxes, avoid probate, and other goals. Lawyers and other professionals like to call the process estate planning, but it really is best to think of it as inheritance planning. That puts the true purpose of the process in the forefront.

To begin the inheritance planning process, take the following steps:

Make a list of all assets and liabilities.   An effective inheritance plan cannot be prepared without this information. And a professional, no matter how skilled, can't do anything without this starting point. Frequently overlooked assets include pension plans, life insurance policies, trusts of which the estate owner is a beneficiary, and inheritances that are likely to be received. Heirs will inherit only net assets, so a list of all debts needs to be compiled, including whether or not the debts are secured by certain property.

Decide the desired distribution of the assets in the future.   The traditional goal is for major assets to be inherited first by the spouse if he or she still is alive, then by the children, usually in equal shares. Smaller amounts or specific items might be designated for special friends, other relatives, and charities. Of course, no one has to follow the traditional route. An owner might want to favor one child over others or want the bulk of the estate to go directly to the children instead of his or her spouse. Many people decide to give a portion of their estates to charity. The only major limits are that a spouse cannot be completely disinherited in most states (unless there is a valid prenuptial or postnuptial agreement) and children can be completely disinherited if the intention is made clear in the will. In addition, an inheritance cannot violate law or public policy.

As part of this step, secondary goals also should be considered. For example, should a spouse inherit everything but only in a way that prevents the property from being subsequently inherited by a second spouse or family instead of by the couple's children? Should property be left to children and grandchildren but with strings attached so that they don't waste the property or so they have to reach certain goals before getting the property? There often are ways of accomplishing both main and secondary goals, as long as the goals are clear.

Decide how much property should be given now, and how much later. As long as both the estate and gift taxes are in place, it is easier to reduce taxes and other costs if the owner is willing and able to part with some wealth now. Some people want to do that, others don't want to or can't afford to.

Work with one or more estate planning professionals to develop an estate plan.   The plan should achieve the desired goals and also take into account estate taxes, probate, and other concerns. An average middle class individual might need to work only with an estate planning attorney. Wealthier individuals and those with businesses or other complicated assets might need to add an accountant, life insurance agent, business appraiser, trustees, and other professionals.

Implement the estate plan after it is fully understood.   Many people have great estate plans designed by skilled professionals, then they fail to fully implement the plans. They don't set up trusts recommended by their planners or fail to transfer assets to the trusts. Maybe life insurance is not purchased as planned, annual gifts to children are not made, or each spouse does not have title to enough assets to take advantage of the estate tax exemption. The result is a lot of time and money spent on estate planning but no effective estate plan in place.

Let heirs know in general what is decided and how things are set up.   An estate owner also should draft a letter of instructions that lists basic information such as where copies of the will are kept, who the financial advisers are, and a summary of assets and liabilities. This document should be updated at least annually and be accompanied by recent tax returns and an outline of your estate plan, at the minimum. The letter should be given to the executor of the estate and to any other key people.

An inheritance plan really involves people more than law, life insurance, trusts, and other legal tools. The focus should be on how to provide for people both now and in the future, and also how one wants to be remembered.

Reducing the Tax Burden

Only after goals for the property are established is tax reduction considered. Once goals are clear, an estate planner usually can present several ways to accomplish those goals and compute the different tax effects of each option. Each option likely has advantages and disadvantages, because estate planning is full of trade-offs. Then the owner decides how to merge the tax plan with the personal plan to come up with one plan that comes closest to meeting the personal goals at the lowest possible tax cost.

Don't fall for the common myth that only the wealthy have to worry about estate taxes. The wealthy do have a potentially large estate tax to be aware of, because the marginal estate tax rate was as high as 50 percent through 2002, then began a steady decline to 45 percent by 2007. But anyone who has greater than $1.5 million in assets in 2004 and 2005 has to be concerned about estate taxes. In addition, the way the IRS counts assets, many people will owe estate taxes. A house, a couple of cars, a modest investment portfolio, a pension or annuity, and someone suddenly is what is known as a modest millionaire. Count in appreciation and inflation between now and 2009, and it is easy to see why most Americans have much larger taxable estates than they think. Without proper planning, money that was intended for loved ones will end up with the IRS.

The estate tax really is fairly simple. First, all the assets in which the deceased had an ownership interest are compiled and valued. The total value of all the assets is known as the gross estate. From the gross estate, several deductions are allowed. Debts are deducted, as are the administrative expenses incurred by the estate, such as lawyer's fees, probate costs, and similar expenses. Another deduction is the marital deduction. Under the marital deduction, all the property transferred to the deceased spouse is deducted from the gross estate. That means all the property that goes to the surviving spouse is free of estate taxes, and the estate tax can be eliminated by giving everything to one's spouse. The final deduction is for charitable contributions.

After the deductions are taken, the remaining amount is the taxable estate. To this are added back lifetime gifts, and the tentative estate tax is computed on that total. Subtracted from that result are prior gift taxes paid, the lifetime estate and gift tax credit, and any state death tax credit. The result is the estate tax payable. There also might be a generation skipping tax for gifts made directly to grandchildren.

This computation reveals several basic ways to reduce estate taxes. All estate tax reduction planning falls into one or more of these strategies:

- Get assets out of the gross estate or reduce the value placed on assets in the estate.
- Maximize use of the marital deduction and charitable contribution deduction.
- Use the lifetime estate and gift tax credit.
- Don't reduce taxes. Instead, buy life insurance to pay the taxes or provide an inheritance.

Now let's take a look at some of the more common strategies that fall under these general strategies.

Basic Tax Reduction Strategies

After the personal goals of the inheritance plan are set and an estimate is made of the estate taxes that would be paid if no tax reduction measures were taken, an estate planner will present tax reduction strategies to consider. The following strategies are likely to be included:

Full use of the marital deduction.   This involves leaving all the property to the surviving spouse. The marital deduction will fully eliminate estate taxes. The problem with this strategy is that it simply defers the taxes until the surviving spouse's death. The surviving spouse must decide how to reduce estate taxes without benefit of a marital deduction or the first spouse's estate tax exemption equivalent. In addition, any appreciation that occurs during the surviving spouse's remaining lifetime increases the value of that estate, making planning and tax reduction more difficult.

Maximize the lifetime estate and gift tax credit.   Everyone gets a credit that in 2004 and 2005 allows $1,500,000 of property to be given or left to the next generation without incurring estate or gift taxes. To take full advantage of this credit, each spouse must have at least $1,500,000 worth of property in his or her name. An estate planner might recommend changing the legal title of some assets so that each spouse will be able to use the credit.

Make lifetime gifts.   Everyone can give any person up to $11,000 worth of property each year without incurring gift taxes, and these annual gifts can be made to as many people as you want. (The $11,000 amount is indexed for inflation.) If spouses give jointly, the exempt amount is $22,000 annually. That means a couple with three children can jointly give the maximum to each child and get up to $66,000 out of their estates annually without incurring gift taxes. More can be removed from the estates tax free if gifts are made to the grandchildren. Gifts can be made directly or through trusts if the trusts have the right language.

Make large lifetime gifts.   The lifetime estate and gift tax credit can be used against either estate taxes at death, gift taxes during life, or a combination of the two. If one can afford to be without the property for life, it is better to use the credit now with large gifts than later through the estate. That's because estate and gift taxes are based on the value of property. If property is appreciating, heirs get more tax-free wealth if the property is given now rather than later when the taxes will be computed on the appreciated value. Also, inflation erodes the value of the credit, and that's another reason to use the credit now if one can afford to do without the property.

Set up a credit shelter trust.   This trust accomplishes several goals. It ensures that full advantage is taken of the lifetime exemption equivalent if it hasn't been used. The trust also allows a surviving spouse full use of the property and its income for life, while ensuring that any remaining property will go to children of the marriage (or other designated beneficiaries) rather than to a potential second family or other objects of the surviving spouse's affection. Under the credit shelter trust strategy, in the will, property up to the lifetime exemption equivalent amount is left to the trust. The surviving spouse is the sole beneficiary of the trust for as long as he or she is alive and is entitled to the income and property of the trust. After that spouse's passing, the children of the marriage inherit the remaining property in the trust.

Use irrevocable trusts.   Property that is transferred during life to an irrevocable trust is excluded from the gross estate. The transferor cannot be a beneficiary of the trust or be able to get the property back. There probably will be gift taxes owed when the trust is set up, but that should be cheaper than paying estate taxes down the road. If a goal is to avoid gift taxes, just enough property can be put in the trust each year to take advantage of the annual gift tax exemption. An irrevocable trust has the additional benefit of allowing the donor to make the gifts with strings attached. Those strings might protect heirs from themselves and also from being spoiled or otherwise damaged by an inheritance.

Buy life insurance to pay taxes or provide an inheritance.   Life insurance is a way to leave an inheritance without altering the ownership of other assets. It is possible that the insurance can provide a larger inheritance than otherwise would be available, especially if a married couple takes out a joint life or survivorship life insurance policy. Life insurance benefits are included in an estate only if the insured had any ownership interests in the policy. Life insurance can be excluded from an estate if the policy is owned either by an irrevocable trust, a limited partnership, or another individual, such as the children.

Give to both charity and heirs.   There are various strategies, such as charitable remainder trusts and charitable lead trusts, which allow an estate or a property owner to take advantage of the charitable contribution deduction while providing income or property to heirs for a period of years.

Use gift tax discounts.   There are strategies that allow one to give all or part of a property away but also pay gift taxes on only a portion of the value. This is known as a discount gift tax strategy, and discounts of 20 percent and higher are available. Family limited partnerships are a popular way to achieve such discounts. Also available are split interest trusts and a few other strategies for reducing gift taxes.

More Than Money

The focus of estate or inheritance planning is on wealth. But there are non-monetary elements to a good plan. A plan should contain a durable power of attorney or revocable trust to ensure assets are managed in case the owner becomes disabled. There should be a health care proxy or power of attorney so that it is clear who will make health care decisions in case of incapacity. A living will or other instructions regarding medical care also need to be considered. An owner also needs to ensure that the estate will have enough cash and liquid assets to pay taxes, debts, specific bequests, and other obligations. Otherwise assets will have to be sold in a hurry to meet obligations. I'll have more to say about the non-tax aspects of estate planning later in this chapter.

Planning in the Transition Period

As discussed, the estate tax is scheduled to be repealed in 2010, but the repeal will last only for one year. The uncertainty caused by that situation paralyzes some people into inaction. They don't want to make irrevocable changes in asset ownership if the estate tax might be repealed permanently. They also don't want to revise their wills every year or two to accommodate changing laws. Let's look at some factors to use when deciding how to deal with the uncertainty.

- Age and health will determine strategy to some extent. Undoubtedly, older individuals or those in poor health should focus on the traditional estate planning strategy of reducing the taxable estate by giving away property. Maximum use should be made of opportunities to give tax free and at gift tax discounts.

- Because the estate tax repeal is well in the future, lasts only one year, and its fate still is uncertain, I recommend that most people plan as though estate tax repeal will not take effect. This means first taking advantage of the annual gift tax exemption and the higher lifetime gift tax exemption of $1 million to the extent that one can afford to give away that much wealth. Additional wealth should be given to the extent it won't reduce one's standard of living. Look for opportunities to make gifts tax free or at a tax discount. As we get nearer 2010, consider deferring some planned gifts if it appears estate tax repeal really will take effect. But in the intervening years it is best to establish a giving plan and stick with it.

- Consider buying term life insurance lasting through at least 2009 to pay any estate taxes that are incurred between now and then. That way, no gifts need to be made in the meantime. One's family will inherit the entire estate, and the life insurance will cover the estate taxes.

- When a home and retirement account are the main assets, the best strategy is to leave most of the assets to one's spouse. That way there is no tax on the death of the first spouse, and the surviving spouse can maintain the standard of living. Then, tax planning or the estate tax repeal can be used to reduce taxes.

- Establish and maintain good records of all assets, even those that have been owned for years. If estate tax repeal takes effect, heirs will need the records to establish the tax basis of inherited assets. Take the time to establish the basis of all the assets.

- Stay flexible. Don't adopt a long-term strategy primarily because of the tax benefits. Gifts should be those one can afford and that meet wealth distribution goals. The estate and gift taxes are almost sure to change in the next 10 years.

Estate Planning Essentials for Everyone

Tom Carvel and his 800 ice cream stores once were familiar to many Americans, especially those in the northeast region where Carvel's gravelly voice was featured in radio and television ads for the stores. In 1989, ill health forced Carvel to sell the business, and in 1990 he died. Carvel's estimated $200 million estate should have been as simple as a $200,000 estate. He wanted his widow taken care of, then the bulk of the estate donated to charity (they had no children).

Carvel made almost every possible estate planning mistake. The result was a disaster. Over a dozen lawyers representing many different interests kept the estate tied up in court. The estate dwindled to $60 million or less because of legal fees. Family members and business associates became estranged and accused each other of various dishonest acts. The whole mess should have ended in 1998 when Carvel's widow, living as a recluse in England, passed away. But her cremation was stopped by an attorney who wanted an autopsy to determine if she was mentally competent at the time of her death, and the disputes continued.

You don't have to be rich to make the mistakes Carvel made. For example, a copy of the will could not be found, and there were reports that the document shredder in Carvel's old office was very busy in the months after his death. The will mysteriously appeared about two years later, after an expensive lost will court proceeding was concluded.

The problems with Carvel's estate, and thousands of other estates, weren't related to the tax law. There are many essential parts of an estate plan that need to be in place even when taxes aren't a factor. To avoid Carvel-like problems, there are key rules that should be followed in every estate plan.

Best Gift to Leave Your Heirs

When Tom Carvel died, his will was not in the filing cabinet that should have contained it. No one had a copy. In addition, his affairs were a web of corporations and other entities through which property frequently was passed. Paperwork for many of the transactions was incomplete. Carvel apparently kept everything straight in his head, but no one else could figure it out.

The best thing one can do for one's heirs is to get things organized and leave a clear guide to the estate. This document has two purposes. One purpose is to make things much easier and less expensive for loved ones. The other purpose is to avoid mistakes, such as overlooked or mismanaged assets.

The ideal way to provide this information is to fill a three-ring notebook with key documents. The first document would be an instruction letter that gives an overview of the estate and the steps that heirs should take right away. The alternative is to have survivors spend weeks or months pulling things together, or perhaps paying a lawyer to do so. At a minimum, the letter should identify who should be contacted, give the location of the will and other important documents, and describe funeral preferences.

The letter should be accompanied by copies of key estate and financial documents. Important documents in this package include:

- A list of legal and financial advisors, including the attorney, executor, accountant, insurance agent, bank, broker or financial planner, and financial institutions at which there are accounts.
- An inventory of assets, including a description of what is owned, where

it is located, an estimate of its value, approximately when it was acquired, and its tax basis.

- Recommendations for the management or disposition of special property should be stated somewhere in the notebook. Items that warrant this treatment include businesses, real estate, art and collectibles, and any investments about which there is a strong personal feeling.
- Current tax returns plus regularly updated copies of the will, personal financial statements, and details of debts. Estimates of estate taxes and cash flow would be helpful.
- Details of financial accounts including Social Security, insurance, pensions, bank accounts, brokerage accounts, mutual funds, and any other assets. In most cases, a copy of a recent account statement is sufficient. Another option is to identify where the files for the accounts are located.

The notebook should be revised at least annually. The estate executor and at least one other person should be aware of the notebook and where it can be located. Remember that no matter how simple and straightforward things appear to an owner, they often are murky to someone who walks right into the situation and has to begin managing the estate. Make things easier for everyone by getting organized. Most people are surprised by what they learn through this organizing process, and it makes them better at managing their wealth.

The 2001 Tax Law and Your Will

Everyone needs a will. Even those who have a living trust need a will. There always are assets that slip through the living trust or other plans. Those who don't anticipate having to pay taxes also need a will. Taxes are only a small part of the estate planning picture. Even modest assets can cause quite a legal tussle if a proper will doesn't settle matters.

Estate tax reform and its transition require special caution. Every will and estate plan needs to be reviewed to ensure it accommodates the changing law.

The common feature all estate plans will need until 2011 is flexibility. Flexibility will avoid extra fees and expenses, and it also will avoid problems with shifts in the tax law.

Beyond that, there are specific parts of an estate plan to consider carefully in light of the 2001 law. The first is asset ownership. The 2001 law raises the exempt amount for each estate. In 2004 and 2005 a married couple can transfer up to $3 million ($1.5 million each) tax free to the next generation. But they can do that only if each spouse has title to at least $1.5 million of assets. The exempt amount will rise to $3.5 million per individual ($7 million per couple) in 2009.

If the family owns more than $1.5 million in assets, be sure legal title is split among the spouses to take full advantage of both estate tax exemptions. If it isn't, shift title of some assets from the "rich" spouse to the "poor" one.

Another important consideration post-2001 is credit shelter trusts. The most critical change in most wills after the 2001 tax law applies to married couples who take advantage of the lifetime estate and gift tax credit through a tactic known as a bypass, credit shelter, or A-B trust.

This was discussed earlier in this chapter. It involves leaving property equal to the estate tax exempt amount in a trust that gives the surviving spouse income for life and also allows the spouse access to the principal during his or her lifetime for certain needs. After that spouse dies, the amount remaining in the trust goes to the children of the marriage. The rest of the estate is left directly to the surviving spouse. This trust allows the couple to get the maximum amount of property to the next generation free of taxes without depriving the surviving spouse.

This simple, standard provision is complicated in several ways by the 2001 law. As mentioned, the exempt amount increases from $1 million in 2002 and 2003, to $3.5 million by 2009, and to no limit in 2010. Many wills provide that a specific amount will be put in the credit shelter trust, usually the exempt amount at the time the will was written. In those wills, the amount will be too low when scheduled tax law changes occur, and even after a revision it will be too low when the next change occurs. The will has to be revised or amended every couple of years to reflect the new exempt amount.

An alternative is for the will to state that the highest amount eligible for the federal estate tax exemption be put in the trust. That avoids a revision every few years.

It could, however, create another problem, depending on the size of the estate. Suppose an estate is $2 million and the owner dies in 2004 when the exemption is $1.5 million. Then the spouse gets only $500,000 outright, and the rest goes to the trust. The spouse might have to live on less than planned or ask the trustee for additional funds when trust income is not sufficient. In this case, the trust is overfunded.

A better solution might be a formula clause. Determine the maximum amount that can be put in the trust to ensure the surviving spouse owns enough assets outright for a comfortable life style. Suppose that amount is $750,000. Then the will might say that the amount to be put in the credit shelter trust will be $750,000 or the maximum federal exempt amount, whichever is lower. This approach won't take advantage of the maximum federal estate tax exemption, but that is secondary to providing for the spouse.

Another option is to put the maximum exempt amount in the trust but make the trust more liberal. The spouse could be co-trustee, giving him or her control over how it is invested, and therefore to some extent determining how much income it will earn. Or the trust can state that the spouse annually can take from the trust up to 5 percent of its value for any reason, with the trustee's permission. This is in addition to being able to get additional amounts for needs such as support, health care, and education.

Still another alternative is for the spouse to be prepared to use what is called a disclaimer. The will would state that any inheritance the spouse disclaims goes to the bypass trust. Here's how it works. Suppose the will says that only $675,000 goes to the bypass trust (it even can say zero). The owner dies in 2004 when the estate tax exempt amount is $1.5 million. After reviewing the estate, the surviving spouse feels comfortable having the trust funded with the entire exempt amount. So he or she disclaims $825,000, which is added to the bypass trust. If the estate were smaller, the spouse could disclaim a smaller amount or even zero. Or if the surviving spouse is confident the estate tax repeal of 2010 will be made permanent, nothing might be disclaimed. That would be the ultimate in flexibility, but it does let the surviving spouse decide how much goes to the trust.

Wills written these days might also need the ultimate in flexibility—a "but if" clause providing that certain provisions are to be ignored if the estate tax is not in effect as of the year of death. This clause could eliminate the bypass trust if there is no estate tax. It also might restructure charitable contributions. For example, the owner might set up a charitable trust if there is an estate tax but leave a smaller amount outright to the charity and the rest outright to the children if the estate tax is repealed.

State Death Tax Alert

The overall estate tax reduction from the 2001 tax law might not be as much as many think. That's because the federal credit for state death taxes paid was reduced immediately, and it is eliminated after 2004. Most states piggyback onto the federal estate tax. That means through the state death tax credit the federal government essentially transfers part of the federal estate tax to these states, without any additional money coming out of the estates. With the ending of the state death tax credit, many states are changing their laws in ways that will increase total taxes on the estate.

Also, the exempt amounts of most states weren't raised when the exempt amount in federal law was raised. It is possible to have an estate that is exempt from federal estate taxes but taxed by the state. The lesson is that most of us have to pay attention to state death taxes for the first time. For many estates, state death taxes will be higher than federal estate taxes.

Writing a Better Will

While we are on the subject of wills, here are some key provisions of wills that often are overlooked and can make a big difference in the results of an estate plan.

- Estate liquidity is often overlooked but vital. An estate might be valuable, but it also needs cash to pay taxes, debts, and other expenses. If there will be a cash shortage, the owner needs to provide life insurance or a schedule of which assets are to be sold first to raise cash. In some wills, the executor is empowered to take out a mortgage on one or more properties to raise cash.
- Avoid specific bequests in a will. A specific bequest is when a certain amount of money or particular assets are given to an individual. This can complicate the estate and cause unintended problems. In Carvel's case from earlier in this chapter, 83 people were left relatively small cash gifts in his will. Most of these were former employees who could have been given bonuses after the business was sold. Instead, the gifts increased the size of the will and the cost of administering the estate. They also greatly increased the number of people involved in the will contest.

  Specific bequests can create other problems. A specific dollar amount might seem small when the will is written. But the value of other assets might fall in a market decline, or there might be unexpected taxes and other expenses. That cash gift suddenly is a bigger part of the estate than was intended. The gift also might use up scarce cash that is needed for taxes and debts.

  A specific property bequest also can have unintended consequences. Suppose a few hundred shares of stock are left to an individual. Suddenly the market likes the stock and it soars in value. This small gift becomes a meaningful part of the estate, and it is going to someone who was supposed to be a minor beneficiary. Or the stock could drop in value, leaving the beneficiary feeling slighted and with less than intended. Or the owner might sell the stock after the will is written. Then, the will has to be rewritten or amended, or the executor can be left to figure out what was intended for the beneficiary. Of course, the asset also might disappear, creating a number of problems.

  Small gifts generally should be made during the owner's lifetime. If they are made in a will, there should be some limits. For example, a cash gift can be made for a specific amount but only up to a certain percentage of the estate's value or its liquid assets. Likewise, a gift of specific property should be limited to a ceiling value or percentage of the estate and only for assets that won't be sold. But the best bet is to make specific bequests only of unique items, and specify that they be part of the residual estate so they won't come out of the estate first.
- Debts and taxes require careful consideration. Without the correct, technical wording, the minor beneficiaries of an estate might receive their bequests without making any contribution to the estate's taxes and debts. The main beneficiaries shoulder the tax and debt burden through their shares. It is a technical issue, but the owner should be aware of who will bear the burden of the taxes and debts.
- Distributing personal property can be the most difficult part of a will.

Oddly enough, it is the personal items, even seemingly insignificant ones, which bring out rivalries among the children and cause the most disagreements. There should be a plan in the will for dividing the personal property. There are several tried and true methods for doing this with a minimum of distress among heirs.

One option is to have the executor divide the property. A non-family member should be executor for this to work. Or the executor can be directed to sell everything and distribute the cash. Another option is to set up a lottery. The oldest child (or the one who picks the lowest number out of a hat) picks an item first. Then the others pick one item in order. For the next round of picks, the order is reversed. Another method is to have the children pick the items they would like while the parents are alive. The children attach their names to the items. These are just a few ideas.

A final point in estate planning is to expect change. An estate plan is not a one-time event. It needs to be updated whenever there is a change in the personal or family situation. A marriage, divorce, or birth in the family should trigger an appointment with the estate planning lawyer. Significant changes in the estate's property or value also should cause reconsideration of the plan. Even when there are no obvious changes, a lawyer should be contacted for a review every 18 months to three years.

CHAPTER

13

How Annuities Can Help or Hurt

Annuities are associated in most people's minds with retirement. For the first generation of retirees, some type of annuity was the bedrock of retirement. In fact, annuitant used to be a common term for a retiree. Annuities fell out of favor during the 1970s, then saw a resurgence in the 1980s as different types of annuities were developed. Research in recent years shows that an annuity can be a more valuable piece of a retirement plan than many people realize.

Initially, annuities were a relatively simple way of guaranteeing lifetime income to the owner. These days there are many different types of annuities. Because of the variations, too many people buy the wrong annuity for themselves. In addition, annuities generally are sold as tax-sheltered savings plans instead of as a source of lifetime income. Too many buyers focus on the tax benefits and don't learn enough about the other qualities of annuities. Also, annuity owners usually don't pay much attention to the many ways money can be withdrawn from an annuity, and they choose the wrong distribution method—a decision that often is irrevocable.

In this chapter we'll explore the world of annuities. We'll discuss the different types of annuities, which annuities are appropriate in different situations, and how to take money from an annuity.

The annuities we'll talk about in this chapter are contracts between the annuity buyer and an insurance company. The buyer invests money with the company in either a lump sum or installment payments. The insurance company promises investment returns, some life insurance benefits, and options for receiving distributions. There are many types of annuities that fit within this broad definition.

Another type of annuity is any fixed, guaranteed series of payments over a period of time. Social Security benefits are an annuity. A traditional pension from a former employer or union also is an annuity. As we've discussed, fewer employers offer these types of pension plan annuities.

This chapter will focus on the commercial insurance annuities in the first definition. Social Security is discussed in Chapter 4. Later in this chapter we'll discuss the different ways money can be taken from an annuity and how to choose the best method. That section also can be used when considering how to take benefits from an employer pension plan, because most employers' defined benefit pension plans offer payment options that are similar to those offered by commercial insurance annuities.

Making Annuities Easy

There are many different types of commercial annuities available. Sorting through them, however, can be made fairly easy. The first step is to understand the features that annuities have in common. Next, learning the differences among the annuities will make them easier to compare.

One common feature of annuities is tax deferral. Income and capital gains earned by the annuity are not taxed while in the annuity. The investment returns compound tax-deferred until they are distributed to the owner.

Another feature is that all distributed income and gains are taxed as ordinary income, even capital gains earned by the annuity. Ordinary income is taxed at the owner's highest tax rate.

The annuity account's value cannot be borrowed or used as collateral for a loan. If either of those events occurs, the amount of money involved is treated as a distribution and is taxable.

There is no tax benefit when contributing money to an annuity. A commercial insurance annuity must be funded with money that already has been taxed, and there is no deduction for the investments. There might be an exception if the annuity is purchased through an IRA or other qualified retirement plan.

Because there are no deductions when contributions are made to the annuity, the owner is not taxed when the contributions are returned to the owner as distributions. Because of this, the owner's preference would be to have accumulated income remain in the annuity while the contributions are distributed first. The tax law doesn't allow this. It imposes a last-in, first-out rule. If distributions are not made on a schedule, then the distributions are considered to have come from income until all the accumulated income has been distributed. Only after that are the distributions considered to be a tax-free return of contributions. When regular periodic distributions are made, a portion of each payment is treated as a tax-free return of contributions and a portion is a taxable distribution of investment returns until all the contributions are returned. A formula issued by the IRS determines how much of each periodic distribution is nontaxable.

Annuity contracts usually have restrictions on withdrawals and distributions. Most annuities have a surrender fee that is imposed if all or part of the money is withdrawn too soon. The most common surrender fee is 7 percent of the annuity's value if the money is withdrawn the first year. The penalty drops by one percentage point each year, until there is no penalty for distributions after the seventh year. Some annuities have surrender fees that last ten or 15 years. Usually an owner can withdraw up to 10 percent of the account each year without paying a surrender fee. A schedule of regular periodic distributions also usually avoids any penalty.

The tax law imposes a penalty when an owner withdraws money before age 59½. The penalty is 10 percent of the amount withdrawn. This penalty is in addition to income taxes imposed on the distribution. The penalty can be avoided when the withdrawal is for certain reasons (such as disability) or is made on a schedule that will last at least for the owner's life expectancy.

Annuities also have a modest life insurance benefit. The benefit usually is that the annuity's beneficiary is guaranteed to receive distributions at least equal to the owner's contributions.

There can be a tax-free exchange of annuities. The tax law does not consider it to be a distribution when an account balance is transferred from one annuity to another. The annuities can be sponsored by the same insurer or by different companies. The annuities don't have to be the same type. For example, a variable annuity can be exchanged for a fixed annuity or an immediate annuity.

Switching annuities is not as easy as it might seem. Insurers are under no obligation to assist in an easy transfer. In addition, for distributions of principal to be tax free, the insurer must have a record of the owner's contributions. After an exchange, the new insurer must receive the record from the original insurer. If the original insurer does not transfer the record, then the new insurer must report all distributions as taxable distributions of income. Some industry sources say that in a large percentage of transfers, the original insurer does not report the contributions to the new insurer.

The Annuity Menu

Now that we've examined the common features of annuities, let's take a look at how they can be customized. Beyond the basic features, annuities are sold under many different names and have a host of different features. Even so, it can be fairly easy to classify the annuities and compare them. Despite all the bells and whistles, a commercial insurance annuity usually can be put into one of three main categories or some combination of two of them.

Variable annuities were the best-selling type of annuity through the 1980s and 1990s until after the bull market peaked in 2000. Variable annuities combine the tax benefits of annuities with mutual funds. The owner of a variable annuity gets to choose how the money in the account is invested from among mutual fund-like accounts selected by the insurer. The insurer determines how often the investments can be changed. Variable annuities also offer a small life insurance feature that guarantees the owner's beneficiary will inherit no less than the contributions made by the owner. That guarantee became more significant after the bear market that began in 2000. Some analysts estimate that it could end up costing insurers a lot of money in the following years.

Fixed annuities are the traditional annuities. The owner's account earns an interest rate that is set by the insurer, usually each year. The interest rate might be set by reference to a market interest rate or it might be determined by the insurer's investment returns. The rate usually is similar to that earned by intermediate-term bonds or by mortgages.

Immediate annuities begin making regular distributions to the owner within a year after the annuity is opened. Both variable and fixed annuities generally are deferred annuities. That means the owner gives money to the insurer now, and that money is invested for at least a year before distributions begin, though usually for much longer. Income and capital gains from the investments are added to the account each year, after deducting expenses. In an immediate annuity, the owner makes a deposit to open the annuity, and the insurer begins payments to the owner within a year.

Most annuities can be put into one of these three categories or are a hybrid of two of these types. For example, an immediate annuity also can be a variable annuity. The owner can choose how the account is invested, and the investment returns will determine the amount of future distributions. Let's look at each of these types of annuities in detail. We'll also look at some special types of annuities. Then we'll examine how to choose from among the distribution options when the time comes to take money from an annuity.

The Tragedy of Variable Annuities

Variable annuities were among the best-selling investment products of the 1980s and 1990s. Unfortunately, the popularity was due more to effective sales methods than to the merits of the annuities. Variable annuities can be valuable financial tools. Too often, however, they are sold to the wrong investors for the wrong reasons.

Variable annuities are complicated. They also pay high commissions, encouraging strong sales efforts. Perhaps that is why about 14 percent of IRA-owners have all or part of their IRAs in variable annuities. Or why 11 percent of variable annuities are invested in assets that pay fixed returns. Or why about half of variable annuities are sold to people over age 65. Let's look at why these are mistakes, and how the benefits of a variable annuity can be maximized.

A variable annuity is a group of mutual funds in a tax-deferred annuity, with some life insurance attached. The owner chooses how the account is invested among the funds offered by the insurer. All income and gains are tax-free in the annuity, and they are taxed as ordinary income when distributed. If the variable annuity provides tax-deferral, why do people buy them through IRAs, which also are tax deferred? Why not simply buy mutual funds directly through IRAs?

One possible reason is the insurance protection. If variable annuity investments lose value after their purchase, as many did after March 2000, the beneficiary is guaranteed to receive at least the amount originally invested. But this protection is overstated. The owner has to die while the annuity's value is below the owner's contributions for the insurance to pay off. The odds of this happening based on history are quite low. The amount insurers have paid on this insurance provision to date is reported to be statistically insignificant. The extended bear market of the early 2000s, however, eventually might make that insurance seem like a good deal for the annuity owners. Annuities that were aggressively invested during that period lost a considerable amount of their value. In 2002, agencies that rate the financial safety of insurers became concerned that in the following few years the insurers might have to pay significant claims under this insurance because the losses in some variable annuity accounts were so steep. It remains to be seen, however, how much insurers will pay under this provision.

In addition, the cost of that insurance is quite high. That is one of the reasons why the annual expenses on variable annuities average 2.1 percent while annual expenses on mutual funds average 1.4 percent. For most people, it is much cheaper to invest in a taxable account and buy term insurance for a few years or until the investments are comfortably above the purchase price.

Another supposed advantage of the variable annuity in an IRA is that the annuity can be annuitized. That means when the owner needs money from the annuity, it can be converted into a stream of fixed payments that are guaranteed to last for life or a period of years, whichever the owner selects.

The owner of mutual funds in an IRA, however, also can annuitize. The IRA owner merely has to sell the mutual funds and buy an immediate annuity. In addition, the IRA owner can shop around for the best annuity deal available. Even if a variable annuity guarantees a minimum annuitization rate, the annuity buyer today doesn't know if that rate will be attractive in the future.

Sales of variable annuities to IRAs are considered so questionable that the National Association of Securities Dealers (NASD), which regulates brokers who sell variable annuities, issued guidelines in 2000. Brokers have to inform buyers that the tax deferral of the annuity is not needed because of the IRA. The brokers also have to prove that the life insurance and annuitization features warrant buying the variable annuity in the IRA.

One also has to wonder why someone would purchase a variable annuity and choose fixed-interest investments for the account. If the owner invests to earn 5 percent to 6 percent interest (or less), expenses of 2 percent or more eat up a major portion of that return. The owner might even get a higher after-tax, after-expense return from an interest-paying bank account. The lower the return expected from an investment, the less sense a variable annuity makes.

More than a high return is needed to justify buying a variable annuity. Time also is needed—a long time. That brings us to those over age 65 who buy variable annuities.

Variable annuities have two big disadvantages. One disadvantage is high expenses. The other is that all gains are taxed to the owner as ordinary income when distributed, even if they were earned as long-term capital gains within the annuity.

To get the tax deferral of an annuity, the owner has to pay mortality and administrative expenses in addition to the regular management expenses for the mutual funds selected. There also might be additional sales expenses. The result is that the average variable annuity has annual expenses of 2.15 percent deducted from the account, while the average stock mutual fund has expenses of approximately 1.4 percent. Those additional expenses are the price for tax deferral.

I've run the numbers many times, comparing variable annuities with purchasing stocks or mutual funds in taxable accounts and managing the taxable accounts to keep taxes low. Before 2003, it always turned out that to make up for the extra expenses, income and gains had to compound in an average-cost variable annuity for about 15 years. That's just the break-even point. For the variable annuity to generate more after-tax wealth than investing through a taxable account, the compounding period needed to be longer than 15 years. My research, which is backed by the research of others, showed that someone who bought a low-expense variable annuity had to let the gains compound for at least ten years for the annuity's advantages to overcome the disadvantages. Low-expense annuities generally are those offered by mutual fund companies (Vanguard has the lowest expenses) or discount brokers (such as Charles Schwab & Co.).

Effects of Tax Cuts

Those were the break-even points before 2003. In 2003, the federal income tax law was changed to reduce the advantages of variable annuities.

Income tax rates were reduced. This was an advantage for the annuities, because all income distributed from them was taxed as capital gains. But the top tax rate on dividends and on long-term capital gains was reduced to 15 percent. These were more significant reductions than the cut in income tax rates. The 2003 law increased the gap on the tax rate imposed on distributions from a variable annuity and on most of the income and gains in a taxable account. The effect of these tax changes is to increase the after-tax return that can be earned from a taxable account.

After the 2003 law, a tax-wise investor in the top tax bracket almost never would benefit from investing through a variable annuity. If the tax-wise investor earns only long-term capital gains and dividends in the portfolio, the maximum tax rate on this investment income is 15 percent. The after-tax value of such a portfolio in a taxable account always would exceed the after-tax value of a variable annuity if the two achieved the same investment returns before expenses and taxes. This conclusion holds true whether the annuity is high cost, average cost, or low cost.

Even a low-cost annuity with annual expenses of only 0.7 percent does not make sense for the tax-wise investor. The higher taxes on distributions and higher expenses are too big a burden for the tax deferral to overcome.

I tried scenarios for less tax-wise investors. Even when 50 percent of the annual returns in a taxable account were taxed at a combination of long-term capital gains and ordinary income tax rates, the taxable account still is a better deal for the top tax bracket investor.

Suppose an investor has 75 percent of the annual returns from a taxable account taxed at the 35 percent rate. Even then, according to my program, it takes 22 years for the tax-deferred compounding of the variable annuity to overcome its higher expenses and higher tax rate. Remember, this result is for a low-cost annuity with 0.70 percent annual expenses.

Suppose the investor is in the 28 percent tax bracket, so there is a smaller gap between the long-term capital gains rate and ordinary income rate. Suppose also that this is not a tax-wise investor, so 75 percent of annual returns in the taxable account are taxed at the 28 percent rate. Even then, it takes 24 years for the variable annuity to have a higher after-tax value than the taxable account.

The break-even point is much shorter for an ultra-low cost annuity with annual expenses of only 0.20 percent. In that case, the annuity comes out ahead after only 13 years of compounding if the investor is not tax-wise and has 75 percent of annual returns taxed at the 28 percent rate. But if the investor is moderately tax-wise and only 35 percent of annual returns are taxed at the 28 percent rate, it takes the ultra-low-cost variable annuity 34 years to have a higher after-tax value than the taxable account.

These conclusions were reached assuming that each portfolio was fully invested in stocks and that the stocks returned 9 percent annually. Are the results different if the variable annuity is in high-yielding investments that would be fully taxable outside the annuity, such as high yield bonds?

I assumed an investor in the 28 percent bracket earns 7 percent annually that is taxed as ordinary income. This return is available from high yield bonds, preferred stock, corporate bonds, real estate investment trusts, and a few other investments. The after-tax income in the taxable account is reinvested and compounded each year.

Here, the variable annuity makes some sense. The ultra-low-cost variable annuity with 0.20 percent annual expenses has a higher after-tax value than the taxable account after only four years. With a $100,000 investment, after ten years the variable annuity's increased after-tax value is about $5,000, after 15 years the advantage is $15,000, and after 20 years the variable annuity is about $34,000 more valuable than the taxable account.

When the annuity's expenses are raised to 1 percent annually, the variable annuity's advantage disappears. In that case, it takes the variable annuity 27 years to have a higher after-tax value than the taxable account. If the investor is in the top 35 percent bracket, the 1 percent expense annuity has a faster payoff—only 22 years.

Keep in mind that even under the old law, a variable annuity needed to own investments with a high return to overcome its additional expenses. A low to moderate return investment, such as a general bond fund, is not a good investment for a variable annuity.

When It Makes Sense

While variable annuities were advantageous only to select investors in the past, they make sense for even fewer investors after the 2003 tax law.

The exact break-even point for the variable annuity depends on several factors. The higher the annual return of the investment, the shorter the break-even period is. Another factor is the turnover (annual sales and purchases) in the taxable account, which determines the annual taxes on the taxable account. If the investor purchases stocks and holds them for many years, or invests in mutual funds with low annual distributions and holds them for many years, it would take an annuity decades to beat the taxable account.

Estate taxes are an overlooked disadvantage of variable annuities. Some surveys show that most variable annuities are purchased with funds the owners don't anticipate needing during their lifetimes. The annuities are considered high-returning emergency funds first, and an inheritance for heirs second. Unfortunately, the heirs would be likely to inherit more if the money were invested outside a variable annuity.

Upon the death of a variable annuity owner, the annuity is included in the owner's estate and subject to estate taxes with the rest of the owner's property. That is one level of taxes. Then, when the beneficiary withdraws earnings from the annuity, the income is taxed at ordinary income tax rates. If the maximum tax is imposed at both stages, the IRS gets about 80 percent of the annuity's value.

Mutual funds also would be included in the owner's estate. The heirs, however, would get to increase the tax basis of the funds to their current fair market value. Then the heirs could sell the funds and incur no taxes. No one would pay capital gains taxes on the appreciation during the owner's lifetime.

All these disadvantages do not mean there is no place for variable annuities in a portfolio. But other steps need to be taken before a variable annuity is purchased.

First, be sure the use of other tax-deferred vehicles, such as IRAs and 401(k)s, is maximized. Also maximize use of the tax-free Roth IRA.

Second, a prospective variable annuity owner should review his or her investment strategy. Someone who invests primarily for safety and income should consider a fixed annuity, tax-free bonds, or regular bond funds instead. Those who will buy and hold quality stocks or stock mutual funds for a long time probably are better off purchasing these investments outside an annuity. In those cases, the tax deferral of the variable annuity won't offset the higher costs and higher taxes on distribution. An investor who sells funds or stocks after less than a year or who seeks top-performing funds and sells them after substantial gains should consider a variable annuity.

Third, determine when the money in the annuity might be needed. If the money won't be needed or wanted for at least 10 or 15 years, consider a variable annuity. Also, the money shouldn't be needed before age 59 1/2. Otherwise, the owner will pay a 10 percent early distribution penalty tax in addition to regular income taxes for any distributions before age 59 1/2.

Fourth, someone who is confident of being in a lower-tax bracket when withdrawals are made than he or she is now in might find a variable annuity attractive.

Fifth, check out fees and expenses. In an average annuity, there will be annual mortality and administrative expenses of over 2 percent of the account and an annual fee of about $25. The lowest expenses are charged by the Vanguard Variable Annuity and by TIAA-CREF's annuity. Of the two, Vanguard offers more investment options. Other mutual fund companies offering low-cost variable annuities include Fidelity and T. Rowe Price & Co. The broker Charles Schwab & Co. offers more options for slightly higher expenses, as do several other brokers.

Take a good look at surrender charges. Many annuities charge 7 percent or more to those who want their money back within a year. Often, surrender charges decline for seven to ten years before being eliminated. Vanguard, TIAA-CREF, and other mutual funds companies have no surrender charges.

Secrets of Annuity U. Exposed

Because of their high commissions, variable annuities are the subject of strong sales efforts. The fact is that variable annuities often aren't purchased as much as they are sold. Because retirees and prospective retirees are the likely candidates for variable annuities and will hear many pitches for them, it is important for them to know how at least some of the annuity sellers are trained.

In the last few years, Americans have received numerous warnings about the inappropriate sales of variable annuities and about annuity sales tactics. A number of financial publications have asserted that few people should buy variable annuities. California Attorney General William Lockyear warned about annuity sales in a February 19, 2003, statement. *The Los Angeles Times* wrote an article detailing the inappropriate sales of annuities and churning of annuities owned by seniors on November 28, 2003. In April 2004, a report was jointly issued by the Securities and Exchange Commission (SEC) and the National Association of Securities Dealers (NASD) that found widespread annuity abuses. In the report, a survey of 125 brokerage firms of all sizes found that customers often weren't told about key features of annuities, such as higher taxes on distributions and penalties on withdrawals.

Perhaps the most disturbing report was published in the *Wall Street Journal* on July 2, 2002. The reporters attended a two-day annuity-selling seminar billed by its sponsors as Annuity University. The firm said it had trained approximately 7,000 agents over 13 years, according to the *Journal*.

At Annuity U., agents are told to attract groups of seniors as prospects by sponsoring an introductory seminar that includes a free meal, because "they like freebies." A goal of the seminar should be to generate fear among the crowd. An annuity can be sold only if it solves a problem, "but you have to create those problems first."

Agents are encouraged to tell seniors that their finances are completely wrong and that they have problems with taxes, asset protection, and investment returns. Annuities are the solution to each and every problem, according to the seminar leaders.

Full solutions should not be offered at these introductory seminars. Instead, agents are urged to tease the audience with hints that annuities will solve their problems without explaining how. Then, the seniors are encouraged to sign up for free follow-up appointments.

The sales seminar gives tips on how to act at seniors' homes during the follow-up appointments, how to earn their trust, and how to garner key financial information.

The *Journal* article said the agents are told to "Treat them [seniors] like they are blind 12-year-olds." The seminar also says seniors buy on emotions such as fear, anger, and greed. Agents are urged to stimulate these emotions instead of intelligently discussing annuities. Annuity U. also teaches agents to say that annuities are safe and guaranteed like bank certificates of deposit.

Governments have reacted to the stories of annuity abuses. Effective January 1, 2004, California enacted new laws covering the sales of annuities to those aged 65 and older. In addition, the NASD proposed new regulations covering the sale of variable annuities in May 2004. The regulations replace "guidelines" that the NASD had issued a couple of years earlier. The regulations require annuity brokers to determine that an annuity is appropriate for a customer before making a sale.

While it is likely that only a few insurance brokers use abusive sales tactics or sell inappropriate annuities to clients, those who do are very aggressive. You need to be aware of the tactics that some brokers use. You also need to know when a variable annuity is an appropriate investment and when it is not.

The Return of Traditional Annuities

Fixed annuities are getting more and more popular. Beaten down by the bear market of the early 2000s, many investors suddenly stopped searching for the highest returns and began looking for a combination of safety and solid income. The safety of fixed annuities has become more attractive after the extended bear market.

Years ago, most retirees could rely on a fixed pension from an employer to cover a large part of their retirement expenses. The employer would send a check for the same amount every month or quarter. Those defined benefit retirement plans largely are disappearing, and retirees are on their own for funding retirement. A good replacement for these plans is an annuity. Shifting part of a retirement nest egg into an annuity gives that safe, guaranteed lifetime income. A price of the safe, guaranteed income is giving up potential capital gains from stocks or bonds.

In a fixed annuity, the insurer invests the owner's contributions however it chooses. Each year, the insurer determines how much interest will be credited to the annuity accounts. The amount might be determined by the insurer's investment experience over the last year. More often, the interest earnings are determined by reference to a market yield, such as the yield on a Lehman Brothers bond market index or the ten-year Treasury bond. Often the index is a gross yield. Only a net yield is credited to the accounts. The net yield is the gross yield reduced by expenses, which usually are listed in the annuity contract.

Fixed annuities often are compared to bonds. The annual interest credited to a fixed annuity should be similar to that earned by intermediate term bonds. Unlike a bond or bond mutual fund, the principal value of a fixed annuity account will not rise or fall with interest rates. The insurer takes the risk of market fluctuations.

A study showed that a fixed annuity offers more than safety and certainty. It also can make wealth last longer. An article in the December 2001 *Journal of Financial Planning* examined the odds of different portfolio combinations lasting for at least 30 years of retirement. The study examined four portfolio combinations, from conservative to aggressive. The conservative portfolio was 20 percent stocks, while the aggressive portfolio was 85 percent stocks. Using the Monte Carlo simulation described in Chapter 3, the study found that for each type of portfolio, putting 25 percent or 50 percent of the fund into a fixed annuity increased the odds of success.

The greatest improvement was in the conservative portfolio. While the annuity also improved the odds of success for the aggressive portfolio, the existence of a lot of stocks in that portfolio already gave it over a 90 percent probability of surviving. Adding the annuity to the aggressive portfolio increased the survival odds only a bit. The odds of survival for the conservative portfolio, however, were 32.6 percent with no annuity, which improved to 53.3 percent when 25 percent of the portfolio was moved into an annuity, and to 81.3 percent when the portfolio was 50 percent in a fixed annuity.

The lesson seems to be that those who are not prepared to invest aggressively all through their retirement should consider adding a fixed annuity to their portfolios.

Buying a Fixed Annuity

The benefits of a fixed annuity won't be available if the wrong annuity is purchased. There are many insurers offering annuities with many different terms. The prospective annuity buyer must shop around and know how to compare annuities in order to get a good deal.

First, consider the financial stability of the insurer.   Earning a high yield doesn't do much good if the insurer goes bankrupt. Annuities are not federally insured. Most states have a modest insurance guarantee fund, but they don't amount to much. The only real guarantee behind the annuity is the financial stability of the insurer. Insurers with lower safety ratings generally offer higher yields. While few insurers go bankrupt and many perk along profitably despite low safety ratings, insurer bankruptcy probably is not a risk to take with retirement money. There are four services that rate insurer safety: A.M. Best, Fitch, Moody's, and Weiss. Examine ratings from all four rating agencies. The Weiss ratings tend to give lower scores than the others. Stick with insurers who are in the top groups of ratings from at least a couple of the raters. Any insurance broker or web site that sells annuities should have the ratings.

Know how interest rates will change.   How often will the rate change and how is the change determined? A fixed annuity usually guarantees a rate for a year. After that, the rate will change, usually annually. Some insurers say the yield will be determined by their investment experience. If so, examine the yields the insurer has credited to similar accounts for at least the last ten years. Compare these yields with intermediate bond yields during the same period. While the history is no guarantee that future yields will be competitive, it does indicate the insurer's investment record and style.

A more reliable system is for the yield to be determined by reference to market interest rates. Be sure the reference is close to that of intermediate bonds, not money market funds or CD yields.

Don't be swayed by promises of bonus yields under certain conditions.
These bonuses are not promised and won't be awarded if the market
changes from what the insurer expected.

Find out the net yield that will be credited to the account.   Insurers
deduct various fees and expenses before the interest finally is credited to
accounts. A prospective buyer should be shown the difference between the
gross yield that is the starting point and the net yield that actually will be
credited. Sometimes it is tough to get the answer, but a buyer wants to
know all the expenses that will be deducted from the gross yield.

Don't be fooled by high teaser first year yields.   Many insurers sell annuities by promising an above-market initial yield, but the yields usually are
guaranteed for only six months or one year. After that, the insurer is likely
to credit the account with below-market yields while continuing to offer
above-market yields to new buyers. Don't be overly concerned with the
first-year yield. Pay more attention to how long that yield will last and to
how future yields will be determined.

Learn about penalties.   Most annuities impose a penalty on investors
who want some or all of the principal back in the early years. The standard
penalty is 7 percent of the account value for withdrawals within one year.
The penalty drops by one percentage point each year until it disappears
after seven years. In addition, most fixed annuities allow owners to withdraw 10 percent to 15 percent of the principal in any year without paying a
penalty. Look for alternatives to any annuity that is more restrictive.

Examine the minimum rate.   Fixed annuities used to guarantee a minimum 3 percent rate. After rates declined significantly in 2002 and 2003, insurers began reducing the guarantee. Most annuities now guarantee less
than 2 percent. After expenses, that kind of return won't amount to much.

Check for payout restrictions.   The ultimate goal is to get a reasonable income from the annuity during retirement. Some annuities offer attractive
terms during the preretirement accumulation phase then take the advantage away during the distribution phase. Avoid a contract that requires the
owner to annuitize at distribution time or that otherwise limits payout options. Also be sure that after the early distribution penalty expires, the annuity can be transferred as a lump sum to another insurer without penalty
in a tax-free exchange.

Guaranteed Income for Life

The immediate annuity is becoming popular again. It fell out of favor in
the 1970s and 1980s because payouts were based on artificially low interest

rates and lost most of their purchasing power in the face of high inflation. In the 1990s, immediate annuities didn't look promising compared to the great bull market in stocks. The immediate annuity, however, begins to look attractive in an era of low interest rates, low stock market returns, and high stock market volatility.

In an immediate annuity, the owner pays a lump sum to an insurance company. The insurer then begins making regular payments to the owner. The payments can be monthly or less frequently, depending on the insurer and the option selected. The payments can continue for life, the joint life of the owner and his or her spouse, or for a period of years. The owner selects the payment period. The longer the payments, the lower each payment will be. When the payment period ends, there is no money left for either the owner or the heirs. If payments for life are selected and the owner dies before his or her life expectancy, the insurance company profits. That's why a popular payment option is life with a guaranteed minimum period of years. If the owner dies before the minimum period ends, payments continue to a beneficiary for the balance of the minimum payment period.

There are tax benefits to an immediate annuity. Income earned by the account is tax deferred as long as it remains in the annuity. Also, part of each payment is a tax-free return of principal and part is taxable interest. Another benefit is creditor protection. In most states, creditors of the owner and beneficiary cannot reach the annuity with their claims.

An immediate annuity protects the owner from one of the greatest fears of retirees. The owner cannot outlive the income or the assets unless the insurer goes out of business. Theoretically at least, an investor doesn't need an annuity. A steady stream of distributions could be received from an investment portfolio. Without the annuity, however, the investor takes the risk of low investment returns and of outliving the portfolio. With an immediate annuity, the insurer assumes these risks.

An immediate annuity also avoids the risk of declining interest rates that reduced the income of many investors after 1982. Investors purchased bonds or certificates of deposit that paid comfortable yields. Market interest rates fell throughout the period. When a bond or CD matured, the owner had to reinvest the principal in new investments that paid much lower yields. Income investors saw their income cut by half or more, even before considering the effects of inflation, during the great bull market. With an immediate annuity, the insurer takes this risk.

There are potential disadvantages to the immediate annuity. The prime disadvantage is that income from the annuity is fixed. That means it will lose purchasing power to inflation each year. Also, if market interest rates rise, the immediate annuity owner won't benefit. The yield prevailing when payments began is locked in. A relatively new option that overcomes these disadvantages is the variable immediate annuity. It adds other risks, as we'll discuss shortly.

An immediate annuity also lacks liquidity. The ability to get additional cash that exceeds the periodic payments usually is limited or nonexistent. Some insurers are loosening their policies in this area. In recent years insurers have issued annuities that allow owners access to 20 percent or more of the account at one time. A cost to this feature is lower initial payments, and taking a large withdrawal reduces future periodic payments.

The immediate annuity can be used anytime after retirement. It provides an income floor during the payment period selected, whether it is life or a period of years. The annuity can be a substitute for bonds or other conservative investments. Most people shouldn't have an entire portfolio in immediate annuities, because the income is fixed. Growth will be needed to offset the effects of inflation. The security of the annuity, however, might let the investor take more risk in other parts of the portfolio than would have been taken without the annuity. That could boost lifetime income if the extra risk is rewarded with higher returns.

An immediate annuity can be purchased with cash. Existing investments can be sold and the after-tax cash used to purchase the annuity. In addition, an existing variable annuity or fixed annuity can be exchanged tax free for an immediate annuity.

A related option is called the split annuity, though it really is two annuities. The investor purchases one immediate annuity to yield a floor of steady, dependable income. At the same time, a fixed, deferred annuity is purchased. This second annuity will earn interest that will compound tax-deferred. When the first annuity runs out, or additional income is needed to make up for lost purchasing power, the deferred annuity is converted to an immediate annuity.

Increase Income by 20 Percent or More

It is important to shop around for an immediate annuity. Even those who plan to annuitize an existing variable annuity or fixed annuity or convert one into an immediate annuity should check what other insurers have to offer. Don't automatically select one of the payout options offered by the current insurer. Each insurer uses its own assumptions about life expectancy and interest rates to determine payouts. Each also has its own level of expenses. Those factors affect the payouts, and those payouts can differ significantly among insurers. Every year or so I check quotes from different insurers. Each time, despite a very competitive insurance market, there are vast differences in payouts. Insurers with comparable safety ratings have payouts that vary as much as 20 percent, a substantial difference. Remember, that is a 20 percent difference in income every month for life.

That's why the most important part of buying annuities wisely is to shop around. Contact local agents and brokers to see what they offer. Then check some national brokers. The Internet has a number of sites that offer comparisons and are listed in the following box.

Annuity Sources' Web Sites

annuityscout.com	immediateannuity.com
brkdirect.com	tiaacref.com
fidelity.com	troweprice.com
topannuities.com	masterquote.com
quotesmith.com	quickquote.com
annuityshopper.com	vanguard.com

National Brokers

Annuity & Life Insurance Shopper	800-872-6684
Quotesmith	800-556-9393

Don't automatically choose the annuity with the highest payout. Safety counts with insurance companies. You might remember that in the 1980s and early 1990s several prominent insurers went bankrupt because of risky investments. Many people had their annuity payments eliminated or reduced when the insurers went under. A broker or web site should give you the safety ratings from the leading rating firms. It's a good idea to stay away from insurers below the top few ratings.

Maximizing Insured Retirement Income

While immediate annuities have increased in popularity, there still is the serious disadvantage of fixed income in the face of inflation. The income does not retain its purchasing power over time. The owner needs another source of funds that will *increase* in purchasing power over time.

There's a relatively new vehicle to consider that tries to offer the combination of steady income with purchasing power protection. It is known as the immediate variable annuity.

I discussed deferred variable annuities earlier in this chapter. Their distinguishing feature is that the owner chooses how the account is invested from among mutual funds offered by the insurer. The owner takes the investment risk but also benefits if the selected investments produce high returns.

The variable immediate annuity (VIA), as might be expected, combines features of the immediate annuity and the variable deferred annuity. It can produce a steady, growing source of retirement income. But these annuities can be very complex.

With the VIA, the investor purchases the annuity and selects how the account will be invested among the investment funds chosen by the insurer. Because this is an immediate annuity, the owner receives an initial monthly income based on his or her age, the amount invested, and the assumed investment return (AIR). The owner selects the AIR from among options offered by the insurer.

The choice of AIR is important, because it determines the initial income. The higher the AIR, the higher the initial income will be.

Income payments in the future are adjusted for the actual investment performance of the account. Strong investment performance means steadily rising retirement income. If investment performance doesn't at least equal the AIR, the income will be reduced. For income to increase, investment returns must exceed the AIR. That's why most people choose a relatively low AIR. They accept a lower initial income in order to reduce the probability that the income will fall in the future. The most common AIR selected, and the one most insurers recommend, is 5 percent.

Obviously the owner takes a risk with a variable immediate annuity. While the retirement income might increase, it also might decline if investment returns don't meet expectations. The insurers offer a guarantee, which I'll discuss shortly, that can reduce this risk.

Another potential disadvantage is that, as with all annuities, income distributions from the VIA are ordinary income. That means capital gains from stocks are converted into ordinary income by purchasing a VIA. Another disadvantage is that there is nothing left for heirs from the annuity.

A number of insurers offer variable immediate annuities. The initial temptation is to purchase the annuity that offers the highest initial monthly income, but that could be a mistake. Other features need to be examined.

First look at total costs. The costs are subtracted from the investment returns. That means high costs will hold down the growth of income in good markets and increase its decline in bad markets. The major costs are mortality and administrative expenses and a general charge for insurance. In addition, there are expenses charged on the investment accounts, such as mutual fund management expenses. There also probably will be a surrender charge if the annuity is canceled within the first five to seven years.

Recently, Fidelity affixed a 1 percent insurance charge, and the average fund expenses were 0.96 percent, for a total cost of 1.96 percent. T. Rowe Price's total expense came to 1.35 percent, and TIAA-CREF's was 0.5 percent. An American Skandia policy, by comparison, had total expenses of about 2.25 percent.

Vanguard doesn't offer a variable immediate annuity. Instead, investors can buy its variable deferred annuity. Then at payout time the owner selects a variable payout option instead of a fixed payout.

Next, look at the guarantees. Fidelity has an option that effectively splits the purchase into a guaranteed immediate annuity and a variable annuity. Of course, the same effect can be achieved by purchasing two separate annuities. Price offers a guarantee that income payments won't decline more than 20 percent from the initial level. But the guarantee costs money. The insurance charge on the regular variable immediate annuity is 0.55 percent. On the guaranteed annuity it is 1.4 percent.

Then, look at surrender fees. Most annuities impose a surrender fee if the annuity is canceled within five to seven years. The Price annuity, for example, charges a 5 percent surrender fee the first year, and the fee declines by one percentage point for each of the next four years.

There also are alternatives to the variable immediate annuity to consider. A traditional immediate annuity can be purchased and supplemented with a portfolio of stocks and bonds. Another option is to purchase an immediate annuity that grows by a stated amount each year, usually 4 percent. A few insurers such as Safeco and Lincoln National offer these growing annuities. The initial payout, of course, will be less than for a traditional immediate annuity.

With all the options available, there is a trade-off among growth potential, security, and costs. There are two more caveats with the VIA. One is that the products are relatively new, so insurers don't have a track record with them. Another is that if all the retiree's money is in the VIA, the ability to take a lump sum for emergency purchases is limited.

The policies can be hard to compare because they offer different AIRs, guarantees, and flexibility. There are directly-sold annuities offered by mutual fund companies Fidelity, T. Rowe Price, and TIAA-CREF in addition to those that might be offered by insurance agents.

A variable immediate annuity probably is best for people who might not have saved enough for retirement. They can buy a VIA that gives them some guaranteed floor on lifetime income that they cannot outlive, but it also has the potential for the income to grow if the investment selections do well.

Stock Returns without Risk?

A relatively new type of annuity that periodically attracts investors is the equity-indexed annuity.

These annuities seem to get popular when the stock market gets in trouble. The annuities offer stock market-linked returns in bull markets and guaranteed minimum returns in bad markets. It sounds like the best of both worlds, the potential of high returns when the stock market rises and a guaranteed minimum yield when stocks fall flat or worse. Of course, the earnings are tax deferred but taxed as ordinary income when distributed.

The equity-indexed annuities are not what everyone expects and are appropriate only for certain types of investors. There are many different forms of equity-indexed annuities, but they do have common features that can be discussed generally.

The return credited to the annuity account can indeed increase if stock market indexes rise. Under most of the annuities, however, the return credited to an account is less than 100 percent of a stock market index's return for the year. Some policies will be straightforward about the limited potential for growth. Others tend to hide the limit in the formula used to calculate the return that will be credited to an account. The return might not be based on the actual rise in a market index but on a computation such as "the average daily closing prices of the index during the year." Such formulas can reduce the return, as the market tends to move in brief bursts both up and down. When a daily average is used, the market's long flat periods and periodic declines are likely to generate a return far lower than the simple percentage difference between the beginning and ending values for the year. Most of these annuities also allow the insurer to change the equity-linked return or index at any time.

After the formula is applied to the stock index returns, most annuities subtract an annuity fee and an asset management fee. Some insurers also put a cap on the return that can be credited to the account each year, no matter how well the stock market does.

A few equity-indexed annuities allow 100 percent participation in the returns of a stock market index. The kicker on these annuities (and even on some of the others) is that there is a surrender fee or vesting schedule or both. For example, with a ten-year vesting period, the owner gets access only to 10 percent of the accumulated return for each year the annuity is owned. Only after ten years is 100 percent of the return vested to the account and available for withdrawal. Surrender the annuity early and all the unvested gains are lost. There usually is the traditional surrender fee along with the vesting schedule.

Before buying an equity-indexed annuity, ask to see the returns that were credited to holders of that type of annuity in the past. Compare those returns with the actual returns of stock index funds. With many indexed annuities, when the stock market indexes had gains of 20 percent or more, the annuities were credited with returns of less than 10 percent.

Taxes can be another disadvantage of equity-linked annuities. Stocks and mutual funds owned outside of a tax-deferred account generate tax-favored long-term capital gains if held for more than one year. But all distributions from an annuity are taxed as ordinary income. Capital gains are converted into ordinary income with an annuity. In addition, in a taxable account, losses can be deducted against gains and other income. Any losses in an equity-indexed annuity cannot be deducted against other income.

The guaranteed return isn't worth getting excited about. On most annuities it is 0 percent to 3 percent, compared to the 3 percent to 5 percent yield on bonds. A better rate is available on traditional fixed annuities. In addition, the guarantee applies to only 90 percent of the investment in most annuities.

These criticisms don't mean equity-linked annuities are a bad product. They can be appropriate for certain investors.

Equity-indexed annuities can be a good idea for investors who fear leaving the safety of certificates of deposit and money market funds but who need some money invested for growth and inflation protection. The annuities also require that investors be able to leave the money in the annuity for at least ten years to get the maximum benefit and avoid the penalties.

Before buying an equity-indexed annuity, however, consider a balanced mutual fund. A good balanced fund will mix quality bonds with quality stocks. The full returns of stocks won't be earned in a bull market, but when the stock market declines the bonds usually cushion the losses. Money is lost in a balanced fund only in rare years, such as 1994, when both stocks and bonds decline or in years when stocks decline far more than bonds appreciate. A balanced fund won't get the tax deferral of an annuity, but most of the appreciation will qualify for long-term capital gains. My recommended balanced funds are Dodge & Cox Balanced, Vanguard Wellesley Income, and Vanguard Wellington.

Another option is for the investor to construct a balanced fund annuity by investing in both a regular fixed-rate annuity and a variable annuity. The variable annuity will give the full stock market gains and losses (after deducting the annuity's fees), and the fixed-rated annuity will give a higher yield than the guarantee in an equity-index annuity. Both annuities will be tax deferred.

Taking Money from Annuities and Pensions

One of the toughest financial decisions most people will ever make is how to take the money out of an annuity or pension plan. How the distributions will be made is one of the keys to managing wealth during retirement. Very often there are many options available, and it is not always clear which is best. There are both tax and nontax factors to consider.

The factors to consider are very similar whether the account is an insurance annuity, IRA, 401(k), or company pension plan. In this section, the focus will be on insurance annuities; variations for employer retirement plans will be explained when they exist. The basic choice is between a lump sum payout and periodic payments. But there are variations of each option. Let's review each of the options, the advantages and disadvantages of each, and how to compare them.

Surrender the Annuity?

One easy option with an insurance annuity is to simply surrender it. In that case the owner receives the cash value. Surrender usually is not a good idea. Many annuities have redemption fees or other charges that are imposed upon surrender. The redemption fee might disappear after the annuity is owned for seven to ten years, but some annuities have redemption fees that never end.

Another reason not to surrender the annuity is the tax treatment. All the accumulated income would be taxed as ordinary income when the cash value is received. If the owner is under age 59 1/2, there also will be a 10 percent federal tax penalty.

The only reasons to consider surrender are when the annuity is extremely bad—because of low returns or high expenses—or there is doubt about the financial health of the insurer. But even in those cases there are other options, such as a tax-free exchange for an annuity at another insurer.

With a retirement plan, taking a lump sum distribution is similar to surrendering an annuity. With a retirement plan, however, there are tax options. The lump sum might be eligible for five-year averaging or for a rollover into an IRA or other qualified retirement plan. These options can reduce or defer taxes in ways that are not available with an insurance annuity.

Annuitize the Annuity

Annuitization is a fixed, guaranteed stream of payments over either the owner's life, the joint lives of the owner and a beneficiary, or over a period of years. This stream of payments presumably is why most annuities are purchased. Also, many 401(k) accounts and employer pension plans can be annuitized. An IRA is annuitized when the account balance is used to purchase an immediate annuity.

With annuitization the owner cannot outlive the guaranteed payments for life, and payments won't be reduced or cut short for years. Again, the greatest fear of most people in retirement is outliving their income or assets. Annuitization prevents this. The only event that could stop the payments is insolvency of the insurer, and in many insolvency cases a state insurance fund or other insurers continue at least a portion of the payments.

Annuitization also provides some tax breaks. A portion of each payment is considered a tax-free return of after-tax principal investments until the principal is recovered. The rest of each payment is taxable income.

Surprisingly, only about 1 percent of annuity holders choose to annuitize. I suspect one reason is that money put into annuities tends to be supplemental or emergency money. The owners generally want the income to compound tax deferred as long as possible and hope never to have to touch it.

But annuitization also might not be used in many cases because it does have some disadvantages. One disadvantage, as we discussed, is that the income payment is fixed and loses purchasing power to inflation over time.

Another disadvantage of annuitization is that it limits the ability to take extra money when needed. Most annuities allow some additional cash to be withdrawn, but this generally is limited to no more than 10 percent of the account balance each year. If money beyond the limits offered by the annuity is needed, there must be other resources to tap. If the annuitization option is not selected, then most annuities will allow one-time withdrawals that exceed 10 percent of the account balance.

Annuitization also prevents the annuity from being part of an estate or inheritance. The payments end when the annuitization period ends. Payments for life end at the owner's death. It doesn't matter if the owner lives six months or 60 years after the payments begin. Take payments for a period of years, and they terminate at the end of the period. Annuitization makes it impossible to make lump sum gifts to heirs or leave them the unspent wealth.

For those who believe the benefits of annuitization outweigh the potential disadvantages, there often are many options. Some annuities offer only a few basic options, but many annuities and retirement plans offer a flexible range of choices. The three most common options are as follows:

Life annuity.   Payments are received for the rest of the owner's life, no matter how long that is. If the owner dies before life expectancy, the insurance company keeps the balance. If the owner lives longer than expected, the owner continues to receive payments and the insurer takes the loss. The younger the owner is, the lower the periodic payment will be. The big disadvantage of the life annuity is that the owner might die prematurely and receive only a portion of the investment and its accumulated income. The wealth won't be available for a spouse or other loved ones.

Joint life annuity.   Under this method, also known as life and survivor, payments are made for the lives of both the owner and a beneficiary. Suppose the owner's spouse is named as the beneficiary. Then, payments are made during the owner's life. If the owner dies first, payments continue to the spouse until he or she also dies. Because two lives are covered, the initial payment will be lower under this method than under the single life annuity.

The advantage of the joint life annuity is that the spouse (or other beneficiary) is ensured of income for life. A disadvantage is that the payment will be less than from a single life annuity. If the spouse predeceases the owner, the owner is stuck with the lower lifetime payment. Another disadvantage is that there is nothing to leave to anyone other than the joint life beneficiary, if he or she survives the owner.

There are a number of variations of joint life annuity. A joint and 100 percent survivor annuity makes the same periodic payment until both the owner and beneficiary are deceased. A joint and 50 percent survivor annuity pays one amount during the life of the annuity owner, then pays half that amount to the beneficiary if the owner dies first. There also might be a joint and 66 percent survivor annuity available. A joint life and term of years annuity guarantees that payments will be made for at least the stated term of years, even if both the owner and the beneficiary die before that period. The payments would continue to another beneficiary named by the owner.

A joint and 100 percent survivor annuity will offer a lower initial payment than the other variations but will leave the beneficiary with a higher income after the owner dies.

Term of years. This annuity ensures that the owner will leave something to heirs if the owner dies early. The guaranteed payments are made for a stated term of years, usually 10, 15, or 20. If the owner dies before that period, the payments continue to a beneficiary until the period has elapsed. If the owner outlives the period, the payments stop and the owner will need other sources of income.

A variation is the life and term of years (or joint life and term of years). If the owner (or the owner and the joint life beneficiary) dies before the term of years, payments continue to another beneficiary until the term of years is up.

Which to Choose?

Some general rules can help decide which annuitization option to use. If the owner is married and the spouse has other sources of income, the owner might want to choose the single life annuity. This maximizes the income while the owner is alive, and the spouse has other assets for income if the owner dies first. A single life annuity also can be a good idea when the owner is likely to outlive the spouse, because of either age or health differences.

The joint and survivor annuity generally is best for most married couples. The tax law requires this option for employer retirement plans unless both spouses sign a consent form to another option. Obviously this option is a good idea when a spouse will not have sufficient other income or assets to maintain the standard of living, especially if the spouse is likely to outlive the owner. The less wealth available to the owner's spouse, the greater the payout to the survivor should be. For example, if the spouse will have some other sources of income, the owner might choose a joint and 50 percent survivor annuity. That provides a higher income while both spouses are alive and a supplement to the surviving spouse. But if the spouse has few other sources of income, a joint and 100 percent survivor annuity is appropriate.

A term of years option is appropriate in several circumstances. If the owner has reason to believe he or she won't live to life expectancy, a term of years can ensure that a loved one benefits from the annuity and might also give a higher lifetime payment than a life annuity. A term of years also is appropriate when there are other resources that can be used if the owner outlives the term.

Periodic Withdrawals

Annuitization usually is not required. The option many people select with an annuity is to withdraw money as needed. Most insurance annuities allow withdrawals of up to 10 percent of the contract's value each year. Many annuities allow for regular withdrawals to be scheduled, known as systematic withdrawals. The insurer sends the same amount on a fixed schedule until the owner tells it to stop or the annuity is depleted.

There are several advantages to periodic withdrawals. Money is withdrawn only when needed. The rest remains in the annuity to compound tax-deferred. Higher withdrawals can be taken when needed, and distributions can be stopped when they aren't needed or there is a desire to conserve the annuity.

Finally, when the owner dies after taking periodic or systematic withdrawals, any money left in the annuity belongs to the beneficiary, who can choose how and when to withdraw the money. That can be an advantage over annuitization.

There are two major disadvantages to periodic withdrawals. The tax disadvantage is that the last in, first out rule applies. The owner is considered to withdraw the accumulated income first. So the periodic withdrawals are fully taxed until all the accumulated income is withdrawn. That contrasts with annuitization, under which part of each payment is a tax-free return of principal.

The second disadvantage is that the owner can outlive the annuity. This method is not very different from taking regular distributions from an IRA or an investment account until the account is exhausted. The main difference is that the annual income from a fixed deferred annuity is guaranteed, unlike income from investments in an IRA or other investment accounts.

Periodic withdrawals make a lot of sense when the annuity is considered a tax-advantaged savings account or a supplement to other retirement income. It also allows the owner to leave the account balance to a beneficiary who will have control over when to withdraw money from the annuity.

Switching Annuities

The tax law lets an annuity owner exchange annuities tax free. The owner can take the balance in the current annuity and use it to buy another annuity, either from the same insurer or a different insurer. This is an annuity version of an IRA rollover. There are several times when a tax-free exchange can be advantageous.

Before undertaking an exchange, check to see if there are redemption fees or other transfer costs imposed by the current insurer.

Definitely consider a tax-free exchange when locked into an unattractive annuity. If it has high expenses or a low yield, check the offerings from other insurers and look into an exchange.

Another time to consider an exchange is when annuitization is desired. There's no reason to take the payment options offered by the current insurer. As discussed earlier in this chapter, I've done considerable research on this over the years and have found that payment amounts differ significantly among insurers. Even among the insurers with top safety ratings, the payouts can vary by 20 percent or more. That is a 20 percent difference in every payment for the rest of the payment period. If the owner wants to assume the risk of using an insurer with less than a top rating, the difference can be even greater. Anyone can compare annuity payouts by using a web site such as annuityshopper.com.

The same principal applies to someone who is considering an annuity from an employer plan. If there is a lump sum option, find out what the lump sum would be and research the annuity that could be purchased from insurers. The employee might very well increase lifetime income by rolling over the lump sum to an IRA and purchasing an immediate annuity.

Payout amounts differ among insurers because the payments are based on assumptions, particularly about expenses, life expectancy, and investment returns. No two insurers use the same assumptions.

When shopping for annuities, be sure to use a number of sources. No insurance agent or broker represents all insurers. Even the web sites do not cover all insurers. Most work with only 20 or fewer insurance companies. Use several brokers and web sites. First, determine the amount of money available to purchase the annuity. Then narrow the annuitization options you will consider. Once those steps are taken it is easy to compare similar policies from different insurers. Be sure to check safety ratings, redemption fees, and other costs.

Consider buying from more than one insurer. To maximize safety and security, invest with at least two highly-rated insurers with comparable payouts.

Before doing a tax-free exchange of annuities, keep in mind that it can be a difficult process. Most insurers drag their feet when they are told to implement a transfer, and there is no law that requires them to complete the transfer in a specific time. Six months or more is not an unusual wait to get the transfer completed. Another problem is that the new insurer needs the premium history from the original insurer to compute how much of each payment is tax free. Without the history, the insurer has to report that each payment is completely taxable. Industry scuttlebutt is that about 50 percent of the time an insurer does not provide the payment history to the new insurer. If an overseas insurer is involved, as with a Swiss annuity, the payment history probably won't be available to the new insurer.

CHAPTER 14

Choosing the Right Retirement Location

The image of the ideal retirement that is ingrained in the imaginations of most Americans includes a home in a sun-drenched retirement community.

Reality often doesn't match the ideal. Not every retiree moves to a sun belt state. Not every retiree who moves to a sun belt state enjoys the experience. Some studies show that 25 percent or more of those who retire to Florida leave the state within five years. I've met retirees who admit to choosing the wrong place to retire. Many people don't realize that despite the publicized exodus of seniors to Florida and other states, most retirees never move from their longtime residences.

There are numerous surveys and ratings of various retirement locations. I advise prospective retirees not to take these too seriously. Research can't be very thorough when a publication claims to investigate and rank hundreds of locations each year. I also find it a bit curious that the rankings change drastically from year to year. More importantly, a generic ranking system of locations cannot determine the best location for you.

One of the most important decisions regarding retirement is where to live. Even someone who gets all the retirement financial decisions right will be unhappy if he or she settles in the wrong place. I know, because I've talked to and counseled retirees. Retirement location questions are among the most common, right after questions about investments and estate planning. Complaints about the chosen retirement location also are very common.

There are some real secrets to finding the right retirement location. Unless you want to move a lot, follow my guidelines to finding your happy retirement home. My recommendations use the published retirement location guides, but use them in a different way. It is not important which areas are ranked best by any particular guide. What is important is why a location received a particular rating and the details about the area that are described in the survey. What is most important is what *your* values are and how you rank a location. You very likely will put a different priority on some qualities of a location than the publishers of the various guides.

Start with You

To start, ignore all the guides and descriptions of retirement locations. Start with you. Make a list of your interests, hobbies, favorite things to do, and things you dislike. Then list the things you expect to do in retirement. I think it is best if you start with a general list of activities. Then try to make it more specific by focusing on what you expect the typical day, week, or month to be like, and on what you would like to do at certain times of the year.

Next, use these interests to compile a list of qualities that are important for the community in which you would like to live. Do you want to live within a certain distance of a golf course, church, shopping, hiking trails, or other activities? Or perhaps you want easy access to libraries, museums, theaters, or racetracks. Most people also have a preference about whether to live in a city, suburb, or rural area.

Consider more than "what." Consider "who." Which people or types of people do you want to be around? If you want to spend a lot of time with the friends you have now or with children and grandchildren, that will greatly influence your decision. Someone who makes friends easily and who looks forward to socializing can consider the whole country. Also consider your neighbors when looking at individual communities. I find that some retirees don't like living in a community that is full of other retirees. They'd rather be in a community of various age groups. Some prefer to be around people of similar education, profession, or intellectual interests. Others like to be around people of varied backgrounds and interests. Which do you prefer?

There also are other characteristics of the area to consider: Climate, terrain, traffic, crime, taxes, job opportunities, and recreational opportunities. Some people have special interests, such as museums or the opera. Some want to be near first class medical facilities. Make your list as comprehensive as possible before considering even one location.

Survey the Country

Using your list of interests and preferences, you can start with the big picture and knock out large portions of the country. If you want to golf in the winter, you won't be living in the northern parts of the country. If you like to ski or hike in the mountains, you probably don't want to live in Florida. The list will help even those who plan to split time between two or more retirement homes, because it will help narrow down where those homes should or should not be.

Refine Your Search

After having narrowed it down to a few regions in the country, it is time to turn to the glossy magazines, books, and friends for ideas on places that are worth examining. When considering each possible location, in addition to the list of qualities already described, consider the following factors that I've found often loom large in a retiree's daily life but are too often over-looked.

Look at all the costs. Sometimes an inexpensive area is not as inexpensive as it seems, at least not for every lifestyle. Every area seems to have its hidden costs. For example, I met a couple who wanted to reduce their expenses in retirement. So they sold their home in a suburban area and used about half the sale price to buy a similar-sized home in a low-cost area. They pocketed the rest of the sale price and thought they were on easy street.

However, the husband was used to going online with his computer every day. Their new low-cost area was too sparsely populated to have local access to an online service, so he had to incur long distance charges to go online. Their new area also did not have the discount superstores or the variety of shopping they were used to, so they would drive for an hour or so to find the shopping they wanted. The list of these little costs and inconveniences went on until they realized the true cost of the location.

It is important to look at the big costs, such as housing, but it is the little daily costs that often surprise retirees. Health insurance and other health care costs vary significantly around the country. There are no reliable rules of thumb, such as "rural areas are always more expensive than urban areas." You have to verify the cost of living in each specific location. Once a specific location is under consideration, ask an insurer what the cost would be for you in that location. Food, utilities, and services also can be eye-openers. I once looked at homes in a community and found that two electric utilities reached the end of their service areas in the middle of the community. One serviced half the community, while the other serviced the other half. Residents said that service and prices differed significantly between the two utilities. In another case, people were surprised about the cost of water when they moved from a suburban area to a semi-rural area with its own water and sewer system.

The tighter your budget, the more important all these costs become. Once an area is under serious consideration, take your proposed retirement activities and budget and see what each item would cost in the new area. To avoid surprises later, actually take a trip to the grocery store and contact the local utilities to find out what they charge.

Make sure low taxes are for real.   There's nothing better for an area's image than to be considered low tax. The label often sticks for decades, even after residents are paying higher taxes. Unfortunately, it often is a false label. For example, many people consider an area to be low tax if it doesn't have an income tax. But the lack of an income tax often is offset by high sales taxes, real estate taxes, personal property taxes, an intangibles tax (which is imposed on investment portfolios), and stiff utility taxes that greatly increase phone and electric bills.

There also are hidden taxes. Some localities have low property taxes, but they don't provide services that are routinely provided in high tax areas. This fools people who come from areas where, for example, trash collection and other services are included in their property taxes. Only after moving do people find out that in addition to property taxes, they must pay separate fees for these other services.

Another tax trap is that there often are high-tax localities within low tax states. Localities often set their own rates for property taxes and can impose their own sales taxes. Sometimes a locality can add its own income tax. In these cases, a difference of only a few miles can make a big difference in tax bills.

Contact the local and state tax departments for details about which taxes are imposed. The Chamber of Commerce might also have good information that summarizes all taxes. Someone who can afford it should meet with a local CPA for details about the taxes and fees. In many areas, real estate agents are required to disclose additional fees imposed on homeowners or they will do so if asked.

Be sure you get information on state and local income taxes, sales taxes, real estate and personal property taxes, and intangibles taxes. Also, take a good look at estate taxes. Sometimes higher inheritance taxes imposed by a retirement relocation can cost your heirs a bundle.

Consider year-round climate and lifestyle.   Once I was golfing in South Carolina. The starter on the course revealed that he was a retiree from New Jersey who had moved south to avoid snow in the winter. But he found he disliked the South Carolina summers even more. "If I had known about the mosquitoes," he said, "I never would have moved here."

One classic mistake is to retire to an area because of a good vacation or short trip there. Soon after moving, the retiree learns that the daily life in the area is not as enjoyable as a short vacation. Another mistake is to move to a warm area to get a break from dealing with winters. Many people who do this eventually change their minds. Sometimes people learn that they really like having four seasons, or at least three. Maybe they don't want to move back to where it is cold nine months of the year, but they also don't want year-round summer. Or they find that while winters can be pleasant in a warm climate, the summers can be unbearably hot.

Find Your Community

By now your choice probably has been narrowed down to a few areas. Now it is time to consider individual communities or subdivisions in these areas. It is possible to pick the perfect area in which to live but to choose a neighborhood or community that causes unhappiness or at least reduces the pleasure of living in the area. Here are a few things to consider when searching for a community.

Demographics.   Florida became a magnet for retirees starting in the 1960s. Now I hear from many near-retirees and new retirees that they don't like Florida and even Arizona retirement communities because the populations are so old. They want to live with a younger, more active group. In addition to age, try to learn about the interests and activities of the community. Some communities have a range of clubs, sports leagues, and social activities. Other communities have more limited activities or have attracted residents who basically stay at home and have a few close friends.

Some people want a leisure-minded retirement community, where the focus is on golf, tennis, and card playing. Others want a learning-oriented atmosphere with a college nearby or with classes, speeches, and lectures. Don't assume every community has all types of activities. Many tend to emphasize one over the other.

Security.   Americans of all ages seem more interested in secure communities each year. Do you want a gated community with its own security patrol? Do you want an active neighborhood watch? Some communities also have security measures built into individual living units.

The association.   In the last few decades, homeowners' and community associations have become another branch of government. State laws usually let an association do pretty much whatever a majority of its members want. That can be good or bad.

An effective association maintains property values and quality of life. But some associations pass detailed, restrictive rules and enforce them to the letter. Rules might encompass the size and design of mailboxes, lawn and patio furniture, and decks. One community association in my area once ordered an entire block of homes to take down their decks because the builder made each one six inches wider than allowed. It is not a bad idea to get a feel for the power and activities of the local association. Some retirement location experts advise you to review association and board meeting minutes for the last year or two to see what the current controversies are and how the group works.

Types of Retirement Housing

Housing for older Americans is a booming industry. There now are many different types of housing available to seniors. There are variations of each type, and some types are common only to some areas of the country, at least for now. Let's take a brief course in the senior housing options.

Choose Your Shelter

Traditional housing. Of course, a retiree can go into any community and rent an apartment or buy a condo, townhouse, or house just as any adult can. In fact, most seniors probably live in traditional housing rather than any special senior housing.

Planned communities.   Some of these are specifically restricted to seniors, while others use pricing and marketing to ensure residents primarily will be seniors. These communities tend to differ from regular subdivisions and developments primarily because they have amenities that are especially desirable to active retirees. Golf and other recreation facilities often are prime features. A community center with an active agenda usually is an important element. Housing usually is single family homes or condominiums or both, with design features that are attractive to seniors (examples include one floor level, door handles instead of knobs, and security). Usually there is no medical care element to these communities. They are for independent, active people who happen to be retired.

Independent living.   In some places this is called congregate care. These facilities are for seniors who need a little bit of help for activities such as cooking, cleaning, and driving or who anticipate needing some help in the near future. Housing usually is in apartments or condominiums. Onsite amenities usually include recreation facilities, a convenience store, dining rooms, meeting rooms, a library, social areas, and television rooms. Often there is a shuttle service to local shopping and medical offices, and regular outings are organized. For many, independent living is like being at college.

The buildings usually feature extra-wide hallways and doorways to accommodate walkers, wheelchairs, and motorized scooters, along with other senior-friendly features. Housecleaning and other services usually are available. But, again, onsite medical facilities are limited. Usually the housing unit is purchased or a large deposit is made, and a monthly fee is paid. Additional fees might be paid based on other services used.

Assisted living.   This often is described as an alternative to nursing homes, but it really is not. Limited medical care is provided at assisted living facilities (which is one reason their basic room rate is considerably less than a nursing home rate). Assisted living facilities are for someone who needs help in one or two daily living activities (dressing, bathing, eating, housekeeping, walking, etc.) but who does not need physical rehabilitation or skilled nursing care. Residents generally live in dormitory-style rooms and have common dining and social areas.

Assisted living facilities generally have to comply with far fewer regulations than nursing homes. Many have a nurse or other licensed medical personnel on site for only part of the day and there are few or no medical facilities on site.

Group homes.   These usually offer assisted living services in homes with 15 or fewer residents. These might be subject to less regulation than larger assisted living facilities.

Nursing homes.   These are for individuals who need physical therapy or skilled nursing care on a regular basis. Usually the care is provided by nurses and other medical professionals under the direction of a physician. Nurses usually are on duty 24 hours a day.

Continuing care retirement communities.   The CCRC is a relatively new but fast-growing type of senior housing. CCRCs attempt to put the main types of senior housing in one community: independent living, assisted living, and a nursing home. Some CCRCs also have townhomes and detached homes in the community.

A resident initially moves to a CCRC when healthy and starts in an independent living apartment, townhome, or detached home. After that, a resident or spouse can move into assisted living and the nursing home as needs require. If a resident never needs either specialized facility, that's fine. But as one ages, there might be the need to move into one of the other facilities. The independent living, assisted living, and nursing home usually are in one building or are connected by walkways so that residents do not need to go outside to visit someone. The community also usually includes the types of amenities found in independent living.

Financing a residence in a CCRC varies. Most often, a large lump sum is paid up front to live in the CCRC. This sum usually is fully or partially refundable to the resident's heirs, though the refund right might disappear after ten years or so. (In some CCRCs the housing unit is purchased outright.) There also is a monthly fee, which might be the same for everyone or might depend on the services received. In return for these payments, the resident is guaranteed care in the appropriate facility for life.

Planned communities generally are suitable for any active retiree. Most senior citizens don't start seeking out the other facilities until their mid-seventies, unless there is a medical problem. So someone younger than 75 who lives in an independent living community or a CCRC might be one of the youngest residents.

Someone considering a move into a planned community or CCRC

should be aware that there has been a building boom among these facilities. It is important to check out the financial stability of the firm that will provide the services and lifetime guarantees. In the 1980s there was some overbuilding in senior housing, and the developers of some communities went bankrupt. It also is important to look at the by-laws, covenants, and other regulations of the community, and know who determines what level of care is needed and when a move into a different level of care can be made.

To learn more about CCRCs consider these sources: "Tips on Continuing Care Retirement Communities," available for $2 and an SASE from the Council of Better Business Bureaus, Dept. 023, Washington, D.C. 20042-2037; "The Continuing Care Retirement Community: A Guide for Consumers," available for $10.50 from the American Association of Homes and Services for the Aging, 901 E Street, N.W., Suite 500, Washington, D.C. 20004-2037; *Retirement Living Communities*, by Deborah Freundlich, published by Macmillan for $24.95.

One final tip: The most attractive CCRCs have waiting lists for entry. Most assisted living facilities and nursing homes find that nobody researches them until there is a problem. Then the children usually select a facility in a hurry. It is a good idea to review the facilities in your area (or near your children) and let them know which ones you prefer, or at least draw up a list of the features you would want.

Avoiding the Boomerang

The boomerang is when someone retires to a location, decides it was a mistake, and moves back to the original location or somewhere else. It occurs when the original decision was made in haste or without considering all the factors. Here is how to avoid the boomerang:

- Start the retirement location decision about two years before a move might actually happen. That allows enough time to take all the steps recommended.
- Don't commit right away. It is a good idea to rent a place in a new location before buying anything. Ideally, the rental should be for at least a year in order to get familiar with year-round weather and activities. It also provides time to locate the most convenient and desirable community in the area. An alternative is to rent for a few months at a time each year for a few years before moving. That might provide enough exposure to the area to make a good final decision and also might make for a smoother transition between the old home and the new one.
- Get involved in the community. Though renting, act like a permanent member of the community. Get involved in your activities of interest, meet people, and learn about the area. Try to develop the kind of routine that is anticipated for the retirement years.

- Decide what size home to have after the move. Be sure to consider factors such as how often family or others will visit, whether an office area is needed, and how many belongings will be in the home.
- Check the financial statements before buying. Many seniors buy in new communities. It is important to be assured that the community and its amenities will be finished as planned. That means checking out the financial condition of the developer. Also check on the condition of the community association. On the financial statement see if the fund balance is positive or negative. Also look to see if there is a reserve for future obligations and maintenance; if there isn't, then the current fees probably are too low. Ask about the current level of dues and about past fee increases. Also, check the current occupancy or sales rates of units. If things are slow, financial trouble could be ahead. Be sure there isn't any outstanding litigation listed in the footnotes to the financial statements. You also might want to review the minutes of board and association meetings for the last year or two to see if maintenance, improvements, or the level of dues have been major issues.
- Finally, determine the full cost of a move and be sure it is acceptable. Moving a household full of goods plus cars and other items can cost $40,000 or more. That expense, plus buying and selling costs, can add up to a stiff price for the relocation.

Most people want to make their retirement location decision only once. To make the right decision, get a head start and be sure to consider all the angles. Finally, consider this option. If there is an area you like for a special reason—say, Florida sunshine for the winter—consider becoming a snowbird. You can rent in that location for a few months during the year and stay in your current home the rest of the year.

New World of Adult Living Choices

Traditional retirement living and housing choices are on the way out. The new generation of retirees is looking for new living experiences. Developers are obliging, giving older Americans more choices than ever. These new choices include building communities outside the traditional retirement havens of Florida and Arizona, but they involve much more than that. The new choices include different types of housing and living arrangements and various types of activities within the communities themselves.

One reason for the new senior living choices is that retirees are relatively young. In many adult communities, about a third of the residents are under age 65. Those under age 55 can amount to 10 percent or more of the residents.

Another reason for the changes is that today's retirements are longer and have more stages than in the past, generally up to three stages. In the first stage of retirement, often at least one spouse continues to work at least part-time. In this stage the retirees might move to a smaller home but want to stay in the same general area to maintain personal and business relationships and living patterns. In the next stage, retirees might move to a completely different area, perhaps somewhere with warmer weather. In the third stage, retirees move closer to family and friends. Each stage has a range of living choices.

When downsizing—moving to a smaller home—the goal is usually to maintain the same contacts and activities while shedding the labor and costs of maintaining the larger home. The retiree decides it is time to stop mowing the lawn, raking leaves, checking the gutters, and maintaining the mechanical systems. It also is time to stop paying for space that isn't being used.

There are several options for downsizing. One is to move to a smaller house, townhouse, or condominium in a regular development. The new neighbors probably will be from most age groups. Another option is to move to a planned senior community, such as the Leisure World or Sun City communities. There are advantages and disadvantages to each.

Some seniors prefer to be around people their own age; others prefer more diversity. A young retiree might want to check the average age in a senior community. In some communities the average age is 75 or older. An adult community also might make one feel isolated from family and friends, though it presents the opportunity to make new friends. A community that includes all ages might be noisier, less well-kept, and maintain later hours.

Each type of community will have its own activities in addition to the activities in the surrounding community. A development built for seniors might provide services that are helpful to seniors, such as laundry, house cleaning, and on-grounds restaurants. Many newer senior communities also have amenities such as spas, golf courses, health clubs, and Internet centers. They can be more like resorts or country clubs than traditional adult communities or regular housing developments.

In making a choice, consider all these factors. Look at the demographics of the community and its appeal. Before deciding, visit several times at different times of the day and week to get a good flavor of the lifestyle. Consider the activities available, both in the housing community and the surrounding community. Also, consider how current relationships and activities would be affected.

The second stage of retirement includes many of the same housing choices but might involve moving to a new area of the country. Traditionally this move is to a warmer weather state, though the trend is for second stage retirees to look outside these traditional retirement havens. While this move is considered a traditional part of retirement, generally only about one third of retirees take this step.

The adult communities outside Florida and Arizona tend to have younger residents than those in the traditional retirement states. Some university towns also are aggressively courting retirees and senior Americans. There might a more varied lifestyle in a senior community that is located in an area that is not a traditional senior haven. Newer communities also have up-to-date features such as wiring for high-speed Internet access.

The third stage often involves moving near friends and family, especially grandchildren, and moving into traditional senior housing with some health care facilities on premises. In this stage, people give serious consideration to one of the four senior-specific communities discussed earlier in this chapter: independent living, assisted living, nursing homes, and continuing care retirement communities.

Hot New Retirement Locations

Many older Americans are becoming "half-backs" instead of snowbirds.

A snowbird is someone who lives most of the year in a cold weather area but spends a few winter months in a warm-weather state. Usually the retiree treks from a midwest or northeastern state to Florida.

But many older Americans are becoming dissatisfied with Florida. They are looking for other areas in which to spend all or part of their time in retirement. The areas they frequently choose are those about halfway between the northern states and Florida. Those states include the Carolinas and Tennessee.

There are many reasons why older Americans are looking at new locations. For many, Florida is becoming too crowded. Others don't care for the hot, humid summers. Some want to experience all four seasons of the year. And others want to be closer to their families than they would be in Florida.

I know people who tried out the traditional retirement havens in Florida and left because there were too many of the "elderly old." They wanted to be around all age groups, not among primarily older people.

The Carolinas and Tennessee have mild winters compared to the north. While they can have intense summers, the summers often don't get as hot and humid in the summer as Florida or routinely hit the 100-degree temperatures of Arizona and Texas.

Major retirement home developers are taking advantage of and even pushing this trend. Del Webb established a Sun City development in Hilton Head, South Carolina, and marketed the community with seminars in Florida retirement havens.

Census data and various surveys also reveal this trend. Florida still has more retirees than any other state. But its share is shrinking. According to one survey, the states that had the highest growth of people age 65 or older in recent years were Nevada, Alaska, Hawaii, Arizona, and Utah. Other states reporting growth in older residents are the mid-Atlantic states, Oregon, and many college towns. In fact, college towns often are catering to the elderly by offering classes at reduced rates as well as other services.

What are the factors that make older Americans choose a retirement location other than Florida? Here are the key considerations:

- Weather is no longer the prime consideration in retirement, though it still matters to some extent to most older Americans. Extremely harsh summers or winters generally are undesirable, but other than that, weather is further down the list for most folks. One growing option is to choose an area that has good weather most of the year, then take a vacation elsewhere for its worst couple of months.
- Lifestyle often is the most important factor. A number of older Americans want physical activities other than golf and tennis. Those who like hiking, visits to the mountains, and similar activities look outside of Florida for retirement homes. Also, retirees generally either love or hate planned retirement communities. Those who don't like them are looking for more diverse communities, usually outside Florida.

  Other activities to consider when researching a location are cultural and community events, entertainment, social groups, and volunteer work. Other qualities to consider are restaurants, stores, public transportation, and medical care.
- Cost of living is a big factor to those who no longer are earning salaries. As Florida has gotten more popular and crowded, the cost of living has increased in many areas. The areas that are starting to attract older Americans have a relatively low cost of living.

  Retirees who want warm weather with a very low cost of living are looking at Texas, which also has no income tax. Other low-cost areas that are starting to attract retirees include Alabama, Idaho, and small towns in the Carolinas.
- Proximity to family, especially grandchildren, is key to many people. Florida is unattractive because it can mean a long drive (or even an airplane ride) to visit family and friends. That is why people are starting to look at places halfway to Florida, making the trip to visit family and friends less arduous.

There are many guides to retirement living locations. Consider *Retire in Style: 50 Affordable Places Across America* by Warren R. Bland, Ph.D. (Next Decade, Inc.; $22.95; 800-595-5440); *Retirement Places Rated* by David Savageau (John Wiley & Sons, 1999), which annually rates about 200 retirement locations; and *Where to Retire*, a magazine published five times annually (1502 Augusta Drive, Suite 145, Houston, TX 77057; www.wheretoretire.com).

True Wealth in Retirement

How is a successful or happy retirement achieved? This book helps create the retirement you desire by focusing on how to build financial security and increase wealth. Financial security is an important foundation of a good retirement. Still, that begs the question: Does financial security ensure a successful retirement, or even happiness in general?

Retirement is a relatively new development, and retirement is changing rapidly. Yet, research has revealed in general the different types of retirements people experience and the factors that influence the retirement experience. Some of these studies captured the experiences from the first generation of retirees through today's retirees. Delving into some of these studies reveals what needs to be combined with sound financial strategies to produce a successful retirement.

Which Type of Retirement?

A fairly exhaustive study released in 2002 revealed some new information about retirees and confirmed some longstanding beliefs. It was conducted by Harris Interactive and gerontologist Ken Dychtwald and sponsored by AIG SunAmerica, Inc. This study confirmed that there are different lifestyles in retirement and different types of retirement. It broke down those lifestyles into four categories.

The Ageless Explorers, comprising about 27 percent of retirees, are youthful, empowered, and optimistic. These retirees generally assert that they never will feel elderly and believe they are extremely knowledgeable about ensuring financial security. They seek personal freedom and flexibility, are in control of their lives, and seek new activities.

Comfortable Contents are like the traditional, first generation of retirees. They are financially secure and live the stereotypical golden years lifestyle of comfort and relaxation. They make up only about 19 percent of current retirees. The Comfortable Contents report being happy and secure, and wouldn't change anything about retirement. They also have the least interest in employment during retirement.

Making up about 22 percent of retirees are the Live for Today crowd. They share many of the same goals and desires of the Ageless Explorers. Unfortunately, they are not as content or secure. They did not take the time to build a financial foundation for their retirement and feel unprepared and anxious about having enough money to last through retirement.

The remaining group, making up 32 percent of retirees, are the Sick and Tired. They are the least happy in retirement and are pessimistic about the future. They report being inactive, unfulfilled, and resigned to an unsatisfying future. They also report being in poorer health than the other groups. These retirees view retirement as a winding down of their lives and say they did little to prepare for retirement.

The study found that no matter which category a retiree reported being in, the biggest key to satisfaction was being financially prepared for retirement. Note the report says being financially prepared, which is not the same as being wealthy. (We'll get to some conflicting information shortly.) While higher net worth individuals tended to be more satisfied than the others, net worth itself wasn't the key factor to happiness. Advance planning was more of a factor. Those who saved for a longer period of time (15 to 24 years for the most satisfied) were happier than those who saved for less than 15 years. The most satisfied generally saved for about 24 years, while the least satisfied saved for 11 years or less. Other factors in happiness were maximizing the use of IRAs and 401(k)s and investing primarily in stocks and stock mutual funds.

When interpreting this study, it helps to keep in mind that it was conducted for and financed by financial services firms. The questions generally focused on finances rather than other issues or aspects of life. Even so, while financial preparedness generally led to retirement happiness, the retirees did not report financial security as being a key to a long and rewarding life. Instead, they counted having supportive friends and family along with strong religious and spiritual beliefs. They also advised future retirees to participate in some physical activity and to remain productive in some way.

Does Money Buy Retirement Happiness?

More detailed research conducted over many years confirms these last conclusions. These nonfinancial factors are the real keys to successful retirement.

A great deal of research has been done over the years on whether or not wealth buys happiness. Not surprisingly, money doesn't really buy happiness. At the lowest levels of wealth, having more money does increase happiness. Once the basic necessities of life are taken care of, however, money doesn't really buy happiness. Some economists believe that the ability of money to increase happiness decreases with age more than with the level of personal wealth. Over the decades, as the wealth of Americans has increased and more Americans are considered wealthy or well off, roughly the same percentage of people report being "very happy" or "satisfied" with their lives. A survey of America's billionaires found that this group had roughly the same percentage of happy and unhappy people as did the population in general. Yet, most people assert that they would be happier with more wealth.

To really turn conventional wisdom on its head, one study actually concluded that more money leads to higher death rates in retirement. The study examined what are known as the "notch babies." For technical reasons, Social Security benefits were reduced by 7 percent to 10 percent for those born after January 2, 1917, compared to the benefits paid to those born earlier, even a day earlier. The group with the reduced benefits was known as the notch babies. The study compared the death rates of those born in the last three months of 1916 to those born in the first three months of 1917. The results were fairly striking. The death rates and other factors were the same for both groups until they reached age 65. Then, those with the higher Social Security benefits actually had a two percent higher death rate than did those with lower benefits. The study also found that those with the lower benefits also tended to work longer. It could be that money wasn't the real factor to longevity and happiness. It could be that staying active in the workplace explains the lower death rate for the lower paid group.

There are many reasons offered as to why money doesn't buy happiness. One theory is that as people acquire more, their goals change. They want to have even more. One study found that at every level of wealth, people believed they needed about a one third to 50 percent increase in wealth to live comfortably and without wants. A middle class family will want a bigger home, a more expensive car, or the ability to take more expensive vacations. A wealthier person might want another home, a private plane, or other toys of the rich. Whatever wealth a person has, the satisfaction from achieving that wealth is transitory. Soon, other material rewards will be sought to maintain the level of happiness.

Another theory is that there are costs to acquiring wealth, and those costs reduce happiness. Longer working hours, less satisfactory family and personal relationships, and other costs of acquiring wealth reduce its satisfaction.

A third theory is that people forget how things were before they had money and take for granted how things are. Today's comforts, technology, and other benefits quickly stop being considered blessings and innovations. They are considered the basic essentials and taken for granted. People forget how their lives used to be and don't realize how much they have improved.

Envy is a factor in another theory. This theory is that people are happy with wealth only if they have more wealth than others do. They keep an eye not only on their own wealth but also on that of friends and neighbors. The theory is that most people aren't happy if other people they know get happy and successful along with them. If their wealth exceeds that of other people they know, the wealth brings happiness. Studies show that this type of wealth and happiness tie-in is more prevalent in Europe than in the United States.

Some theorize that happiness is programmed in our genes. Everyone has a set point of satisfaction or happiness. Some people naturally are grumpy; others are happy and optimistic. During brief periods individuals will deviate from their set points because of events, but the changes are short term. If someone is unpleasant and unhappy when poor, the theory goes, having wealth will not change that.

Still another theory is that Americans enjoy the process of seeking wealth. Whether it is building a business or becoming a skilled professional, Americans get pleasure from the accomplishment rather than the wealth it generates. After a level of accomplishment is reached, the satisfaction begins to fade. People get bored with the new things purchased from the fruits of their success, and they are ready to seek new accomplishments that result in more satisfaction.

Once we get beyond the statistics of whether or not people are happy with their wealth, the rest is just theory. Fortunately, there are other studies that give us a good idea of what really makes for a successful retirement.

How to Age Well

If money by itself cannot ensure a happy and successful retirement, what can?

Aging and the elderly are well studied in the medical profession. The most valuable studies probably are those published in *Aging Well* by Dr. George E. Vaillant. The book contains the findings of three decades-long studies. In these studies, people were tracked starting in their college years. Those conducting the studies interviewed the participants every decade or so and collected significant other information on the participants to compare against their statements in the interviews. The participants are old enough now that the study can help determine who aged successfully and what qualities they had in common.

The most successful retirees were grouped into a category called the Happy-Well. These people were emotionally satisfied and also physically well. These contrast with the Sad-Sick. The people in this group were both emotionally dissatisfied and not physically well. These studies found that income, wealth, and social status were not good indicators of aging well.

Let's look first at which factors destroy happiness in retirement. A key to successful aging is to avoid both alcohol and tobacco. Alcohol abuse and smoking are the factors most likely to contribute to chronic illness during the later years or to premature death. Good mental health also is a key to successful aging. It is possible that the three factors are tied together. Alcohol and tobacco might interfere with the normal maturing that contributes to good mental health. Whether that is true or not, the studies make clear that the first and easiest key to a happy retirement is to avoid tobacco use and the overuse of alcohol.

Let's also take a look at what does not seem to contribute to successful aging. Some of these findings will surprise you, because they are contrary to conventional wisdom.

- Genes apparently don't count for much. In the early years and up to about age 60, the longevity of one's ancestors can determine one's own longevity. At age 75, however, the studies found that genes and family history didn't influence longevity. In addition, the life spans of ancestors did not influence whether an older person was a Happy-Well or Sad-Sick retiree. Other factors were more important.
- Despite the promises of diet and exercise book authors, cholesterol levels don't seem to be a deciding factor. A person's cholesterol level at age 50 did not influence whether he became a Happy-Well or a Sad-Sick older person.
- Stress during the earlier years also did not influence successful aging. Dr. Vaillant hypothesizes that the illnesses and physical symptoms that stress can cause will disappear in time as the stress is reduced or eliminated.
- Parents also were not a major factor. The type of parents a person has can have an influence earlier in life. But the effects of parenting, whether good or bad, decline over time.
- Childhood temperament is another factor that can influence early adulthood but its importance declines with time.
- Another factor that has an influence earlier in life is general social ease. Yet, this is another factor whose influence on happiness declines in the later years.

Things that Matter

The studies do reveal factors that influence one's happiness after age 60. The more of these factors one has at age 50, the more likely one is to be among the Happy-Well later in life. Some of these factors are not surprising. But some of the key indicators will surprise many people.

We've already covered tobacco and alcohol. Heavy smoking and alcohol abuse definitely increase the likelihood that the years after 60 won't be healthy and happy ones. There always are exceptions, but the odds are against those who are heavy users of alcohol and tobacco.

A well-publicized factor that is supported by these studies is a stable marriage. Scientists disagree on the explanation for this. For example, does a stable marriage really contribute to a healthy life? Or do the behaviors that provide a stable marriage also provide for a healthy, happy life in general? Whatever the reason, the Happy-Well in their later years tend to have stable marriages.

Another factor: The more years of education one has, the more likely one is to be among the Happy-Well. Again, the reasons are disputed. It is likely that more educated people are more likely to take care of themselves and to have more perseverance than others. Education might be a result of other qualities that contribute to a satisfying retirement rather than of a cause.

Two obvious factors that contribute to a positive retirement are getting some exercise and having a stable weight. Obviously, the odds of being physically well are lower if one is obese. Exercise appears to influence both physical and mental health.

The surprising, little-known factor that contributes to happiness for many older people is defined as having mature defenses or an adaptive coping style. In fact, Vaillant found this to be the most powerful predictor of being among the Happy-Well.

Life involves a lot of changes, and not all of them are pleasant. Those who are most likely to be Happy-Well after 60 tend to be those with mature coping mechanisms for dealing with and responding to change. These mechanisms include humor, altruism, suppression, and sublimation. The first two mechanisms are well-known and do not require discussion. Vaillant says suppression is different from repression. Suppression involves postponing one's desires when forces intervene to make them unattainable for now. But the desires and the hopes of realizing them are not forgotten. Repression, on the other hand, is foregoing the desire for or gratification of achieving new goals and satisfying new desires. Sublimation essentially involves turning lemons into lemonade. For example, a painful experience could be used to create a new work of art in an artistically inclined person.

There are actions that indicate whether one has developed the mature coping mechanisms that lead to emotional well-being and satisfaction. Psychologists identify what they call six life tasks for adults. Two of these are key indicators of successful aging. They are known as Generativity and Keeper of the Meaning.

Generativity is one of the predictors of being among the Happy-Well and having a successful life after 60. The quality involves taking care of the next generation. Older people who look after younger ones in some way tend to have more satisfaction and believe they have more of a purpose in life. It doesn't matter if they are helping their adult children, grandchildren, or unrelated people.

Keeper of the Meaning is similar though less personal. This task involves preserving traditions and institutions and trying to pass them on to the next generation. It can involve leading a group, organization, or institution.

Those who undertake one or both of these tasks report having a reason to get up in the morning and to look forward to each day. Those without these social views tend to be unhappy in their later years.

Does Retirement Kill?

Many people say they don't want to retire, because people die shortly after they retire. Everyone knows a seemingly healthy person who passed away within a few years after retiring. That sequence of events was likely for the first generation of retirees, when the average life expectancy was about 70.

Vaillant reports, however, that today there is no support for the theory that retiring or not retiring affects life expectancy. What matters is whether one has the mature coping mechanisms already described, and also what one does in retirement.

People who become bored and unhappy in retirement do so because their jobs and things related to their jobs were the major focus of their lives. To remain happy and to feel valued, they need to replace the benefits and activities that their jobs provided. They need to engage in the four activities that, unknown to most people, work provided for them.

A social network has to be developed. Someone who is not going into work five days a week needs to develop new contacts and friends. This can be done by getting involved in new activities, joining clubs, becoming more active in church, or through other activities that create a new network.

New ways to play, especially competitive play, also are important. Work gives one something to strive for and a sense of accomplishment. A host of new activities can replace this. The new retiree needs to find activities that he or she can enjoy, achieve something while doing them, and become a bit better at the activities.

Creativity and lifelong learning are two other aspects of work that need to be replaced. These traits might be found in the same activities that form the new social network and competitive play, or they might be found in other activities.

Another key factor to successful aging is that retirement should be voluntary. People who enjoy work should continue it as long as their health allows. Once one retires, it will not affect one's health as long as the four important aspects of work are replaced.

Pyramid of Success

Money alone will not ensure a successful retirement. It is, however, a foundation to creating the retirement you desire. No matter which activities one chooses to engage in during retirement, financial security can make it easier to engage in those activities one truly enjoys and that contribute to a successful retirement.

Financial security allows a retiree the time to exercise and stay active. Financial security also can reduce stress and help a person better cope with the stressful events that will occur. Financial security enables one to spend more time building those important relationships with family and friends. With financial security, a retiree can choose to work during retirement, if that is desired. The work is more likely to be something that is fulfilling and enjoyable instead of something that is done to generate desperately needed funds.

No, money won't guarantee a happy and successful retirement. But having one's financial house in order will help. Being financially prepared for retirement does have some correlation to being satisfied with the retirement years, according to the SunAmerica study. Freedom and flexibility are important to most Americans. The earlier one starts preparing for retirement and the more steps one takes to ensure financial security and independence, the more likely it is that retirement will be a satisfying time.

Retirement will hold something different for everyone. Some will work until late in life. Others won't. Some will live in retirement communities and enjoy traveling. Others will remain in the same home and community in which they spent most of their adult years. There are many other variables in retirement, and within a very broad range there is no right or wrong retirement lifestyle. Retirement has changed and will change again. Whether you are 40 or 80, plan your retirement, and then stay on top of and adjust to the changes that are going to occur. This kind of flexibility is essential to a happy and successful retirement.

INDEX